Dynamic Techniques of

Sales Management

Dynamic Techniques of
Sales Management

Vinod Patel
Girish Rana

Oxford Book Company
Jaipur ▪ New Delhi

Oxford Book Company

Regd. Off. "Bony Residency", Gate No. 2
Opp. Tilak Public School, Vishweswariya Nagar,
Gopalpura Road, Jaipur - 302018, India
Ph: 0141 - 2761280, Telefax: 2761381
email - oxfordbookjpr@gmail.com
website - oxfordbookcompany.com

Delhi Office: 102, 1st Floor, Satyam House,
4327/3, Ansari Road, Darya Ganj,
New Delhi - 110002, India
Ph: 011-45652440

Edition, 2025

ISBN : 9788189473020

Price : ₹ 2500.00

Typeset by Shivangi Computers, Jaipur

Printed and bound in India by Thomson Press Ltd.,
New Delhi

PREFACE

Production in modern era is in anticipation of demand. Large varieties of goods are produced on mass scale to be sold to customers. However, it is important to note that some of the guidelines must be set up by the management within which the business firm is to seek to reach its selling objectives. The sales management or department has to consider three important policies before venturing into any production work—what to sell, i.e., production policy; whom and how to sell, i.e., distribution policy; and at what price to sell, i.e., pricing policy. In modern time, the nature of the sales policies in effect directly influences the job of sales managers. Sales managers provide them with a sense of direction as they plan how the business undertaking will reach its selling objectives, as they organise the sales efforts, as they manage the sales force and as they control and promote sales.

In addition to taking demand as an important consideration for production, management must look into highly competitiveness of modern economy. Hence, every producer and dealer will have to try to capture the market by appealing to tastes, preferences and general desires of buyers. Hence, in addition to product, pricing and distribution, promotion of the product is the fourth important factor in the successful sales effort. Its importance lies in the fact that it helps the product to sell quickly and therefore increases business efficiency and prosperity. The need to increase the turnover of goods in a competitive market has given rise to the art of salesmanship and publicity.

Since the success of sales department depends on efficient and hardworking salesmen, their proper management is of utmost importance for every business organisation. Therefore, recruitment and selection of sales force must be based on sound principles. Through training good quality traits are inculcated in the salesmen to make them efficient and successful. Thus aware of sound principles of sales and product promotion, salesmen are able in a better way to not only achieve the sales targets but also to exceed them.

Vinod Patel
Girish Rana

CONTENTS

1

The Motivation

Motivation and Frustration

In many respects, the problems that we meet in life are even more important than our motives, because it is the problems that compel us to change our behaviour—that make us learn. The psychologist often refers to these problems as frustration, and to the tense feeling that arises when problems are encountered as a feeling of frustration. Figure 1 shows us the three general types of frustration that can block our motives.

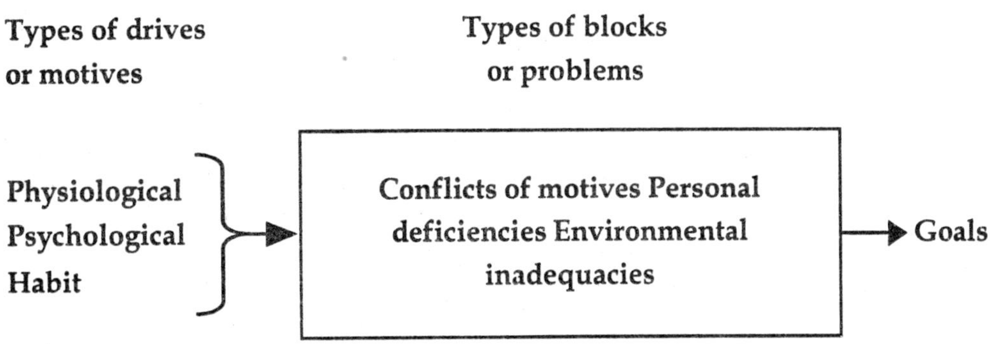

Fig. 1 The Motivation and Frustration in Human Behaviour

Conflict between Motives

As you have often been told, "You cannot eat your cake and have it too." You have to resolve the conflict between two or more motives. You want to save your money for future needs, but a new suit of clothes or an evening at a nightclub seems desirable too. You want to attend school during the summer to prepare yourself for a better position, but travel or a summer at a resort offers more opportunity for new experiences. The child in the classroom wants to win your approval, but he finds that in order to do so he must earn the disapproval of some of his fellow students.

Personal Deficiencies

Personal deficiencies make up a second general class of frustration. Because of insufficient size, strength, or agility, a child is unable to compete successfully with his fellows in rough-and-tumble play. Because of some lack of attractiveness, such as being too large or having a poor complexion, a girl is rejected by members of either her own or the opposite sex; because on insufficient intellectual ability, a child fails to attain success in the classroom; because he has suffered the loss of an arm or a leg, or is afflicted by muscular paralysis or some other disability, a child may lose security and self-esteem.

Environmental Inadequacies

Our third class of frustration includes those that arise from a deficiency in the environment. A sailor is unable to obtain fresh drinking water. An explorer cannot find enough game to live on. A boy cannot secure spending money or clothing that meets the standards set by his fellows. A girl is ashamed of her clothes, her home, or the neighbourhood in which she lives. Frequently the home, the school, and the peer group make social, intellectual, or emotional demands on the child that he is unable to meet. A personal defect that would be insignificant in one environment poses an insoluble problem in another. The race, nationality, and religion of the child become serious problem in one group and highly acceptable characteristic in another.

As long as we are able to satisfy our motives, we have no real need and are faced with no real problem. If we can eat when we are hungry, drink when we are thirsty, receive the praise of our fellows, feel secure in our job and family, and brush our teeth if we are in the habit of so doing, we are scarcely aware of the potential power of our motives.

But when we are unable to satisfy our motives immediately, our contentment vanishes and we become tense. Mentally or physically, we spring into motion. Motion is typical of all animals in problem situations. We may learn to suppress physical motion by finding that mental activity is more likely to lead us to a solution of our problems, but the tendency to move remains with us. This tendency appears to arise from a heightened muscular tension that is typical of our behaviour whenever we encounter a problem that we cannot solve immediately. This type of reaction has had survival value through the long period of animal and human development. If our ancestors has felt contented ad released when they grew hungry, they would have starved and we would not have been born. If they had become sleepy when their motives were frustrated, they would have failed to avoid pain or to seek warmth. In short, the restlessness, aggression, and wakefulness that we experience when we are frustrated are natural responses, and, at least until recent times, have contributed to the preservation of the individual and the survival of the species.

As we move about in our search for a solution, our behaviour may be based on trial and error, or it may progress through a planned series of attempts to investigate the various possibilities for solving the problem.

But we can plan and carry out an intelligent campaign only if the present obstacle resembles one that we have overcome in the past. Our physical tension mounts and our search for a solution becomes more random when we feel that we are faced with a problem that is really insurmountable. The tension may lead to digestive disturbances and to acts of aggression towards individuals or other objects in our environment. Problem-solving behaviour is a highly active process.

This pattern is typical of human behaviour. The problems that stand between us and the satisfaction of our needs compel us to search actively for solution. If a high-school girl feels that she needs a new party dress, she may be willing to take a job to earn extra money even though she has to sacrifice sleep and recreation. In the classroom, this same need for social approval may compel a child to a sacrifice play time so that he can keep up with his classmates in spelling or algebra.

Personality is shaped by the problems encountered and by the individual's solution to those problems. If the girl who felt the need for anew party dress had chosen instead to pinch money from her mothers purse, or if the schoolchild had copied from his neighbour's paper, and if these actions had resulted in general satisfaction, each child would have taken a serious step toward developing an unsavoury personality. Thus motives are the life force, but the problems encountered shape life's course.

Fortunately, our civilisation forbids the use of physical force to compel children to learn. The teacher is not permitted to block physiological motives intentionally in order to force a child to master a mathematical problem or the parts of speech. Instead, we rely almost exclusively on psychological motives and on habit motives to encourage learning in the classroom.

And these are important motivational forces. The child needs the approval of both his teacher and his classmates. He wants to receive good marks to show to his parent and to convince himself of his own adequacy. By guiding and rewarding his curiosity, which is primarily a desire for new experiences, we can encourage him to move on from one valuable learning experience to another.

The habits of work and attention that we help the child to develop will carry him through many tasks for which he fells no immediate need. Once developed, correct habits of learning are perpetuated by two very strong forces: (1) the motivational value possessed by all habits and (2) the efficiency and ease of effort that they carry with them.

A general principle of behaviour is that the individual tends to eliminate unnecessary motion. As he practices a task, he becomes more efficient. For example, if a child attempts to find information in a book, he flounders about. But after he is taught to use the index, he goes directly to the proper place and finds what he wants. With practice, he forms the habit of using the index and, since this leads him most directly to his goal, he has an added reason for retaining his habit. We must consider this factor of efficiency when we seek to break habits that have become well established. If we have learned to operate the typewriter by the hunt-and-peck system, we are not likely to change to the more effective touch system without considerable motivation and instruction. To make a change would interfere with our existing habits would result, at least for a time, in a loss in efficiency. However, once we do make the change and grow competent under the new method, our efficiency supplements the force of our new habit to guarantee that we will maintain it. Thus, though it is difficult to discard old habits of work and to adopt new ones, if we can once find better methods and practice them for a time, they will be retained.

Motive and Goals

In a sense, striving toward goals is nothing more than an attempt to satisfy motives that have been blocked by obstacles or problems. Once we have reached our goal, we tell ourselves, the tension created by our present failure to overcome our problems will be reduced.

The effort that we expend to achieve a given goal is determined by a number of factors, some of which are more powerful than the importance of the goal itself. We strive harder for a small satisfaction that we can attain now than for a much larger goal that we can attain only at the end of a long period of time. A dime held near to the eye appears to be larger than the sun; a small reward attainable now may loom larger, and many induce more effort, than a great reward that can be obtained only in the indefinite future. When we set out on a 20-mile hike, the thought of arriving at our destination hours later furnishes us with little immediate satisfaction. Instead, we pick out a tree or a hill a mile or so away and then watch as our footsteps make the distance dwindle.

And so the child strives far harder for a gold star or a word of praise that he can get this morning or this afternoon than he does for a Ph.D. that will not be with in his reach for twenty years. But notice that the higher his level of intellectual development, the longer he is willing to wait for rewards. The mature student is quite content to work for goals that are in the far-distant future. He is able to break his major goals down into the smaller steps of a book read, a paper completed, a few pages written, or a semester of study accomplished.

But immature students have not yet learned that the only way to reach important goals is by moving forward a step at a time. As a matter of fact, since their experience is so limited, they may not even be aware of the existence of distant goals. So one of your big jobs in working with these pupils is to break down the large but relatively unattainable goals of life into small, attainable goals. At the end of each small unit of accomplishment, you will want to provide opportunities for reward through a sense of accomplishment, through a satisfaction of curiosity, or through a felling of teacher or group approval. The child cannot work for a mastery of arithmetic simply because he may need it when he becomes an engineer many years later. Each small step in the long-range plan must prove rewarding to his curiosity, his security, his self-esteem, his esteem in the eyes of others, or to some other motive.

Only by making sure that every unit of work will satisfy some need of every child, can we create a good learning situation. Pupils and more likely to strive toward vital goals when they themselves feel that the goals are important than when they are produced by a taskmaster.

When the school provides for the satisfaction of needs, pupil motivation soars to the same high level that exist in out-of-school, informal, child-directed learning situation. What is more, the learning is directed toward a planned end. To the values of out-of-school learning, we add adult assistance and planning, the facilitates of the library, well-lighted classrooms, and carefully chosen laboratory equipment.

But here is where our thinking about education so often goes astray. True—the tasks to be performed must fulfil a felt need of the child. But this alone is not enough. The tasks must also point toward definite and wisely chosen goals that posses social utility and that prepares the child to meet future problems of life. The school must be child-centred, but the child must be deserted by the teacher and the curriculum maker and left to chart his course unassisted. Since he cannot appreciate how great his future need will be for certain-skills and knowledge, he is entitled to the very best guidance that educational experts can offer him. It will be your duty, as a teacher, to see that the child's activity takes him in a desirable direction and at the same time fulfills needs that he feels at the moment. As you grow in experience, you will discover that goals with high social utility can be made as rewarding to the needs of the child as goals with little or not utility.

Levels of Aspiration

Different persons aspire to different levels of attainment. If we are to make an accurate estimate of how valuable a goal is to a specific child, we must think not only of how important it seems to us as adults, or of how soon the child can attain it, but also of how attractive it seems to the child. Goals that seem to us to have the same apparent size and to be the same distance from attainment may differ greatly in attractiveness from child to child. One reason is that individual children have individual needs. Some children are most in need of security, others of self-esteem, and still others of new experiences. These needs arise from, the life problems that the child is encountering at the moment and from the level of aspiration that has been determined by himself, his family, and his associates.

His race, his religion, his family, his teachers, and his friends have taught him what values to place on various goals. One family places a high value on scholarship and assumes that its children will do well in school and will enter a profession. A child from such a family will need high marks to maintain his security, self-esteem, and esteem in the eyes of others. Another family places a higher value upon material possessions and urges its children to get a good job as soon as possible. The members of a minority group who have had few educational and cultural opportunities may expect relatively little from their offspring, whereas the members of another group may expect a great deal. One religious group may place high value on conformity to moral codes; persons who do not belong to any religious group may emphasise the importance of attaining a large share of worldly goods. A child's friends may be interested in music, art, and books, or in baseball and fishing. All these and many other aspects of the child's experience and of his present environment help to determine how attractive various goals will seem to him.

If the child sets up goals that are in proportion to his abilities he will probably succeed in reaching them. But if his goals are so high and his abilities so low that his efforts are not rewarded, he will be forced either to set a lower goal for himself or to choose quite different goals—goals that may even be socially unacceptable.

You will want to help each pupil to set his levels of aspiration low enough to guarantee some measure of success as he strives toward them, yet high enough to produce enough frustration to call forth effort and to stimulate learning. The level of aspiration is one determinant or how much frustration he will encounter. Since we find little or no motivation without frustration, and since no learning occurs without both motivation and frustration, the level of aspiration must not be too low. On the other hand, if the goal seems unattainable, the child may be driven into despair, unhappiness, random activity and aggression. Ideally, the goal should be attainable but high enough to be difficult. Such a goal fosters high motivation and stimulates the child to make logical exploratory efforts.

How the 'Personality' Determines Values

Each of us behaves with some degree of consistency and stability. Our individual pattern of behaviour is controlled by our habits, by our levels of aspiration, and by our past experiences in achieving success or suffering failure. This pattern is a major portion of what we call 'personality'.

Though we usually think of our personality as affecting others, its effect upon our own behaviour is no less important. One person—through habit, level of aspiration, and successful experiences in the past—places a high value on honesty; another seeks immediate successes without regard for the methods that he must employ to attain them. One child must aim for the praise of parents and teachers; another for the attention of his peer group. And still another must find his successes and excitement in a dream world. One adolescent may fell the need of having a camera, a coin collection, or the security and prestige of a good job; another needs a fast car or flashy clothes.

Thus, when you make an assignment, show a film, or give a demonstration, each pupil views this classroom experience from an entirely different vantage point from that of every other pupil each seeks different goals. In reading a story, one child's past experiences and levels of aspiration make him identify himself with the hero, another with the heroine, and still another with the villain. One child gains his greatest pleasure from the wealth or physical traits of the hero (or the villain), another from his romantic successes or power over others.

The Learning

A teacher is interested in how motivation influences the acquisition of skills and knowledge in a school situation. We shall look closely at the problem of learning in the classroom. Here we shall discuss some aspects of motivation that are not directly a part of the classroom situation.

'Plateaus' in Learning

Over a long period of time, the development of a motor skill, such as typewriting working on an assembly lime, or sending code message, follows a fairly predictable pattern. At first, the individual shows a rather rapid increase in efficiency. This is followed by a period of slow improvement and then by a long period in which little or no improvement is made. When a secretary first learns to typewrite by means of the tough system, for example, her speed develops during the first year of practice from zero to perhaps 50 words per minute. The next year or so of practice may bring her speed up to 60 or 65 words per minute. After that, she will probably maintain the same level of skill for many years, with slight day-to-day fluctuation. This will be true even though she receives a certain set fee per page typed and it is to her advantage to type as rapidly as possible. We might decide that she has reached her physiological limit. However, psychologists discovered long ago that although individual do reach a level beyond which they do not progress as long as their need remains the same, a substantial increase in need will result in progress far beyond what originally appeared to be their limit. When sufficient additional motivation arises, further improvement takes place and the individual may continue to improve for a substantial period of time.

If our typist, for example, is promised a promotion that involves prestige and money if she can attain a level of speed well beyond her present maximum, there is a good chance that she will succeed-assuming, of course, that the goal is not actually beyond her abilities. Habits of working at a speed that satisfies the individual's present motivation will not be broken until his motivation is substantially increased. He is content with his presently performance even though it is well below his physiological limits. Each individual's level of performance is determined by a combination of his abilities, his level of aspiration, and the habits of work that have proved adequate to satisfy his current needs.

Of course, the ability to attain various levels of skill does vary from person to person. But regardless of our real physiological limit, we seldom come very near to attaining it. And the nearness with which we do approach it is determined by the extent of our needs.

Although, we have been talking here only of simple motor skills, there is evidence that other types of learning, problem-solving, and competence in doing complex tasks, such as reading with speed and understanding also depend on the amount of motivation furnished by our present needs.

The Use of Incentives

Rewards designed to influence behaviour are often called incentives. To influence behaviour significantly, however, the reward must be needed. It must serve to satisfy some motive. In the school we offer the child interesting experiences and opportunities to satisfy his curiosity and to achieve status and self-esteem. For example, a child can have numerous incentives for reading about the pioneers. His curiosity concerning what solution they will find to each problem acts as an incentive. And he identifies himself with Daniel Boone or David Crockett and obtains interesting experiences. He is able to share his experiences with his classmates and gain their attention and approval. He gains a word of praise or a sense of security from his teacher. His reading may result in a better grade and heightened self-esteem and esteem in the eyes of his parents.

In business and industry a bonus or a promotion may be offered as a reward for extra effort. In any situation, the most successful incentives are those that appeal to one or all of the psychological motives.

Positive and Negative Incentives

Educators have stated repeatedly that praise is stronger than reproof. But before we accept such a broad generalisation, we should look closely at what is known about these common incentives.

Both praise and reproof are strong drugs. If praise is administered constantly over a period of time, it loses much of its potency. In addition, how effective it is depends a good bit on the personality of the person who administers it. We expect praise from some individuals and accept it almost as we would accept silence from another. And if we hear little but praise from everyone, we grow to value it less and less.

The same is true of reproof, if a teacher constantly berates his students, they come to expect it. In fact, a student fails to receive his fair measure of reproof for the day, he may lose status with his fellows. And so it is in the home. A child who receives little but reproof from his parents comes to expect and accept it. Its sting becomes dulled. But give such a child an unexpected word of praise and he will grasp it as a jewel. He will treasure it as a rare source of satisfaction.

Both praise and blame, like certain drugs, lose their effectiveness as we become tolerant of them, but our tolerance varies in relation to the individual from whom we receive them. We strive for a word of praise from one person either because he rarely gives praise or because his good opinion is necessary for our security. A word of reproof from another person may fail to stir us either because we have come to expect it or because his good opinion is of little importance for our feeling of security. If praise or blame is to affect our behaviour, it must either satisfy or threaten our security, our self-esteem, our esteem in the eyes of others, or some other motive.

The varying effect that praise and blame have on different individuals has been well demonstrated by experiments. During one learning experiment, a group of introverted children and a group of extroverted children were praised at certain times and blamed at others. The extroverted children made more improvement when they received blame than when they were praised, but the opposite was true of the introverted group. Other studies suggest that the extrovert tends to come from an environment where praise is more common than blame and that the opposite is true for the introvert. Typically, the introvert's development has been marked by strong respiration whereas the extrovert has been encouraged to express himself and has often been the centre of favourable attention.

Other things being equal, then which has the more powerful effect on classroom learning—praise or blame? As you might expect, praise seems to be somewhat more praiseful in actual practice. However, the evidence indicates that both serve to stimulate learning, since either one seems to produce better results than no comment whatsoever.

Praise and blame are examples of positive and negative incentives. Although individuals may react somewhat differently because of different past experiences, it is more pleasant to all of us to strive for positive rewards than it is to escape from negative threats. We strive either to improve our status or to prevent loss of our present status. Which motivation will result in greater effort depends somewhat on the nature of the individual and on the nature of the promised gain or possible loss.

Quite apart from the actual effort induced by different motivating situations, we as teachers must also be interested in the mental health of each child. Striving for advancement, particularly when it leads to success, is accompanied by happy, pleasant feeling. Striving to prevent a threat to our present status, however, even of it is eventually successful, is accompanied by an unhappy, unpleasant feeling and by worry. The maladjustment evidenced in 'nervous breakdowns' is more closely related to overworry than to overwork. Positive incentives in them selves, then, contribute more to the mental and emotional well-being of children than negative incentives do.

Interests as Motivation

Interests are a specific type of positive incentive. They are capable of arousing and sustaining concentrated effort. For this reason, we shall want to study them carefully. How much appeal the classroom material has to a child's interests determines to a considerable extent how hard and how long he will be willing to concentrate on it. For the most part, study fatigue is created by nothing more than disinterest or boredom.

Why People Differ in Interests

Since people learn new things in order to satisfy physiological and psychological motives biological factors have a strong influence on the development of their interests. If a child is large and agile, he is likely to gain selfesteem and the esteem of others from physical competition; if he is small or awkward, his security and prestige are likely to be threatened. If a child finds that experiences in the classroom nurture his security, he comes to enjoy being a worker and to spend more time and effort in his pursuits. If adolescent girl finds that boys admire her, she is likely to enjoy dancing and similar activities in which she can receive their attention; if boys do not seek her out, she will find other activities to nurture self-esteem.

Most interests are the product of past experiences. The goals that a person discovers to be approved by his concern and his community, the experiences he has had with employers and companions, and the experiments he has made in the world about him determine the direction that interests will take.

Some differences in interests are caused by differences in chronological age. If for no reason other than the desire for social acceptability, the boy of 16 must shun some activities that are quite appropriate to the boy of eight.

Other differences in interest are related to sex. The fact that parents tend to approve one type of play activity for girls and another for boys is especially important to younger children. A girl receives favourable recognition when she spends time with dolls, plays house, or learns ballet dancing, but a boy who does the same things finds that his security and self-esteem are threatened.

Since girls, on the average, reach maturity at an earlier age than boys do, they show an earlier interest in dancing and on other in physical maturation among members of the same sex have a strong effect on interests. As we have seen, some boys of 14 are sexually mature and others are immature. For both boys and girls, the attainment of sexual maturity results in new forms of motivation and in new problems. It is reflected in their choice of reading matter, conversational topics, heroes, movies, and radio and television programmes.

Actually, the specific interests that a child develops depend directly on how clearly he has been able to identify the types of activity that satisfy his motives. His desires for security, self-esteem, the esteem of others, and new experiences, and the success of failure that he meets in attempting to satisfy these desires, play a major part in determining what his interests will be. In other words, psychological motives, as well as physiological motives are significant.

And once interests are formed, the habit motives tend to perpetuate them. A boy may retain an interest in coin-collecting, fishing, football, or photography long after they cease to satisfy the motives that they originally satisfied. Habit motives and the desire to be with friends who have the same interests may be sufficient. Or, as we trace interests throughout life, we may find that an activity remains the same but that the motives satisfied by in change greatly. For example, a boy may take up golf because it makes him feel mature and because it has social prestige; as a young man, he gains group and self-esteem from his proficiency; later he continues the game for the business contacts that come from it; and still later he follows it for reasons of health and to satisfy habit motives.

As a teacher, you will need a deep understanding of what interests are typical of both sexes at each developmental level, and of the range of interests that you can expect to find within groups of the same age and sex. Then you can translate your information into specific, practical terms, such as the games, books, movies, and songs that will be most appealing to a particular group of children.

What techniques can we use to determine specific interests? And how can we use interests in developing an effective learning situation?

Leisure-time Activities due to Interests

When children work and play under the direct supervision of adults, they have a natural tendency to display the interests they feel are expected of them. They are more interested in winning approval than they are in following their other inclinations. But in their freely chosen, leisure-time activities, they unwillingly provide us with valuable dues to what their interests really are. So you will want to take advantage of every opportunity to observe children after school hours, to talk with them about how they spend their evenings, and to enter into their social activities whenever you can do it unobtrusively and without embarrassment to the children and to yourself.

Try to find out what books they like to read, what radio and television programmes appeal to them, what movies they go to, what friends they spend their time with, what hobbies they follow, and what they do when they are with the family group. In the classroom itself you can gain insight into children's interests by encouraging them to exercise self-direction in attacking problems or in choosing assignments.

Each time you discover a new interest, remember that it has real importance in the life of the child. It represents to him a possible way of finding satisfaction for his motives and a solution to his problems. If you can manage to accommodate classroom activities to a real interest that the child himself has shown, you will succeed in creating a stimulating, effective learning situation. The secret is to enlist children's interests in the classroom rather than to oppose and reject them.

With the information you gather by observing children's leisure-time activities, you can do more than just appeal to their current interests. You can encourage them to enlarge and extend their interests in new, more rewarding directions. Since interests are the child's way of satisfying his motives, he will welcome sincere attempts to help him develop more satisfying activities. Of course when you attempt to build up new interests, you will have to be much more careful than when you appeal to interest that already exist. But once a child has discovered that a new activity provides him with satisfaction, he will adopt it as a new interest.

Never worry about creating motivation in children. Every child has a tremendous amount of motivation that he is eager to satisfy every hour of the day. If you can suggest desirable educational goals that appeal to the child's motives, and if you can give him frequent opportunities to succeed in his attempts to reach those goals, you will have harnessed one of the most powerful learning forces known.

Since frustrating problems are as essential to the learning situation as motives them selves, you will want to be careful not to remove every difficulty from the child's path. Problems are a necessary condition of learning. They must be great enough to call forth serious effort, but not so great that they lead to defeat and a retreat from important goals.

As you help children in their attempts to satisfy their motives always remember that individual children vary in their ability to achieve. No child will strive after an impossible goal for very long. He must find his tasks challenging but not discouraging. They must be tailored to fit his individual abilities. By providing him with opportunities to succeed in winning security, self-esteem, the esteem, of others, and new experiences, you will make the classroom the scene of significant learning.

Be careful about how you approach the needs and interests of the child. Your task is not so much to let each child do just what he wants to do, but rather to encourage him to strive for significant long-range goals by appealing to the needs and motives that he already possesses. In short, you will help the child to choose what he is to learn. You will not force him to do things that he finds objectionable, but you must guide him in the directions that the curriculum-maker and the school as a whole find desirable.

There is much for the child to learn, and only a short time in which to learn it. You can increase both the speed and the quality of his learning by appealing to the motives that he brings with him into the classroom.

Learning and Motivation

The Process

Another question, how does learning take place? What are the conditions which favour learning? What external conditions result in improved performance by an individual? These questions are of great interest to the teachers, parents, students and the educationists. Psychologists have defined learning as any relatively permanent changes in behaviour as a result of practice or experience. It modifies or changes the behaviour of the students in terms of achieving the goals. It is the process by which the student profits from past experiences. It is an inference from behaviour and must be distinguished from it, for learning can occur without behaviour being affected. We may learn that a certain petrol-station is open twenty four hours a day without influencing our observable behaviour, unless and until we need petrol-station during the night. It is inferred that learning has occurred if in such circumstances we patronise the petrol station concerned whereas previously we would not have done so. Thus learning is a change in behaviour potential rather than in behaviour itself. Such changes can occur for many reasons, including maturation, fatigue, injury or the effects of drugs. But the term learning is applied only to those resulting from pasty experience. Further, it is restricted to changes of relatively permanent nature. Once having learned to ride a bicycle or drive a car, we quite soon regain former attainments in these skills after even long periods of disuse. Long term changes in behaviour potential of this sort are to be distinguished from shorter term changes which are often the result of temporary states in the learner such as variation in motivations.

The Concept

From the above discussion, it is understood that learning is the modification of behaviour potential as a function of experience. A simpler definition, most frequently found in ordinary dictionaries, is that learning involves the acquisition of information. This is often the case, but there are a number of situations in which individual learn without acquiring any new information. This is obvious in the development of certain motor skills where practice rather than information leads to gradual modifications in behaviour.

In addition, affective learning (learning involving emotional behaviour) does not necessarily involve the acquisition of information as it is ordinarily defined as a behaviour change due to experience including all affective motor and cognitive (intellectual) changes that do not result from other causes. For example, behaviour can change as a result of fatigue, drags or maturation; but these changes are of transient nature resulting from genetic forces, or are induced artificially. They are not considered to involve learning.

Man learns new methods and skills to successfully do, think reason and adjust to any forthcoming problem. Learning is associated with acquisition of new behaviour of modification of old behaviour. Psychologists from their own viewpoints have defined learning in various ways. Let us discuss some important definitions given by eminent psychologists.

While a student wants to learn more and more new ideas, a teacher tries to make his teaching effective and fruitful. Similarly, a doctor is interested to know about new medicines, and an engineer wants to invent new ideas of construction. An industrialist puts into use new methods of production. A politician sticks to new methods of propaganda to attract people towards him. In the same way a housewife prepares new items of food, while children want to make themselves attractive by wearing dresses of new designs. Priests and prophets adopt new tricks to make their views popular. They manipulate methods to attract more and more persons and to have more and more followers. So it is clear from the above discussion that everybody is inclined to learn new methods for his way of life. Then a question arises spontaneously as to, how does learning take place? What is learning? What is nature and what are its principles? Now let us discuss the definitions and nature of learning.

Learning can be defined as any relatively permanent change in behaviour which occurs as a results of practice or experience. This definition has three important elements. (1) learning is a change in behaviour, for better or worse. (2) It is the change that takes place through practice or experience, changes due to growth, maturation, or injury are not learning. This part of the definition distinguishes learning from innately controlled, species specific behaviour of the sort. (3) Before it can be called learning, the change must be relatively permanent, it must last a fairly long time. This rules out changes in behaviour due to motivation, fatigue, adaptation, or sensitively of the organism.

According to Skinner, "Learning is not acquiring knowledge or skill by mere mechanical repetitions. It is a process in which the learner organises different elements and experiences to reach a particular goal."

In the view of Hilgard, "Learning refers to the change in a subject's behaviour to a given situation brought about by his repeated experiences in that situation, provided that the behaviour change cannot be explained on the basis of native response tendencies, maturation or temporary states of the subject (e.g., fatigue, drugs, etc)."

In the opinion of King Ley and Gray, "Learning is the process by which an organism in satisfying its motivation adopts and adjusts its behaviour in order to overcome obstacles or barriers."

According to Eason, "Learning includes changes in behaviour that are determined primarily by the individuals interaction with his, environment."

H.J. Klausmeireir writes, "Learning is a process whereby a change in behaviour results from some form of experience, activity, training, observation and the like change in some behaviour which results from such forces as bodily injury, disease, fatigue or use of drugs is not considered learning."

According to Cornerback, "Learning is shown by a change in behaviour as a result of experience."

Blair, Jones and Simpson are of the view that "any change of behaviour which is a result of experience, and which causes people to face later situations differently may be called learning".

According to W.C. Morse and G.M. Wingo, "Learning can be defined as changing one's potential for seeing, feeling and doing through experiences partly perceptual, partly intellectual, partly emotional and partly motor".

According to Morris L. Bigge, "Learning is a change in a living individual which is not heralded by genetic inheritance, it may be a change in insights, behaviour, perception or motivation or a combination of them."

Guthrie in *Psychology of Learning* says, "Learning is the ability to learn, that is, to respond differently to a situation because of past response to the situation."

Hall opines, "the essential nature of learning process may, however, be stated quite simply. Just as the inherited equipment of reaction tendencies consists of receptor effector corrections, so the process of learning consists in the strengthening of certain of these connections as contrasted with others or in the setting up of quite new connections."

One of the shortest definitions was given by J.P. Guilford. It reads, "Learning is change in behaviour resulting from behaviour."

According to Garret, "Learning is an organisation of behaviour, It is the activity by virtue of which we organise our responses with new habits."

Murphy states that "Learning is a modification of both behaviour and the way of perceiving."

The Nature

Man not only learns but also trains the lower animals. For example in a circus, wild animals like tiger, elephant, and bear perform many tricks. So also a pigeon can be trained to carry letters from one place to another, and a trained dog can identify a thief. Psychologist Hays brought up a chimpanzee from his babyhood just like a human child. By providing him with special learning experience certain changes in his behaviour were marked. As a result of his learning his latter days he preferred more to live among human beings than among other chimpanzees. He was able to clean the dishes, polish and colour the furniture, clean the room and sharpen the pencil, etc. He was even able to attend psychological non-verbal tests with human children of his age. But in spite of all the attempts of the researchers, he could not develop his skill in language. It is because, the vocal center of animals lacks something, which human begins possess. While human beings are able to read, play, dance and gather knowledge, about various things, the animals fail to do these. The mind of human beings is a developed on and that is why they are able to master the knowledge of higher level. What learning does for a human child and how it affects his lifestyle is clear from the following discussions:

(1) Learning is Modification of Behaviour: Learning produces change in behaviour. Learning is often described as the modification of behaviour. The child learns ideas, rules, customs, etc., from his surroundings in order to adjust himself with his environment and different required behaviour and predicted activities though no one teaches him, to do so. Gradually this modification of behaviour becomes permanent and goes on developing and changing day by day.

(2) Learning Helps to Reach the Goal: Learning not only brings change in behaviour but also helps one in meeting the desires of one's life. Again, goals and ambitions can be achieved only with appropriate and positive learning in a particular direction. It directly or indirectly helps the individual to reach his goal. Learning of speech, learning to laugh, cry in the case of a child, is organised deliberately. They are not accidental. Hence learning is accepted by all as an internalising process.

(3) Learning Creates Interest to Know New Things: A deep desire or thirst for knowledge is often marked in some individuals. Even in case of children, it is observed that they show interest and are anxious to do new works to find out new facts and engage themselves in small and simple researches. This helps them to learn more and more.

(4) Environmental Influence Brings Difference in Learning: All children are not reared up in similar environments. A particular child is brought up in different environments during his lifetime. Hence learning process and its effects on one child may be different from that of another on the basis of their difference in environment in which their learning experience takes place. Children coming from adverse environments such as poverty, sometimes show amazing results in learning. So also the ones coming from a proper environment sometimes show the same originality in learning. Children coming from villages and undeveloped localities, in spite of their intelligence, fail to become successful in learning due to their undeveloped environment. On the other hand, children in urban area, in spite of their low I.Q., are successful in better learning performance. It is because their environment helps them learn better. Hence it can be said that a proper and adequate environment is very much necessary for a fruitful learning of the child. Especially the house and the school should provide the necessary stimulus for learning experience.

(5) Learning is a Problem-solving Activity: Society is dynamic. An individual has to adjust himself with every change and he has to face many novel and unexpected situations. There are some problems that cannot be solved by means of age old customary methods. The novel situations should be met with new ideas, and at this point learning helps him. Changing problems in changing circumstances can only be solved with new forms of learning.

(6) Learning is Matter of Habit: From this proposition one may conclude that doing a work habitually is learning. Learning is the display of mastered personal reaction to a given situation. Man has to react in the right way to his stimulus. By habit formation, he can do away with incorrect ways of reaction formation. Secondly, learning makes habit not only to be formed in the correct way but also be organised.

(7) Learning is an Automatic Process: Learning takes place when the child becomes active. He has to indulge himself in the process of learning. In course of performing daily activities he automatically gathers experience. And that is the process of learning. When he himself becomes aware of his requirements—mental, physical, social and emotional, etc.—he becomes active. Its requirements stimulate his will and produces response. If he is easily motivated by some other factors, then learning can also take place even without a teacher. The child learns when he feels the requirement for it. So this process is always directed to a particular goal.

(8) Learning is not Knowledge about Subjects: Learning is not confined to the four walls of an educational institution. Reading and remembering books is also not learning. All round development of a person is learning and by learning only, one's personality matures. Studying different branches of knowledge in schools and colleges is generally termed as learning. But apart from this there are so many things such as knowledge about God, language, literature, philosophy, art, sculpture, social values, personal traits, which are also learned by human beings. So it should not be misunderstood that learning implies only traducing books.

(9) Learning may be Correct or Incorrect: Though learning is defined as modification of behaviour, the modification itself may be correct or incorrect. It may be socially acceptable or unacceptable. We learn both good behaviour and bad behaviour in our day to day experiences. But true learning warns us against bad behaviour and this is right learning.

(10) Learning Occurs both in Formal and Informal Situations: Process of learning starts from the birth of a child. He learns many things through social interaction with other in his environment. New habits are formed and skills mastered. Many novel ideals also occur in his own mind. New choices, new beliefs and new interests are aroused in him. Then he comes to school and learns what he is taught. He is aware of what he is learning. So all the above learning processes can be termed as formal learning. Apart from these, he also learns informally from his various other experiences. Various institution such as family, club, gymnasium, religious place, playground, excursion, etc, render informal learning to him.

(11) Higher Learning Depends upon Capacity of Individual and Complexity of Learning Material: For successful and effective learning, so many personal factors are responsible. They are our individual capabilities. They include our memory, interest, understanding, emotion, controlling capacity, etc. Make learning effective, the child takes the help of two processes. One is that he tries to solve some of his problems with already acquired knowledge and skills and the second is that he discovers new methods and skills to face some personal problems. In order to solve some complex problems, he needs higher and more learning.

(12) Learning is a Function of Maturation: Learning to an extent is also a function of maturation. One cannot teach a new born baby to walk or to pick up any object with his fingers however much one may try. Before anything is learnt by a person, his sensory, motor and also the nervous system including brain must reach a certain level of maturity.

The predetermined sequential stage of maturity of the sensory motor and nervous system of an animal is called maturation. Individuals of different species undergo different sequential patterns of development and maturation. It has been observed that unless an individual attains a particular level of maturation, he cannot learn a particular skill of learning. Different learning require different levels of maturation. Acquisition of simple motor skills is possible in early infancy. But complex activities like reading and writing, etc., which require a developed brain has to be postponed for pre-school and early-school period.

Important in this content is the concept of 'critical periods' for learning. If it has not been learnt at a particular stage of child's maturational development, it becomes difficult for him to master it at a later period. Harlow made an experiment in 1962 on monkeys regarding this. He raised some monkeys in isolation, without letting them to mix or play with other monkeys. He found that if the isolation is upto 90 days the resultant abnormal social and sexual behaviour is short lived, but if isolation is more than that period, the abnormally persist throughout life. This made him conclude that the first 90 days is the circle period for learning of social and sexual behaviour in monkeys.

(13) Learning is Dependent on Nervous System: Learning is also dependent on the nervous systems which includes the brain. It has been found that the animals with more complex nervous systems learn faster and acquire more complex skills than those with simpler nervous systems. An experimenter reared a chimpanzee just like a human baby soon after its birth. He also gave it special training wherever necessary. As a result of this she learnt to perform simple acts like dusting, washing dishes and painting furnitures, etc. But she could not talk because of the deficiency in the language or speech center of her brain. Thus, limitations of the brain is an important factor in the learning ability of a child or an animal.

As to human learning, the growth of cerebral cortex plays a very important role. Growth of learning ability during childhood and adolescence is directly related to maturation of the cerebral cortex. The decline of learning ability in old age is probably due to the decay of the tissues of this part of the brain.

Lashley conducted an experiment on white rats. His three important finding about learning and the brain are that learning is related to the amount of cortical tissue, available inside the brain of the subject. The greater the amount of cortical tissue, the quicker will be his learning. He proved this by taking away various percentages of cortical tissue from the brains of rats and then making them learn the maze. The second conclusion is that learning is related to the location of specific cortical tissues in the brain of the subject. He proved that removal of specified cortical tissues led to the loss of sensitivity to visual details, removing another, to the loss of sensitivity to different odours, and so on. Thus, there are functional specialsatiation inside the brain. A brain has different centres for different abilities. If the subject's brain lacks a particular centre, say speech centre, he cannot learn that ability. Lashley also came to another conclusion. He found that if a particular centre in the brain of the subject, relating to some particular ability is destroyed, then it results only in temporary loss of the ability. Gradually other parts of the cerebral cortex take up the function of the destroyed centre. Hence the lost ability of the subject reappears from this. He propounded his theory of mass action, which means that cerebrum function as mass.

(14) Learning is a Self-acting Process: Learning is also a self-active process. Learning involves the subjects. If a child has to learn, he has to be involved in the process of learning. He has to participate in his experiences and has to learn from them. There cannot be any learning without the involvement of his self. To learn, a child or a subject has not only to involve his senses but he has also to use the higher centre of his brain, which will import pattern, meaning and significance to his sensory inputs.

The Characteristics

We can conclude that learning is a process that provides impetus for new behaviour or through interaction with the environment brings change in the already existing behaviour. Learning brings a permanent change in behaviour, hence the changes in behaviour caused by regular exercise, games, habitual walks, are permanent change. The intensity of emotion may also bring change in behaviour. So it is right to conclude that human behaviour is the central point of learning process. Here behaviour does not mean physiological activities only, but inner process like thinking, memory, power, causality and emotional reaction.

❑❑❑

2

Sales Policy

Introduction

It is important to note that some of the guidelines must be set up by the managing director within which the business firm is to seek to reach its personal selling objectives. There are three important policies of modern sales department:

(1) What to sell?

(2) Whom to sell?

(3) At what price to sell?

Sales managers' role in the determination of sales policy vary considerably from organisation to organisation. At one extreme, in some organisations, this role is not to determine, but to administer, sales policies laid down by chief executive of organisation. At the opposite extreme, in other organisations, the sales manager alone is responsible for determining sales policies of the organisation. In our country, however, the sales manager participates as a member of a executive board charged with responsibility for making sales policy. In modern time, the nature of the sales policies in effect directly influences the jobs of sales managers. Sales managers provide them with a sense of direction, as they plan how the business undertaking will reach its personal selling objectives, as they organise the sales efforts, as they manage the sales force and as they control the sales efforts.

The basic nature of a business organisation is determined by the product it has to sell. A business organisation comes into existence because its organisers visualise an opportunity to make and sell some goods. As the organisation grows, management must make many key decisions on products whether to drop old products, whether to add new products, whether to expand the current product lines or add new product lines and on product design and product quality as well as on such product related matters as product guarantees and product services. Sales policies are the general rules set up management of an organisation to guide itself in taking important sales decisions. They should derive from and by wholly consistent with product objectives.

Policies relating to the width of a product line are classified as either short-line or full-line. The organisation following a short-line policy handles only a portion of a line, while the organisation with a full-line policy handles all-or-most of the items making up a line. The business organisations after use short-line policies for some goods and full-line policies for others. The head of sales department must decide for each goods whether the basis of competition should be short-line or full-line.

All items in a product line should be subjected to continuing evaluation and reappraisals should occur at regular intervals. The reappraisal serves two main purposes: (1) to decide whether each commodity item is still in turn with market demand, and (2) to find such commodities that should be dropped from or added to the line. Unless each product item is reappraised fairly regularly, market demand may shift, and more alert competitors may succeed in capturing large share in market. Regardless of which manager or group in an organisation is responsible for determining product policies, sales manager should participate in product line appraisals. Compared with other management executives, they have the closest contract procedures exist for receiving communications on customer product acceptance from the salesmen and should make this information available regularly to those responsible for making product policies.

Production Policy: What to Sell?

Appraising the Product Line

Every item in the product line should be compared with similar and competing items in the lines of other manufacturers. The focus should be upon identifying relative strengths and weaknesses, especially with regard to which features of each item consumers consider to be desirable or undesirable. During the appraisal process, too, special attention should be paid to significant trends in usage. Management should seek the answers to several question: How much of the item is used? What is it used for? When is it used? Where is it used? The answers to these questions may have supplemental benefits of importance of sales executives; they may provide insights useful in the construction of sales presentations and in the motivation of the sales force and dealer organisation.

By all odds, however, the most critical factor in analysing the individual items in a product line is profitability. Generally, an item should not be retained in the line unless it meets management's standards for profitability, or shows promise of meeting those standards. Nevertheless, before an item is dropped because of its poor profitability showing, other factors need considering. Will modifications in price policy or in promotion cause the item to improve in profitability? Even if the item would continue with a poor profit showing regardless of changes in price or promotion, do other factors dictate its retention? Some companies cater to customers and dealers who, logically or not, expect a full-line offering. If distribution is through exclusive agencies, for instance, dealers often insist that the manufacturer provide them with a complete line. Also, certain items, such as repair and replacement parts, are by nature unprofitable for many manufacturers; but, because of the need for providing service on major products, most manufacturers find they must retain such items in their product offerings. Furthermore, since markets are not characteristically homogeneous but are made up of various segments with unique tastes and preferences, many companies find that some unprofitable products must be retained in order to help sell profitable products. This happens, for instance, when customers combine individual products into 'product systems,' as in the case of sprayer fixtures used with insecticides. Subject to exceptions such as those mentioned, however, unprofitable products should be eliminated from the line.

Under certain conditions, it is appropriate even to drop some profitable products. A product should be dropped if the resources involved in marketing it could be used to better advantage in behalf of a product which has a brighter future or in which the company has a greater investment. An item should also be dropped if it causes sales personnel to divert their efforts from more profitable items. Products with slow turnover rates should be discontinued if dealers might then place more emphasis on the better-selling products in the line. Finally, any item that does not fit logically into the basic line is always a likely candidate for elimination.

Appraising the Product Line and Line Diversification

Management also needs to make periodic appraisals of the product line relative to the company's growth objectives. These objectives are necessarily restricted as an established product line approaches the point of market saturation. Such objectives are restricted, too, when the industry is slowly dying, or when competitors have succeeded in making permanent inroads in a company's 'natural' market. In fact, if action in the product policy area is long delayed in such situations, the survival of the firm itself is at stake. In most cases of this kind, the indicated action is to diversify by adding new products or even entirely new product lines.

Although some firms diversify to survive, others diversify to expand or to reduce costs. For example, a decision to shorten marketing channels almost always causes parallel consideration to be given to widening the line. If sales personnel are to write orders large enough to justify the higher costs of direct selling, addition of new products may be necessary. On occasion, too, top management assigns the sales organisation a substantially larger task than previously. When sales volume must be expanded greatly, one solution is to add new products. Sometimes, too, new products are added to stimulate the sales force or dealer organisation. An addition to the line not only has news value, it may help sales-people earn larger commissions, and assist dealers in increasing sales and profits.

Furthermore, circumstances elsewhere in the company may result in adding new products. The production department may initiate the search for new products if there are unused plant facilities or if seasonal sales fluctuations cause manufacturing irregularities. The treasurer may advocate diversification if idle funds cause financial criticism of the company or if there is an opportunity for profitable acquisition of a firm manufacturing related products. The purchasing department sometimes suggests the addition of new products, particularly when difficulty is experienced in procuring adequate supplies of materials for the fabrication of existing products. Pressure for line diversification may originate in the scientific research division, which may discover or perfect a new product, or in the marking research department, which may uncover natural additions to the line as an additional result of other studies. Occasionally, too, either through research or by chance, uses for industrial waste materials are found which result in net addition to the product line.

The sales department is often the division that pushes hardest for line diversification. Its intimate contact with the market enables it to keep close watch on the degree of market acceptance enjoyed by new products of other manufacturers. Therefore, with the objective of holding or improving an established market position, sales executives exert strong pressure for the addition of new products. Consequently, any significant shift in customer's buying patterns may be a signal for line diversification.

Ideas for New Products

Once management decides to add new products or new product lines, it faces the problem of finding candidates for addition. Progressively managed companies seek to tap both internal and external sources of new-product ideas. Ideas for products that come from within the company generally are related to the company's regular operations. The sales department, for instance, may identify unsatisfied market needs in its day-to-day contacts with customers and prospects. Or the production department may develop improvements in existing products, and the research and development department may turn up ideas for new products as a routine part of its activities.

Because they represent thinking undulled by close association with the established product line, ideas from outside the company are often unique. Here are a few examples: A pottery company got its idea for a new vase from a museum exhibit. One plastics manufacturer secured an idea for a film-viewing device from an unsolicited outside suggestion, and another plastics manufacturer got an idea for a similar device from a list of needed inventions published by a bank. A chemical company picked up an idea for an insecticide from a list of government-owned patents available for licensing. Thus, product ideas from external sources often result in the addition of items that otherwise might never have been considered.

Appraisal of Proposed New Products

What criteria should be used for appraising products or product lines proposed as candidates for addition? As in the evaluation of established product offerings, the key question is: Will this item (line) add to the profitability of the company? The next factors to be considered include the nature and size of likely markets, competition, price policy, sales programmes, and legal implications.

The marketing and production characteristics of a proposed product should be compared with those of items in the existing line. Ideally, any addition should be in alignment on both the marketing and production sides. Such products are natural additions; they round out the line and make marketing and production efforts more efficient and more profitable. From the marketing standpoint, the same sales force can sell the product, and distribution can be through existing channels. Also, the ideal product reaps the benefits of goodwill previously built up for other items in the line; its seasonal sales dovetail with the present sales patterns; and it broadens the market base (diversifies the company's business by adding new classes of customers).

Product Design Policy

Manufacturers have two main policy decisions to make with respect to product design: (1) the frequency with which designs will be changed, and (2) the extent to which product designs should be protected from the copying of competitors.

Frequent introduction and promotion of design changes and design improvements has become an important marketing factor in many industries, such as in clothing, automobiles, home appliances, and office machines. Through design changes that make the product more attractive, for example, users are persuaded to replace old models, which in many instances are still usable, with new models. In addition to weakening the sales resistance of buyers, changes in design reduce to emphasis on price, assist in the stimulation of salespeople and dealers, and provide new inspiration for the advertising department. However, this design change policy is not appropriate for all companies or for all types of products, since the successful promotion of a design change (especially if it involves only the product's external appearance) requires not only a high degree of skill in design but exceptional skill in the planning and execution of promotional programmes.

A company's policy with respect to design protection is closely related to its policy on frequency of design change. In certain industries in which designs change very rapidly, such as in the women's apparel field, it is usually impractical to attempt to a produce a new design. In fact, the rapid rate of fashion change in most areas of the apparel industry makes legal protection impractical. Indeed, success in high-fashion fields partially depends upon the extent to which designs are adopted by competing firms so that the style becomes fashionable. In other industries, where design changes occur less frequently, design protection is practical and desirable. This is true, for instance, in the home appliance, furniture, and jewelry industries. Legal protection is affected through design patents granted by the Patent Office for terms of up to fourteen years. While they are in force, these patents protect a company against use of the design by others.

Product Quality and Service Policy

For consumer durables, and most industrial goods, product quality and the amount of service rendered in connection with the sale are closely related. Generally speaking, in other words, high-quality products tend to require less service and low-quality products, more service. Since buyers ordinarily expect the performance of different products to vary with their quality, manufacturers marketing high-quality products usually have the more liberal service policies. Often, too, product quality is largely a matter of those characteristics built into a product that the buyer is unable to judge until after he has made the purchase and begun to use the product. Since such technical features are apt to be deeply hidden, a liberal service policy helps reduce customer's reluctance to buy items whose quality cannot be judged in advance of actual purchase. The maintenance and, if feasible, the improvement of product quality are also important matters for the sales department – if quality deteriorates, for example, the sales department bears the brunt of customers and middlemen dissatisfaction.

Manufacturers' service policies take a variety of forms. The simplest merely provides for education of the buyer in the use and care of the product. Other service policies – particularly for industrial products and such consumer lines as air-conditioning and heating equipment – provide for installation, inspection, and repair of the product. When a company adopts a formal service policy, sales management should make it an integral part of the promotional programme. An appropriate service policy not only facilitates the making of initial sales but also helps in keeping products sold, stimulating repeat sales, and building customer goodwill. There is no legitimate place in a promotional programme for a service policy that fails to accomplish these aims. Success of failure of service policies depends on sales management, since the chief sales executive is responsible for their administration.

Many manufacturers, at least for a specified period after sale of the product, do not charge for service. This 'free' service may be provided either under the terms of a written guarantee or as a matter of policy. When the buyer requests service a considerable time after the date of purchase, most manufacturers charge for it. Firms maintaining centralised service facilities, or operating their own service stations, generally make the charge a nominal one. Such a charge pays part of the costs of service and handling and eliminates many unreasonable demands by buyers. Companies that depend upon dealers or distributors to provide service have less control over the size of the charge. It may be a nominal amount, with the manufacturer absorbing part and the user the remainder; or it may be larger, and borne entirely by the user. Unless the manufacturer pays some portion of the cost, middlemen hesitate to assume responsibility for service.

Guarantee Policy

Guarantees, or *warranties* as they are sometimes called, serve as sales promotional devices and as a protection to limit liability and guard against abuses of the service policy. If the product does not perform as represented, the guarantor may promise to replace it, to refund the purchase price or a multiple of that price, to furnish the purchaser with a competitive product at no expense, or to remedy defects free of charge or for a small fee. When a guarantee is used for promotional purposes, its terms are likely to be extremely liberal. When used a protection, its terms are not only less generous but are hedged with various conditions and restrictions. It is unusual for a guarantee to serve both purposes satisfactorily. The guarantee is weakened as a tool for sales promotion when clauses are inserted to protect the manufacturer; and the absence of such clauses makes it less effective as a protective device. However, this does not mean that a promotional guarantee should be without some protective provisions. Nor does it mean that a protective guarantee should be absolutely useless for promotional purposes. But the guarantee must emphasise one purpose, not both.

Distribution Policies - Whom to Sell?

The distribution policies of a company are important determinants of the functions of its sales department. The decision to utilise a particular marketing channel, or channels, set the pattern for sales-force operations, both geographically and from the standpoint of the kinds and classes of customers from whom sales personnel solicit orders. The decision with respect to the number of outlets that are to handle the product at each distribution level affects the size and nature of the manufacturer's sales organisation and the scope of its activities. Related decisions concerning the cooperation that is extended to and expected from the various middlemen also strongly influence both the nature of the sales department's operations and the sales persons' jobs.

Policies on Marketing Channels

One of the most basic of all marketing decisions is that of choosing the most appropriate marketing channels. The principal choices normally available, of course, omits many channel variations that see less common use. Detailed descriptions of these channels would be superfluous here, since the conditions under which each is an appropriate choice, the problems met and the advantages gained through using each, and descriptions of the service rendered by different middlemen are exhaustively covered in most basic marketing texts. Manufacturers selling goods to the consumer market have a choice of five main channels, and those selling to the industrial market have four main options. Few manufacturers use only one marketing channel; most use combinations of two or more. Firms that sell to both the consumer and industrial market are in this classification, as are the many manufacturers who sell through both chain and independent outlets. Recognise, of course, that the actual situation is commonly more complex than that depicted in the diagram. The typical manufacturer of toothpaste, for instance, sells through both chain and independent outlets in the drug, grocery, variety, and department store fields.

Decisions concerning the selection of marketing channels are required more often than is commonly supposed. The obvious occasions are those following the initial organisation of a manufacturing enterprise, and when additions to the product line are made. At such times, the relative desirability and appropriateness of the various channel options are discussed, and the selection is made (or should be) only after all factors influencing it are evaluated. However, at other times – even though the product line remains unchanged – continuous review and reappraisal of the channel system are advisable. Frequent shifts occur in the nature and comparative importance of the factors that governed the original selection. New market institutions appear, marketing innovations develop, the characteristics of markets change, and so on. Marketing is highly dynamic and the relative effectiveness of various marketing channels is always changing. Consequently, one of the chief sales executive's responsibilities is not only to keep higher management fully apprised of changes in the factors affecting the marketing channels (both those currently used and those available), but also to call attention to the need for policy decisions.

The initial selection, or subsequent re-evaluation, of marketing channels is essentially a problem in determining which channel, or channels, affords the opportunity for returning the greatest net profit to the enterprise. Channels, in other words, should be so chosen as to obtain the optimum combination of profit factors. This is no simple task. Neither maximum sales volume, nor minimum cost, should be considered alone; the most profitable combination of both must be sought. Furthermore, the time dimension also must be considered – management must look to the probable long-run effect as well as to the short-term impact upon net profits. The policymakers, then, should keep in mind all three profit factors - sales volume, costs, and resultant net profits - and they should consider the effect of different channel options and combinations on each factor over both short and long periods.

Sales-Volume Potential

For each channel option, the basic question is: Can enough potential buyers be reached to absorb the desired quantity of product? The answers to such questions are found through market analysis. The raw data are secured from the company's own records, external sources of market statistics, and field investigations. When these data are analysed, and after allowances have been made of the strengths of competitors, the potential sales volume of each channel option can be estimated. Among the most important factors influencing any channel's sales potential are the ability of the company's sales management, the excellence of its planning and the skill with which it implements sales programmes and campaigns. In appraising the sales potentials of alternative channels, therefore, one must assume that, regardless of the channel chosen, the sales-management functions will be performed with the same degree of managerial competence. In the absence of this assumption, comparisons of alternative channels have little meaning. It makes little sense, for instance, to compare a well-designed and skilfully executed plan for selling through wholesalers with a poorly designed and awkwardly executed plan for selling direct to retailers.

Comparative Distribution Costs

Most distribution-cost studies have shown that the costliest channels are the shortest ones. For instance, when a manufacturer decides to sell directly to the consumer, it assumes responsibility for the additional performance of marketing functions. It incurs larger expenses as it steps up its performance of such functions as selling, transportation, storage, financing, and risk bearing. If the manufacturer chooses to use the door-to-door direct-selling method, it faces, in addition, problems related to the selection, training, supervision, and general management of this class of sales personnel. If the manufacturer decides instead to open its own retail outlets, it has such added problems as selecting store locations and buildings, negotiating for leases, designing store fronts, obtaining equipment, arranging interior store layouts, managing retail personnel, conducting retail advertising, and procuring executives who are retail-minded. The manufacturer using short distribution channels has a higher gross margin to compensate for additional selling costs; but its net profits are often lower, because it may perform these functions less efficiently than the middleman. Most middlemen carry a broader line of merchandise, and their fixed costs are spread over more products. However, direct distribution has important nonfinancial advantages resulting from more intimate contacts with consumers and closer control over the conditions under which the product is sold. Nevertheless, before a manufacturer decides in favour of direct-to-the consumer selling in any form, it should recognise that it will face a broader range of problems and incur additional distribution expenses. Furthermore, the shorter the channel, the more the manufacturer's selling costs will tend to be of fixed rather than of variable nature. This is important, especially in times of fluctuating sales volumes, because the break-even point is almost higher when short marketing channels are used.

Direct sale is more common in the industrial field than in the consumer field. But the costs of selling directly, even to large buyers, are still high. In the industrial market, for example, many direct-to-user sales personnel need to possess considerable technical education; their training is long and expensive; and necessarily their compensation is high when compared to that of less-qualified persons. Nevertheless, selling directly to industrial users enables the manufacturer to provide special attention to each customer's needs. In many cases, this advantage more than offsets the additional expenses involved.

The longer marketing channels result in lower selling costs for the manufacturer. When middlemen are used, they perform some functions that would otherwise be performed by the manufacturer. It is necessary to compensate the middlemen for performance of these functions and to provide them with the opportunity for net profit. Consequently, when a manufacturer switches from short to longer channels, its own gross margins are reduced. However, this usually is accompanied by a reduction in selling expense more than offsetting the loss in gross margin. Thus, the result of using indirect distribution is often higher profit per unit of product sold. In addition, the manufacturer shifts a wide range of problems to the middlemen and, in most situations, operates with a lower break-even point. However, the disadvantages of indirect distribution are (1) greater remoteness from final consumers, and (2) less control over the conditions under which the product is sold to them, which may produce lower sales volume.

Net-Profit Possibilities

Sales-volume potentials for various channels are meaningful only when considered in relation to the respective distribution costs. A channel with high sales potential might conveivably involve distribution costs so high that net profit is extremely low. A second channel might not produce a worthwhile sales volume, even though it involves extremely low distribution costs. For each alternative, total costs of distribution should be deducted from the estimated sales potential to determine the net-profit possibility present.

Those formulating policy on marketing channels must keep in mind the relation among gross margin, expenses, and net profit. High gross margins, such as those obtained by manufacturers using short channels, do not always mean higher net profits. Expenses of distribution, in the final analysis, are incurred for the performance of marketing activities. Choosing marketing channels, in essence, is a matter of determining the extent to which the manufacturer should perform these activities and the extent to which their performance should be delegated to middlemen. The rule should be: Determine which agency—the manufacturer or the middleman—can perform this particular activity most efficiently. If this rule is followed, the manufacturer's total costs of moving the product to final buyers should be lower, and its net profits are almost certain to be higher.

Policies on Distribution Intensity

The manufacturer's choice of marketing channels affects, and is affected by, its policy on distribution intensity. At each level of distribution making up the channel, decisions must be made concerning the number of outlets to be utilised. Ordinarily, it is advisable to decide first upon the policy to be followed at the distribution level nearest the final buyer, because that decision generally requires application of the same policy at other distribution levels. Once the policy on distribution intensity has been set, the chief sales executive's responsibility is to interpret and implement it. The chief sales executive, subordinate sales executives, and often even the sales personnel in the field must make decisions to use or not to use particular distributive outlets.

Mass Distribution

The company following a policy of mass distribution obtains maximum sales exposure by securing distribution through all those outlets from which final buyers might expect to purchase the product. This is the policy used in distributing many consumer convenience items. Cigarettes, candy and chewing gum, for instance, can be bought by consumers in food stores, drugstores, cigar stores, candy shops, variety stores, restaurants, theatre and hotel lobbies, at newstands, and from vending machines in numerous other types of locations. Often, the manufacturer using this policy needs not one but several marketing channels. But even though the manufacturer may maintain a sizable sales organisation, its sales personnel cannot possibly sell directly to all retail outlets. Consequently, the manufacturer must determine how large each account must be before it is sold directly. In areas where retail outlets are concentrated, the manufacturer may find that it can sell directly to all accounts, large and small; but, in other markets, such manufacturers generally find it necessary to secure distribution through wholesalers.

Selective Distribution

Selective distribution involves selecting only those outlets that can best serve the manufacturer's interests. In a firm following a selective distribution policy, the chief sales executive sees to it that criteria are set up to provide guidance to subordinate sales executives and the company's sales personnel in their selection of accounts. These criteria relate to such matters as sizes of orders, volume of purchases, profitability, type of operation, and geographical location. In practice, the policy of selective distribution almost always represents, directly or indirectly, an attempt to make every account a contributor to net profit.

The basic procedure in applying a policy of selective distribution, then, it is to set up criteria for the selection of accounts. An account analysis helps to identify the characteristics that differentiate profitable from unprofitable accounts. It may reveal that a fairly small percentage of the customers contribute a relatively large proportion of the total net sales and profits. It is not unusual for 20 per cent of the account to be responsible for 80 per cent of the net sales, and an even higher percentage of the net profits. But there are exceptions to the general rule that only profitable accounts should be retained or solicited. Some losing accounts may be retained because of long-standing relationships, and others because of their future promise. Furthermore, unprofitable accounts, if they contribute to the payment of overhead expenses, may add enough to sales volume to enable the firm to realise certain economies in manufacturing. Usually, however, it is possible to make savings through the elimination of most unprofitable accounts. One manufacturer of industrial tools, for example, found that it was losing money on almost one-third of its dealers. By discounting sales to these dealers, it was possible to reduce the number of salespeople by almost one half. Through more effective use of the remaining sales staff and the surviving dealers, this manufacturer reduced selling costs from 30 per cent of sales to 10 per cent.

Exclusive Agency Distribution

Exclusive agency distribution is an extreme form of selective distribution. To implement a policy of exclusive agency distribution the manufacturer makes an agreement, either written or oral, with a middleman in each market area stipulating that the distribution of the manufacturer's product or products within that area is to be confined solely to that middleman. Exclusive agencies are common in marketing such lines as automobiles, musical instruments, household appliances, machine tools, high-quality men's and women's shoes, and branded men's clothing and furnishings. In return for the exclusive right to sell the product line, the middleman is expected to provide more aggressive selling (and sometimes product service, as in the case of appliances) than under milder forms of selective distribution or under mass distribution.

For many years, most such agreements were mutually exclusive; that is, they required the exclusive dealer to refrain from selling competitive lines. Section three of the Clayton Antitrust Act prohibits exclusive dealing when the effect is "to substantially lessen competition or tend to create a monopoly in any line of commerce." Until 1949, court interpretation of Section three was that exclusive dealing was not illegal unless the actual or probable monopolistic consequences of the agreements could be shown in court. However, in the Standard Oil Company of California case, the court made it clear that exclusive dealing contracts employed by the larger firms in an industry could result in a 'substantial lessening of competition' and would likely constitute a violation of the antitrust laws. The result has been to weaken the status of exclusive distribution, particularly of mutually exclusive contracts.

Implementing a policy of exclusive agency distribution present a number of problems for the sales executive. In some markets the most desirable dealers may be under agreement with another supplier, and the company may have to select a second or third rate dealer or open up its own outlet. Furthermore, some middlemen want no part of an exclusive agency contract, perhaps because of the history of exclusive agencies in the food field. If exclusive distribution is used at the wholesale level, the wholesaler may not reach certain highly desirable outlets on the dealer level. In addition, it is sometimes difficult to sever relations with a middleman whose performance is unsatisfactory, and some middlemen accept an exclusive agency merely to deprive a competitor it.

A policy of using exclusive agency distributors does, however, have a number of attractive features from the sales executive's standpoint. It should be fairly easy to develop distributor enthusiasm for the product and stimulate them to sell it aggressively. The manufacturer should be able to persuade the exclusive outlets to stock a more complete line and to service the product or handle repair and replacement parts. Relations between company sales personnel and the middlemen are likely to be of long duration and, after the agreements have been reached, salespeople can focus more on 'servicing' and less on 'selling.' The sales force should, therefore, be able to spend more time assisting dealers in planning local promotions of the product. Not to be overlooked either is the fact that with exclusive distribution, the sales force can be smaller and subject to more effective supervision and control.

Pricing Policies

Although the chief sales executive's role in formulating pricing policies generally is solely an advisory one, in almost all companies they bear the primary responsibility for implementation of pricing policies. The sales personnel in the field are, after all, the company employees whose jobs consist most directly of persuading buyers to accept the company's products at the prices asked by the company.

We shall discuss next the main types of pricing policies of direct interest to the sales department.

Policy on Pricing Relative to the Competition

Every company has a policy regarding the level at which its products are priced relative to the competition. If competition is principally price-based, a company generally sells its products at the same price as its competitors. If there is non price competition, each company chooses from among one of three alternative policies, discussed next.

Meeting the Competition

Meeting the competition is the most widely used policy. Companies competing on a nonprice basis simply meet competitor's prices, hoping thereby to minimise the use of price as a competitive weapon. A meeting-competition price policy does not mean meeting every competitor's prices, only the prices of important competitors-'important' in the sense that what such competitors do in their pricing may lure customers away.

Pricing above the Competition

Pricing above the competition is a less common policy but is appropriate in certain situations. Sometimes higher-than-average prices convey an impression of above-average product quality or prestige. Many buyers relate a product's quality to its price, especially when it is difficult to judge quality before actually buying. Almost always, the policy of pricing above the competition needs the support of strong promotion (both advertising and personal selling) by both the manufacturer and the middlemen.

One way in which the manufacturer using this policy obtains the strong promotional support of its dealers is, by setting relatively high list prices on its products. These prices, the prices which the manufacturer suggests the dealers use in reselling the products, are set at levels that include above-average markups. Middlemen pass the higher markups on to final buyers in the form of higher prices, but increased support by the dealers of the manufacturer's product often more than offsets the sales-depressing tendency of the higher prices and may even increase total unit sales. For a product to compete successfully at a price above the competition, it must generally either be so strongly differentiated that buyers believe it to be superior to competitor's offerings, or middlemen must enthusiastically and heavily promote it. The manufacturer's sales personnel play key roles, of course, in securing this kind of promotion from the middlemen.

Pricing under the Competition

Not many manufacturers, at least those with sales forces, willingly follow a policy of pricing under the competition. However, some manufacturers, such as a number in the clothing industry, price under their competitors and appear to have demonstrated, at least to their own satisfaction, that aggressive pricing increases market demand appreciably and helps to keep new competitors from entering the field. Sales executives, quite generally, dislike this type of pricing policy and contend that it tends to cause sales personnel to sell price more than the product.

Policy on Pricing Relative to Costs

Every company has a policy regarding the relationships between its products' prices and the underlying costs. Long-run sales revenues must cover all long-run costs, but short-run prices do not necessarily have to cover short-run costs. There are two main policy alternatives:

Full-cost Pricing

Under a full-cost pricing policy, no sale is made at a price lower than that covering total costs, including both variable costs and an allocated share of fixed costs. The reasoning is that if prices cover short-run costs, they will also cover long-run costs. Nevertheless, rigid adherence to this policy is not only difficult but often ridiculously stupid: the price buyers are willing to pay may bear little or no relationship to the seller's costs, and there are complex problems involved in determining 'real' costs. Furthermore, prices on items already in the inventory often must be cut below full cost in order to sell at all. Although most companies should seek to keep prices above short-run costs in *most* situations, they should also permit below-cost prices under certain conditions.

Contribution Pricing

A company with a contribution-pricing policy uses full-cost pricing whenever possible but will price, under certain conditions, at any level above the relevant incremental costs. Suppose, for instance, that a seller is offered a special contract to supply a large buyer, who will not pay the going price. The buyer may argue that the price differential is justified because of savings to the seller in selling time, credit costs, handling expenses, and the like. Still, the demanded price concession may exceed the likely savings, so that total sales dollars from the proposed transaction is not enough to cover total costs. In most such situations, the seller should accept the order if the resulting sales dollars are sufficient not only to cover all incremental costs but to make a contribution to fixed costs and/or profits. After all, current sales at the going price may already be large enough to cover the fixed costs, and the proposed sale at a special price will not raise fixed costs (assuming the incremental costs are all variable ones), so this sale need not bear an allocated share of fixed costs to yield net profit. In other words, as long as the proposed price more than covers the out-of-pocket costs of the transaction, the excess over these costs is profit. However, two important conditions should both be present for such offers to be accepted: (1) the company has the capacity and can put it to no more profitable use, and (2) the portion of the output sold below full cost is destined for a different market segment. Both conditions are important, but the second is critical to the continuance of prices at full cost or above for the bulk of the output.

Policy on Uniformity of Prices to Different Buyers

Concerning the prices charged to different buyers, companies make a choice between following (1) a one-price policy, under which an item is offered for sale to all similar buyers at the same price, or (2) a variable-price policy, under which the price to each buyer is determined by individual bargaining. In the United States, most marketers of consumer goods adhere to a one-price policy, even though many do vary their prices among different classes of customers and from one geographic region to the next. The variable-price policy, however, is in common use wherever individual sales transactions involve large sums, as characteristically happens in marketing many industrial goods. The bargaining power of individual buyers varies with the size of the transaction and, as in the industrial market, a large buyer generally represents a greater potential for future business than a small buyer, so a seller may make price concessions to gain or retain the large buyer's patronage.

There are two main reasons why sales executives consider the one-price policy attractive: (1) since prices are not negotiated with individual customers, sales personnel need to spend only a minimum amount of time discussing price and can devote nearly all their time to 'creative selling'; and (2) there is less risk of alienating customers because of preferential prices given others. Furthermore, the existence of laws prohibiting price discrimination, such as the Robinson-Patman Act, make it safer legally for a marketer to apply a one-price policy than a variable-price policy.

Policy on Resale Price Maintenance

A marketer distributing its products through middlemen follows a policy of (1) not attempting to suggest or maintain standardised resale prices on its products, or (2) seeking to control the prices at which middlemen resell its products. Such 'resale price maintenance' may be either informal or formal. Informal resale price maintenance takes the form of suggesting resale prices to middlemen - perhaps by printing the price on the package or through suggestions made by the manufacturer's sales personnel. Formal resale price maintenance is affected by using the provisions of various states 'fair-trade' laws. Informal price maintenance is easiest to implement when the marketer utilises some form of selective distribution, in as much as the difficulties of enforcement of suggested prices tend to multiply with increases in the number of middlemen handling the product. Marketers following policies of mass distribution, if they desire to maintain resale prices at all, generally find that they must take formal advantage of the resale-price maintenance (fair-trade) laws of the various states.

Policy on Use of Discounts

Trade Discounts

A manufacturer selling to more than one class of middleman, such as both to wholesalers and retailers, may quote different prices, that is, offer different 'trade discounts,' to each class of customer. Under the federal laws prohibiting price discriminations, discounts, to be legal, must be made available on proportionately equal terms to all similar customers. Wholesalers and retailers are not similar customers; each group performs a different distributive function. For this reason, the law permits a manufacturer to charge a higher price to retailers than to wholesalers, even though some buyers in each class may buy in the same quantities. A company's policy on trade discounts depends on the importance (to the manufacturer) of each class of buyer and on the relative bargaining power of each class of buyer as a whole.

Quantity Discounts

Quantity discounts are price reductions granted for purchases in a stated quantity or quantities, and are normally aimed to increase the quantities customers buy. Through such price reductions, sellers try to increase sales by passing on to buyers part of the savings that can result from large purchases. These savings can be considerable, for it may take little, if any, more of a salesperson's time to sell a very large order than to sell a small one. The same holds for order processing, order filling, billing and transportation costs.

The firm using a quantity discount policy must keep two legal restrictions in mind: (1) the discounts must reflect actual savings - the price reduction can be no greater than the actual savings resulting from the larger quantity ordered; and (2) the discounts must be available on proportionately equal terms to all similar purchasers.

Geographical Pricing Policies

One type of pricing policy of particular interest to sales executives is that regarding "who should pay the freight for delivering the product to buyers." The company's answer to this question is important to the sales executive, because it directly affects price quotations given to buyers in different geographical areas. In general, the farther away the customer is from the factory, the greater are the freight charges for a given size of order. No matter what policy the company adopts on this matter, freight differentials are reflected one way or another in price quotations. Likewise, regardless of the company's policy on payment of shipping charges, its administration is the sales executive's responsibility. There are three policy alternatives: (1) F.O.B., or 'free on board' pricing, under which the customer pays the freight; (2) delivered pricing, under which the seller pays the freight; and (3) freight absorption, a compromise between F.O.B. and delivered pricing used in certain competitive situations but not described here in detail.

F.O.B. Pricing

The marketer using this policy quotes its selling prices at the factory (or other point from which it makes sales), and buyers pay all the freight charges. Each buyer, in other words, adds the appropriate freight charges to the quoted F.O.B. factory price and, thus, determines the total delivered cost. Thus, F.O.B. pricing results in variations in the resale price that middlemen put on the product in different geographical areas. In consumer-goods marketing, F.O.B. pricing is widely used for items that are heavy or bulky relative to their value - for example, canned foods and fresh vegetables. In marketing such industrial goods as raw materials and heavy machinery, F.O.B. pricing is also in widespread use.

Delivered Pricing

The marketer using a delivered pricing policy pays all freight charges and includes them in its price quotations to buyers. In other words, the price is really on 'F.O.B.

destination' price, and the net return to the seller varies with the buyer's location. Delivered pricing generally is most appropriate when freight charges account for only a small part of the product's price. It is also usually a necessary policy when a marketer attempts to suggest or maintain resale prices. Standardised resale prices are most likely to be obtained if middlemen and assured of uniform markups, regardless of their location.

The simple form of delivered pricing policy provides a uniform nationwide delivered price - sometimes called a 'postage stamp' price. Makers of chewing gum, candy bars, and many drug items, particularly patent medicines, use postage stamp pricing. Because under this policy all middlemen pay the same price to the manufacturer, the resale price should be roughly the same figure throughout the entire market.

A variation of delivered pricing is zone pricing, under which the market is divided into zones and different prices quoted to buyers in each zone, depending upon the zone's distance from the factory. The manufacturer still builds the freight charges into its quoted price (as in any delivered pricing policy), but it quotes different prices to buyers situated in different geographical zones.

Policy on Price Leadership

All marketers should decide whether, as a matter of policy, they will initiate or follow price changes. In some industries there are well-established patterns of price leadership and following. In selling basic industrial materials, such as steel and cement, one company is the price leader and is usually the first to raise or cut prices; other industry members simply follow - or, sometimes, fail to follow, as sometimes happens in the case of a price increase, thus causing the leader to reconsider and perhaps to cancel the announced increase. Similar patterns exist in marketing such consumer products as gasoline and bakery goods, where usually market by market, one company serves as the price leader and others follow. Generally, price leaders have rather large market shares and price followers, small market shares.

Even when final buyers (for example, ultimate consumers) are not particularly price conscious, most producers know that the middlemen handling their products are extremely sensitive to price changes. In response to even very small price changes, up or down, they will consider switching suppliers. Thus, even the marketer of a consumer product competing on a nonprice basis must be alert to impending price changes; the important policy question is whether to initiate or simply to follow price changes. The answer depends upon the marketer's relative market position and the image of leadership that it desires to build and maintain.

Product-line Pricing Policy

Pricing the individual members of a product line calls for certain policy decisions. The different items in a product line tend to 'compete' with each other; that is, a buyer buying one member of the line usually does so to the exclusion of others. One policy decision relates to the amount of 'price space' that should exist between the prices of individual members of the line. Having the right amount of price space is critical; too little may confuse buyers, and too much may leave 'gaps' into which competitors can move and make sales. Sales executives contribute major inputs to this decision through their knowledge of the market, of buyers' motivations, and of competitors' offerings and prices.

Other important policy decisions concern the pricing of the 'top' (highest priced item) and the 'bottom' (lowest priced item) in the line. Generally, companies try to price the 'in-between' members of the line so that they account for the greatest sales volume, using the bottom of the line as a traffic builder and the top of the line as a prestige builder. As the traffic builder, the lowest-priced item ordinarily affects the line's total sales far more than the price of any other item in the line. Price changes on it tend to directly affect the sales of other item in the line. Price changes on it tend to directly affect the sales of other line members. A price increase on the traffic builder tends to cause higher sales on other line members. The same is true for the prestige builder; a change in the price of the top of the line tends to strongly influence sales of other line members.

Competitive-bidding Policy

In purchasing certain products, industrial and governmental buyers customarily solicit competitive bids from several potential suppliers and award the business to the bidder offering the best proposal. A proposal may be selected as best for a number of reasons (for example, price, delivery dates, reputation for quality), depending on which is most important to the buyer. In some industries, competitive bidding is the general rule, and individual manufacturers have virtually no choice but to participate. But in other industries, only a part of the volume is sold on this basis, and each manufacturer must decide whether it is to its advantage to participate. For example, a typewriter manufacturer who sells to industry on a uniform price basis must participate in competitive bidding if it wants orders from governmental agencies (since government purchasing agents at all levels of government are ordinarily required to request competitive bids on most of their purchases). However, many manufacturers believe that competitive bidding reduces competition to almost entirely a price basis; consequently, they prefer to avoid this kind of business, unless the share of the total market involved is too large to ignore.

In companies that do participate in competitive bidding, the sales executive and the sales personnel play particularly important roles. Their close contact with the market puts them in a good position to estimate just how low a particular price must be to obtain the order. Furthermore, the long-term relationships developed between salespersons and their customers are very important in giving the company a chance to make a 'second bid' in those cases where industrial buyers give favoured suppliers the chance to meet lower bids submitted by competitors. This chance does not exist in competitive bidding for government business, where closed bids are usually specified (that is, all bids are opened at the same time and there is no chance for high bidders to adjust their quotes downward). But an effective salesperson can often remove competition from closed government bids by persuading the purchasing agent of the value of a differentiating characteristic of the product so that the purchasing agent will include this characteristic in the written specification supplied to potential bidders.

❑❑❑

3

Personal - Selling

Selling under Different Market Settings

An organisation's competitive posture in the market place is determined both by its overall sales policy and by the effectiveness with which this policy is implemented. Sales policies provide the general guidelines for taking decisions on the personal-selling effort, while personal selling strategies are adoptions of sales policies, individualised tailorings of personal-selling decisions to fit specific sales situations.

Different industries provide different types of competitive settings within which individual firms must work. From industry to industry, there are important differences with respect to whether the industry is new or old and whether the number of competitors is small or large. Management experts identify four basic kinds of competitive settings:

(1) Monopoly

(2) Competition

(3) Monopolistic Competition

(4) Oligopolistic Competition.

Different components of overall selling strategy assume different levels of importance in each of above competitive settings. In the following discussion, we study the personal selling component of overall selling strategy with each kind of competitive setting.

Monopoly

In this market situation neither the monopolist nor the organisation selling a radically new and different product in its market-pioneering life-cycle stage has direct competitors. But both the monopolist and the innovating marketer have indirect competitors; both must via with sellers in other industries for the same prospects' interest and buying decisions, the monopolist on a long-term basis and the innovating marketer for the limited period it has free from direct competition. Both the monopolist and the innovating marketer must initiate and stimulate primary demand - that is, demand for the product category - through promotional (personal selling and advertising) strategies aimed to influence final buyers and middlemen. Both need distribution strategies providing for marketing channels, middlemen's cooperation, and the product's physical distribution; and the putting into effect of these distribution strategies requires the effective implementation of personal-selling strategy in terms of both kind and number of sales personnel. Both require a pricing strategy; the monopolist (at least in theory) being free to maximise profit through 'charging what the traffic will bear,' the innovating marketer choosing between either a price-skimming or a penetration-pricing strategy, depending mainly upon how soon it expects direct competitors to enter the market. Here, too, putting into effect the chosen pricing strategy calls for the effective implementation of personal-selling strategy by sales executives and sales personnel alike. Further, both the monopolist and the innovating marketer seek to integrate their individual product, distribution, promotion (including personal selling and advertising), and pricing strategies into overall marketing strategies (that is, competitive postures) consistent with their long-term goals. Such consistency is obtained only when all elements of overall strategy are 'in balance.'

Pure Competition

Economists define pure competition as a market setting with large numbers of buyers and sellers, none of whom is powerful enough to control or to influence the prevailing market price. In this definition, the economist assumes, among other things, that (1) no single buyer or seller is so large relative to the market that it can appreciably affect the product's total demand or supply; (2) all seller's products are identical in every respect, so buyers are indifferent as to which seller they buy from; (3) no artificial restraints on prices of any kind exist (there is no governmental price fixing or administering of prices by individual companies, trade associations, labour unions, or others); and (4) all buyers are always informed about all seller's prices.

If these assumptions held true in the real world, there would be no need for a company to concern itself with marketing strategies of any kind. Each seller would be too small to gain business through price cutting at the expense of its competitors, and if it did cut the price, they would immediately match the cut. No seller could compete by offering a 'better' product, because product differentiation is ruled out. It would be futile for a seller to push its product through personal selling or stimulate its sale through advertising or other promotion, inasmuch as all potential buyers are already fully informed and buy only on the basis of price. Because the economist also implicitly assumes that sellers and buyers are in direct contact, no seller would need to worry about marketing channels or physical distribution. Under the type of competitive setting visualised in the economist's definition of pure competition, there would be no need for marketing strategies of any kind. In this competitive setting, then, there also would be no need for personal-selling strategy or for sales personnel. The real world contains no known instances of industries operating under conditions of pure competition, and we need not concern ourselves further here with this kind of competitive setting.

Monopolistic Competition

Most modern marketers in most situations operate in competitive settings under conditions that approximate monopolistic competition, which means that some or all of the assumptions of pure competition do no hold. More precisely, monopolistic competition exists when there is a large number of sellers of a generic kind of product but each seller's brand is in some way differentiated from every other seller's brand. Furthermore, under monopolistic competition, it is comparatively easy for additional competitors to enter the market, such as for retailers to enter as private-level competitors. This competitive setting describes that of many products during late phases of their market growth and during much of their market-maturity life-cycle stages.

Nearly every seller's brand of product, whether it be nailpolish remover or pet food, can be differentiated (at least in final buyers's minds) from competing brands. Most ultimate consumers appear convinced that different brands of even such 'identical' products as aspirin, table salt, and flour are not exactly alike, providing individual marketers with opportunities to build brand preferences among buyers and hence to control a share of the market. Furthermore, most ultimate consumers (and even many industrial users) are not really fully informed – frequently not even adequately informed – about the offerings of competing sellers. Seller of such products seek to differentiate their 'market offerings' through individualising one or several components of overall marketing strategy. Unique packaging may serve to differentiate the product (for example, table or picnic-sized shakers of salt); an unusual distribution method, such as house-to-house selling of cosmetics, may serve to differentiate the product's distribution; various pricing gimmicks, such as 'cents-off' pricing and fair-trade pricing, may differentiate the product's pricing; but usually the main way in which sellers of products that are in the market-growth and market-maturity stages differentiate them is through promotional strategy. Advertising is used to differentiate the brand in the minds of final buyers and to stimulate selective demand, while personal selling sees to it that the desired distribution intensity is secured and maintained and that middlemen provide the needed 'push' in the product's behalf.

Competitive settings characterised by monopolistic competition provide not only marketing opportunities but clearly require skill in planning and implementing overall marketing strategy. Whereas the key element in the overall marketing strategy for such products is the ability to differentiate the product, even if ever so slightly, in some way(s), appropriate promotional strategy (usually some blend of advertising and personal selling) is the critical element in implementing such an overall marketing strategy. In this type of competitive setting, advertising's role appears most often to be that of relating market messages to final buyers, while personal selling's role is that of servicing the distribution network and stimulating promotional efforts by the middlemen.

Oligopolistic Competition

Increasing numbers of marketers operate under conditions approximating oligopolistic competition, a competitive setting within which the number of competitors is small enough that they are individually identified and known to each other and it is difficult for new competitors to enter the market. Each competitor is a large-enough organisation and has a large-enough market share that changes in its overall marketing strategy have direct repercussions on the others. Each marketer in an oligopolistic industry must weigh the possible reactions of each of its competitors in formulating and implementing its own overall marketing strategy. Oligopolistic competition tends to develop in the marketing of many products either during a late phase of their market growth or an early phase of their market maturity.

In the United States oligopolies exist in such industries as automobiles, appliances, soap and detergents, and shoes in the consumer-goods field, and in steel, aluminum, textile machinery, and machine tools in the industrial-goods field. There is a strong trend for the more successful firms to keep on growing, and for the less successful to fail or disappear (through merger). The soap and auto industries provide dramatic examples, both having been reduced from numerous competitors to a very small group in fairly recent times. Although governmental authorities try continually to discourage the merger movement as a threat to 'free competition,' the drift toward oligopoly continues but through the slower process of expansion by the successful, and failure or withdrawal by the others.

Oligopoly produces the most aggressive kind of competition. When a few large companies dominate an industry, the competitive moves of any one can significantly affect the entire market. When, for instance, one competitor introduces a new variation of a basic product (such as a new scent in hand soap), the other competitors risk a rapid loss in market share if they do not respond appropriately and almost at once. For this reason, competitors' actions are watched closely, and marketing changes by one firm are almost certain to be matched or otherwise countered by its competitors. Changes in one competitor's product, in its distribution, in its promotion – if they hold some promise of increasing its market share – are imitated, improved upon, or otherwise countered by its competitors as rapidly as they can launch their counter offensives. Price changes by individual industry members can be and often are matched by others almost immediately. Industry-wide price adjustments are often made so quickly that they appear to result from collusion, when, in fact, there has been none whatever. Personal selling strategy under oligopolistic competition plays important roles in building and maintaining dealer cooperation, in servicing the distribution network, and in gathering information on competitors' activities. Again, as happens under monopolistic competition, promotional strategy generally features both advertising and personal selling, with both playing highly critical roles, particularly with respect to the successful implementation of overall marketing strategy.

Objectives and Strategy of Personal-Selling

Objectives

Personal-selling objectives are of two broad types, qualitative and quantitative. The qualitative objectives vary importantly and directly with the kind of competitive setting and mainly concern the nature of the contribution management expects personal selling to make in achieving overall long-term company objectives. Qualitative personal-selling objectives influence both the nature of the sales job (that is, the kind of sales personnel needed) and the size of the sales force. For instance, a company that expects its salespeople to do the entire selling job (as when it has no other elements in its promotional mix) needs a different kind of sales staff, and a larger staff, than a company which expects its salespeople only to 'service' already existing accounts and back them up with heavy advertising. Qualitative objectives usually are long-term objectives and are carried over from one promotional period to the next. But when a qualitative objective is changed, it involves changing the nature of the sales job and usually the size of the sales force as well.

In contrast to the qualitative personal-selling objectives, the quantitative objectives assigned to personal selling are short-term and are adjusted from promotional period to promotional period. The sales-volume objective – the dollar or unit sales volume that management expects the company to obtain during a particular promotional period – is by far the most critical quantitative personal-selling objective. Regardless of the competitive setting within which a company operates, if it has a quantitative personal-selling objective at all, it will be one relating to the sales volume desired for the period. Most companies, too, benefit from assigning other types of quantitative objectives to personal selling, as, for instance, one directing that sales volume be obtained in ways that contribute to profit objectives (for example, by selling the 'proper' mix of products). In monopolistic and oligopolistic competitive settings, most companies assign still other types of quantitative objectives, including ones specifying the securing and/or retaining of a certain market share. Quantitative personal-selling objectives have direct implications both for the nature of the sales job and the number of sales personnel needed. For instance, a company that increases its sales-volume objective significantly must also expect its sales force to do a more effective selling job (that is, to change the nature of their job) or expect to increase the number of salespeople or, perhaps, expect to do both.

Personal-Selling Strategy

Sales policies are the guidelines set up by management within which the company is to seek to reach both its qualitative and quantitative personal-selling objectives. They provide general guidance with respect to what to sell (product policies), whom to sell to (distribution policies), and the terms of sales (pricing policies). Decisions on what to sell and who to sell to not only shape the fundamental nature of a company but are important determinants both of the kind of sales personnel needed and their total number (the two components of personal-selling strategy). Pricing policies, too, have an important impact, especially on the kind of sales staff needed - salespeople in the field are the ones who have to persuade target buyers not only to accept the company's products but at the prices asked. The exact nature of sales policies, like personal-selling objectives, vary somewhat with the competitive setting of the industry, but it is of critical importance that they be appropriate to a company's particular situation under conditions of monopolistic or oligopolistic competition.

Determining the Kind of Sales Personnel Needed

Management makes one of its two key decisions on personal selling strategy when it decides the kind of sales force that the company should employ. A clear determination of the kind of salesperson required is an important prerequisite to recruitment and selection. There is a great diversity among selling jobs, ranging from truck-driver route selling to selling complex industrial installations such as lathes and presses. Different selling jobs require different levels of selling ability, training, and technical knowledge, and unique marketing factors (such as the nature of the products, buying practices and motivations of customers and prospects, and strengths and weaknesses of competitors) cause each company in each industry to have individualised requirements as to the kind of sales-person best fitted to serve its needs.

In determining the kind of sales staff best fitted to serve a company's marketing needs, we must thoroughly understand what its salespeople will be expected to accomplish - objectives of their jobs and the tasks necessary to achieve them. Knowing the sales-person's job means knowing the particular job for the particular salesperson, knowledge that enables management to avoid "putting square pegs into round holes." It helps management, in other words, in fitting the job to the person and the person to the job.

Product-Market Analysis

No one person is capable of selling all kinds of products to all kinds of customers. In one situation, an individual may be trained to sell one or a few products to many kinds of customers. In a second situation, the same individual may be trained to sell a wide line of products to one or a few kinds of customers. It is possible to hire, or to hire and train, salespeople either as product specialists or as market specialists. An advisable step in analysing the sales job, then, is to delineate the precise nature of product-market interactions. One way is to construct a 'product-market grid.' In actual use, of course, such grids are constructed showing much finer details of product-market interactions; this demands thorough analysis and classification both of markets and products. Note that the various product-market 'boxes' on the grid indicate the different customers who might be sold the different products. As management decides which customers should be sold which products, some boxes are blacked in, others left empty. The result helps answer the question: Should our sales personnel be product specialists, market specialists, or a combination? Product specialisation usually is indicated when the product is highly technical, requiring salespeople to advise on uses and applications. Market specialisation generally is called for when the product is nontechnical but different kinds of customers have unique buying problems, require special sales approaches, or need special service. In many cases detailed study of product-market grids reveals that sales personnel need not only considerable knowledge of the product line and its applications but skill in dealing with various kinds of customers.

In addition to product-market interactions, other elements in a company's marketing situation may affect the calibre of salesperson required. If most customers are large, for instance, salespeople may need different talents than if most customers are small. Sometimes, too, the geographical location of a territory has a bearing on the best type of sales-person for it, particularly where local prejudice exists in favour of 'native,' as opposed to 'outsiders.' If management considers these or similar elements important, it may be advisable to construct appropriate grids to assist in the analysis.

Analysis of Salesperson's Role in Securing Orders

The nature of the role that a company expects its sales personnel to play in securing orders influences the kind of sales staff it should have. Even though all salespeople must seek orders aggressively in some situations while in others they need only take orders coming their way, the relative emphasis on order taking and order getting varies in different kinds of selling environments. The driver-salesperson for a soft drink bottling company is primarily an order taker, because the product has been strongly presold to consumers and retailers reorder automatically. The encyclopaedia salesperson calling on householders most often functions as an order getter, since getting the order is this sales-person's main goal. If the promotional strategy of a manufacturer is to rely heavily upon advertising to attract business and build demand, marketing channels are likely to include several layers of middlemen, and the role of the manufacturer's salesperson is likely to be that of order taker primarily and order getter only incidentally. The opposite situation obtains when advertising is used mainly to back up personal selling – marketing channels contain a minimum number of layers of middlemen, and the salesperson's role is chiefly one of order getting. Depending on whether promotional strategy places major reliance on personal selling or advertising, salespeople may be either active or passive forces in securing orders.

There are cases both in consumer-goods and industrial-goods marketing in which the salesperson plays only a minor and indirect role in securing orders, the salesperson's major role being concerned with other matters. In consumer-goods marketing, the missionary salesperson's major role is to assist middlemen in their efforts to make sales to their customers. Orders from customers, then, result indirectly, rather than directly, from the missionary salesperson's efforts. In industrial-goods marketing, the 'sales engineer' plays two major roles: (1) advisor to middlemen and customers on technical-product features and applications, and (2) design consultant to middlemen and industrial users on installations or processes incorporating the manufacturer's products. Sales engineers also secure orders indirectly, rather than directly, and as the result of playing their major role as advisors and design consultants.

Choice of Basic Selling Style

Differences in many marketing factors cause each company to have rather individualised requirements as to the kind of salesperson that is best for it to have in its employ. These differences cause each company to expect its own sales staff to play somewhat unique roles (at least in some respects) even relative to 'similar' companies employing 'similar' kinds of sales personnel. Nevertheless, it is revealing to group sales job roles into a limited number of categories. Specifically, sales roles can be grouped into four basic styles of selling that cut, to a large degree, across industry and company boundaries: trade selling, missionary selling, technical selling, and new-business selling.

Trade Selling

The trade sales-person develops long-term relations with a relatively stable group of customers. For the most part, this style of selling is low key with little or no pressure, and the job tends to be rather dull and routine. This selling style, which predominates in marketing food and apparel and in wholesaling, applies primarily to products that have well-established markets. In such case, advertising and other forms of promotion are often more important components of overall marketing strategy than is personal selling. One important responsibility of the trade salesperson is to help customers build up their volume through giving them promotional assistance. For example, the salesperson for a line of breakfast cereals devoted much time to promotional work with retailers and wholesalers - taking inventory, refilling shelves, suggesting reorders, setting up displays, and the like.

Missionary Selling

The missionary salesperson's responsibility is to increase the company's sales volume by assisting customers with their selling efforts. The missionary salesperson is concerned only incidentally with securing orders, since the orders obtained result from the missionary's primary public relations and promotional efforts with customers of the customers (indirect customers). The missionary salesperson's job is to persuade indirect customers to buy from the company's direct customers. For example, the salesperson for a pharmaceutical manufacturer calls on retail druggists to acquaint them with a new product and to urge them to stock it. Thus, the missionary seeks to persuade them to buy from drug wholesalers, who are the company's direct customers. In some situations, missionary sales staff members call on individuals and institutions who do not buy the product themselves but who influence its purchases by others. The medical 'detail man' who calls on doctors and hospitals to acquaint them with new drugs is an example. Missionary selling, like trade selling, is low key and generally does not require high-level technical training or ability.

Technical Selling

The technical salesperson deals primarily with the company's established accounts, and the main job objective is to increase their volume of purchase by providing technical advice and assistance. The technical salesperson performs advisory functions similar to those of the missionary salesperson but, in addition, this type of sales-person normally sells direct to industrial users and other buyers. The technical salesperson devotes considerable time to acquainting industrial users with technical characteristics of products and with product applications and to helping them design installations or processes that incorporate the company's products. In this style of selling, the ability to identify, analyse, and solve customer's problems is important. Technical salespeople often specialise, either by products or markets. In selling heavy made-to-order installations, such as steam turbines and electric generators, different technical salespersons work with different items in the product line. Other technical salespeople specialise in servicing either industrial accounts or government procurement agencies.

New-business Selling

The new-business salesperson's main responsibility is to find new customers - that is, to convert prospects into customers. The salesperson specialising in new-business selling needs to be unusually creative and ingenious and possesses a high degree of resourcefulness. Few companies, however, have sales personnel who do nothing but new-business selling; most firms expect their regular sales staff, who primarily do trade selling, to do new-business selling also. However, since it is rare for the same individual to possess both needed sets of talents and because there is a common tendency for salespeople to neglect new-business selling in favour of servicing established accounts, some experts advocate the specialisation of sales personnel into two separate groups, one to concentrate on retaining existing accounts, and the other to focus on converting prospects into customers.

Determining the Size of the Sales Force

Management makes the second of its two key decisions on personal selling strategy when it decides the size of the sales force that the company should have. Having determined the kind of salesperson that should best fit the company's needs, management must now determine how many such salespersons should be employed to meet the company's sales volume and profit objectives. If the company employs too few salespersons, opportunities for sales and profits go unexploited, and if it employs too many, excessive expenditures for personal selling (even though they may bring in additional sales) reduce net profits. In practice, it is extremely difficult, perhaps impossible, to determine the exact number of salespersons that a particular company should have; however, there are three basic approaches used in approximating this number: (1) the workload method, (2) the sales-potential method, and (3) the incremental method. Each approach provides needed insights on the 'right size' of sales force, although none produces a definitive answer to the 'how-many-salespersons' question.

Workload Method

In the workload method of determining sales-force size, the basic assumption is that all sales personnel should shoulder equal workloads. Management first estimates the total workload involved in covering the company's entire market, then divides by the work load that an individual salesperson should be able to handle, thus determining the total number of salespeople required. Companies applying this approach generally assume that the interactions of three major factors - customer size, sales-volume potential, and travel load - determine the total work load involved in covering the entire market. There are six steps involved in applying the workload approach, as shown in the following example:

(1) *Classify customers, both present and prospective, into sales-volume-potential categories:* (Classification criteria, other than sales volume or sales-volume potential, can be used as long as it is possible to distinguish the differences in selling effort required for each class). For purposes of this example, assume that there are 880 present and prospective customers, classified by sales-volume potential as follows:

Class A - large	150 accounts
Class B - medium	220
Class C - small	510

(2) *Decide on the length of time per sales call and desired all frequencies on each class:* (Several inputs are used in making these two decisions - for example, personal judgement, the opinions of sales personnel, and actual time studies). For purposes of this example, assume that both present and prospective customers require the same amounts of time per sales call and the same frequencies per year as follows:

Class A : 60 minutes/call × 48 calls/year = 48 hours/year
Class B : 30 minutes/call × 24 calls/year = 12 hours/year
Class C : 15 minutes/call × 12 calls/year = 3 hours/year

(3) *Calculate the total work load involved in covering the entire market:* In our example, this calculation is:

Class A : 150 accounts × 48 hours/year	=	7,200 hours
Class B : 220 accounts × 12 hours/year	=	2,640 hours
Class C : 510 accounts × 3 hours/year	=	1,530 hours
Total		11,370 hours

(4) *Determine the total work time available per salesperson:* Suppose that management decides that salespeople should work 40 hours per week, 48 weeks per year (allowing 4 weeks for vacations, holidays, sickness, etc.), then each salesperson has available:

40 hours/week × 48 weeks = 1,920 hours/year

(5) *Divide the total work time available per salesperson by task:* Assume that management specifies that sales personnel should apportion their time as follows:

Selling tasks	45%	864 hours
Nonselling tasks	30	576
Travelling	25	480
	100%	1,920 hours

(6) *Calculate the total number of salespeople needed:* This is a matter of dividing the total market workload by the total selling time available per salesperson:

$$\frac{11{,}370 \text{ hours}}{864 \text{ hours}} = 13 + \text{sales people needed}$$

The workload approach to determining the size of the sales force is attractive to practicing sales executives. Perhaps, the main reasons are that it is easy to understand and easy to apply to practical situations. Such large firms as Celanese, IBM and AT&T all have been reported to use this approach.

However, there is an inherent flaw in the workload approach. As usually applied, this approach disregards profit as an explicit consideration; but, of course, it is possible for management to take profit criteria into account in determining lengths and frequencies of sales calls. In appraising this approach, P. Kotler concludes that:

> The optimality of the overall solution depends upon management's accuracy in estimating appropriate call frequencies for different-size accounts. Actually, desirable all frequencies

> depend on aspects other than account size, such as the probable response of the account to additional effort, the costs of servicing, and the gross margin on the product mix purchased by the account.

Still another shortcoming inherent in this approach lies in the assumption that not only all sales personnel should have the same work load but that they all can and will utilise their time with equal efficiency. Although a relation exists between the amount of time spent on calling on an account and the size of the order received, some salespeople are able to accomplish more in a shorter time than others can. In other words, as experienced sales executives assert, the "quality of time invested in a sales call" is at least as important as the "quantity of time spent on a sales call."

Sales-potential Method

The sales-potential method of determining the size of the sales force is based on the assumption that performance of the set of activities contained in the salesperson's job description represents one sales-personnel unit, not necessarily that of any particular sales-person. A particular salesperson may represent either more or less than one sales-personnel unit. If the individual's performance is excellent, that individual may do the job of more than one unit; if the individual's performance is below par, he or she may do less. However, if management expects all company sales personnel to perform as specified in the job description, then the number of salespersons required equal the number of units of sales personnel required. Generally, it must be noted, sales job descriptions are constructed on management's assumption that they describe what the average salesperson with average performance will accomplish. With what assumption, then, one can estimate the number of dollars of sales volume that each salesperson (that is, each sales-personnel unit) should produce. Dividing this amount into forecasted sales volume—the company's sales-volume objective—and allowing for sales-force turnover results in an estimate of the number of salespeople needed. These relationships are summarised in the equation

$$N = \frac{S}{P} + T(S/P)$$

This reduces to $$N = \frac{S}{P}(1 + T)$$

Where

N = number of sales-personnel unit.

S = forecasted sales volume.

P = estimated sales productivity of one sales-personnel unit.

T = allowance for rate of sales-force turnover.

Consider, for example, a firm with forecasted sales of Rs. 1 million, estimated sales productivity per sales-personnel unit of Rs. 1,00,000 and an estimated annual rate of sales-force turnover of 10 per cent. Inserting these figures in the equation, we have

$$N = \frac{\text{Rs. } 10{,}00{,}000}{\text{Rs. } 1{,}00{,}000} \times 1.10$$

$$N = 11 \text{ sales-personnel units}$$

This is a highly simplified model for determining the size of a sales force. It does not, for instance, include the lead times required for seeking out, hiring, and training salespeople up to the desired level of sales productivity. Actual planning models have built-in lead and lag relations to allow for such requirements. If two months of full-time training are required to bring a new salesperson up to the desired productivity, recruiting must lead actual need for the new salesperson by two months. Another assumption implicit in this simple model is that sales potentials are identical in all territories, which is similar to the assumption that the number of sales-personnel units required is the same as the number of salespersons needed; where this assumption does not hold, the model should be adjusted accordingly.

Difficulties in making estimates for this model vary both with the factor being estimated (N, S, P, or T) and with the company. The crucial estimate for the sales productivity of one unit of sales manpower relies heavily on the accuracy and completeness of the sales job description; it depends also on management's appraisal of what reasonably may be expected of those who fill the position. Estimating the sales-force-turnover rate is mainly a matter of reviewing previous experience and anticipating such changes as retirements and promotions. Both the estimates for unit sales productivity and the sales-force-turnover rate require management to have some means of evaluating the efficiency of individual salespersons, and of determining the probabilities that individuals will remain with or leave the sales force during the planning period.

The estimate for forecasted sales volume deserves special comment. In many situations, the magnitude of the sales forecast is itself influenced by the planned size of the sales force. Indeed, since it takes time to add significant numbers to the sales force, a realistic sales forecast must take into account the number of salespersons (or sales-personnel units) likely to be at management's disposal during the planning period. In a new and rapidly growing company, potential sales volume often depends chiefly on the number and ability of its sales staff. Then management actually may derive its sales forecast by multiplying the estimated sales productivity of its average salesperson by the number it has, can expect to keep, and can recruit and train during the planning period. By contrast, as a company expands distribution geographically and its growth rate slows down, the procedure reverses itself. Under these circumstances, the number of salespersonnel units required is determined by making the sales forecast first, and dividing this by the expected sales productivity of an individual salesperson, making adjustments in the process for anticipated sales-force turnover, lead times for recruiting and training, and other relevant factors.

Incremental Method

The incremental method represents the most conceptually correct approach to the problem of determining the size of the sales force. It is based on one main proposition: net profits will increase when additional sales personnel are added *if* the incremental sales revenues exceed the incremental costs incurred. Thus, to apply this method, one needs two important items of information, incremental revenue and incremental costs.

To illustrate the application of the incremental method, assume this situation. A certain company has found that its total sales volume varies directly and significantly with the number of salespeople it has in the field. Its costs of goods sold do not vary significantly with increases in sales, but hold steady at 65 per cent of sales. All company sales personnel receive a straight salary (Rs. 10,000 annually per person) and in addition are paid commissions of 5 per cent on the sales volume they generate. In addition, each salesperson receives a travel and expense allowance of Rs. 6,000 per year, that is Rs. 500 per month. The company now has 15 people on its sales force and wants to determine whether it should add additional staff. Its sales executives have estimated that the following increases in sales volume, costs of goods sold, and gross margin would result from the addition of the sixteenth, seventeenth, eighteenth, and nineteenth salespersons:

With the Addition	*There will be Additional*				
of Salesperson No:	*[Sales Volume of:]*	–	*[Cost of Goods Sold of:]*	=	*Gross Margin of:*
16	Rs. 2,00,000	–	Rs. 1,30,000	=	Rs. 70,000
17	1,50,000	–	97,500	=	52,500
18	1,00,000	–	65,000	=	35,000
19	50,000	–	32,500	=	17,500

The next step is to calculate the *net profit contribution* resulting from the addition of each salesperson, as summarised in the following table:

With the Addition of Salesperson No.:	*Gross Margin of:*	–	*Sales Salaries of:*	+	*Commissions of:*	+	*Travel and Expenses Allowances of:*	=	*Net Profit Contribution of:*
16	Rs.70, 000	–	(Rs.10,000	+	Rs.10,000	+	Rs.6,000)	=	Rs. 44,000
17	52,500	–	(10,000	+	7,500	+	6,000)	=	29,000
18	35,000	–	(10,000	+	5,000	+	6,000)	=	14,000
19	17,500	–	(10,000	+	2,500	+	6,000)	=	-1,000

Adding the eighteenth salesperson results in an additional net profit contribution of Rs. 14,000, but adding the nineteenth salesperson produces a negative net profit contribution of Rs. 1,000. Thus, in this illustration the optimal size of sales force is 18 people.

Although this method is the most conceptually correct, it is also the most difficult to apply in the real world. It requires, first, that the company develops a sales-response function which can be used to approximate (in terms of sales volume) the market's behaviour in relation to alternative levels of personal-selling effort. A sales-response function is a quantitative expression which describes the relationship between the amount of personal-selling effort and the resulting sales volume. For the response function to be a useful tool in setting the size of the sales force, sales volume must be sensitive to changes in the number of sales personnel. Not many companies yet have the degree of research sophistication required for the development of sales-response functions, but there is some evidences that companies are beginning to apply the basic concept. Furthermore, doubt exists that the incremental method is applicable in situations where personal selling is not the primary means of making sales – that is, in cases where other forms of promotion, such as advertising, have stronger influences on sales volume than does personal selling effort. Two additional problems in applying this approach are noted by T.R. Wotruba, "It fails to account for possible competitive reactions as well as for the long-term 'investment' effect of personal selling effort."

Individualising Selling Strategies for Each Customer

Ultimately, the acid test of the basic appropriateness of personal-selling strategy comes when particular salespeople interact with particular customers. From the composite of all such interactions evolves the company's achievement of its personal-selling objectives. Management makes one critical decision on personal-selling strategy when it determines the kind of salesperson best fitted to serve the company's marketing needs. It makes another critical decision when it determines the number of salespeople that should make up the company sales force. But after these two key decisions are implemented - after the desired number of the field - each salesperson must individualise his or her own dealings with each customer. The job, when boiled down to its essentials, is to influence customer behaviour in ways that both benefit the customer and contribute to the achievement of the company's personal-selling objectives.

Regardless of whether the salesperson's major role is that of order getter or order taker and regardless of the 'basic selling style,' the extent of the salesperson's success (in performing the job) still depends on the outcome of interactions with the customers. Each time the salesperson comes into contact with a customer, the salesperson says certain things, does certain things, and behaves and reacts in certain ways to what the customer says and does. What the salesperson says and does and how the salesperson behaves and reacts to the customers' behaviour should, and generally does, vary from one sales call to the next. The nature of the variation in the salesperson's approach to each customer, of course, is a matter of selling skill. This skill is a function of both how good the salesperson's preplanning of each sales call has been and performance on the call itself. In doing the preplanning, the highly skilled salesperson analyses a great deal of information about the customer and the nature of its business. What are its key objectives and problems? Who in the customer's organisation makes and influences buying decisions, and what are their aspirations, needs, motives, fears, anxieties, drives, and the like? What rival sales personnel from what companies compete for the account's order, and what are they like? After analysing these and similar items of information, the skilled salesperson sets definite goals to accomplish on each call made to each customer. Next, the skilled salesperson plots the selling strategy to use on each successive call in an effort to achieve these definite goals - that is, what the salesperson plans to do and when. Then the salesperson makes the scheduled sales call. If all go on according to plan, the salesperson achieves the goals set for each call, and thus the salesperson contributes to the achievement of the company's overall personal-selling objectives.

While the individual members of the sales force ultimately determine the success or failure of the company's overall personal-selling strategy, sales management has the important responsibility for helping them develop and improve their selling skills. How effectively salespeople perform their assigned tasks, in other words, is closely related to sales management's effectiveness in providing them with instruction on sales techniques.

❑❑❑

4

Pricing Decisions

Introduction

Pricing is one of the most important determinants in the marketing strategy of any organisation. It is one of the first attributes of the marketing mix of any product that is noticed by the customers including prospective buyers, who might be influenced by it to decide one way or the other about buying a given product. In the absence of any other more readily noticeable and quantifiable attribute of the product, many times consumer's perception about quality of any product is also found to be influenced by the price at which it is being offered. From the organisation's point of view, price is the component which has a considerable bearing on the revenue and profits made by it and, in the final analysis substantially contributes to the success or failure of the organisation's enterprise.

On a closer look, it can be seen that pricing policies followed by any organisation will have an important bearing on almost every aspect of its activities. It will decide the quantum and pattern of wages it can pay to its labour force, the commission or discounts it can offer to its distributors, the prices it can pay to its suppliers for the raw materials and intermediate products, the expenses it can incur on advertising, publicity and sales promotion and so on. Even a consumer's confidence in an organisation's fairness and integrity may be influenced by, say, the stability or frequent changes it makes in the prices of its products or services during times of shortages, inflation or such other difficult circumstances.

Then again, prices, more than any other aspect of a company's marketing programme are likely to be subject to government control, consumer resistance or competitor's actions. The allocation of resources for the development or promotion of any given product, the possibility of the entry of competitors in the field and also the success of those who enter, the types of retail outlets or other distribution channels and pre-sale or post-sale services offered will also be favourably or otherwise affected by the price at which a product can be sold.

What is Price?

While, thus, it can be seen that price holds a unique importance in the overall marketing, it is rather difficult to define price in specific terms. It is also to be viewed as compensation or exchange a seller received in return for some combination of goods and services which make up the product when its ownership is transferred to the customer. The perception of the product differs widely between one group of customers and another and, within the same group also, from one point of time or set of circumstances to another. As a wag has said, "the price of your product is what someone is prepared to pay for it." Therefore, the concept of price has to be understood in some broad relief and terms.

In addition to such considerations as "what somebody is prepared to pay for a product" or the cost of manufacture, etc., prices are always subject to such pressures and considerations as government intervention, competition and its effects, consumerism and its impact, etc. While deciding the price of any product including service, all the above and several other related considerations need to be kept in view and properly accounted for, failing which the success of any marketing effort is likely to be in severe jeopardy. Even such commonly accepted beliefs as "the price of product primarily affects the buyer's decision to buy," "an increase in the price of a product will adversely affect its sale" are found to be open to question and need to be carefully examined in the context of one's product and marketing strategy rather than being accepted as axiomatic truths.

It must always be remembered that the buyer's perception of any variation in the price of a product may be substantially different from that of the marketer. "Customers will not always put the most straight-forward interpretation on a price change when it occurs. A price reduction, which would normally attract more buyers could mean other things to the buyers:

> The item is likely to be superceded by the later model. The item has some fault and is not selling well. The firm is in financial trouble and may not stay in business to supply future

parts. The price will come down even further and it pays to wait. The quality has been reduced.

A price increase which would normally deter sales, may carry a variety of different meaning to the buyers:

The item is very 'hot' and may be unobtainable unless it is bought soon. The item represents an unusually good value. The seller is greedy and is charging what the traffic will bear."

In this context, it may be pointed out that the introduction of its Money Back Policy by the Life Insurance Corporation of India at some extra premium as compared to the Anticipated Endowment Policy, which was withdrawn simultaneously, initially gave a setback to its sale as compared to that of the Anticipated Endowment Policy during the corresponding period of the previous year. As a marketing tactic, if this price rise could have been projected as a sign of the unusually good value for the customer's money, some of the lost ground could, presumably, be protected. Some individual agents did request their clients to consider what could have prompted the Life Insurance Corporation to increase the price of this particular plan when, otherwise, premiums were being reduced across the board on the same three bases of mortality, interest and expenses and succeeded in covering those with whom they had opened negotiations for the purchase of Anticipated Endowment Policies to the new plan without much sales resistance.

Price Affects Products

Apart from the effect of price change, even a low price initially fixed at the time of introducing a product in the market can sometimes become a handicap rather than an asset. Here the example of a newly introduced brand of lipstick in the market will help to illustrate the point. The lipstick which was manufactured by a new process which enabled the organisation to make considerable saving in the manufacturing costs, was introduced at a moderate price, which was markedly lower than most other brands. To its chagrin, the organisation found that all its estimates of sales based on careful quality testing, market potential analysis, etc., were totally believed. Further studies revealed that even those customers to whom their usual stores recommended the new brand of lipstick were reluctant to try it out, because of pre-conceived notion that the lipstick selling at that price was likely to be of an inferior quality. The same lipstick, however, took off after the brand name and packaging were changed and with a proper promotional programme it was marketed, at a considerably higher price. Similarly, unless a proper communication programme precedes and accompanies any price reduction of a premium product, the buyers are quite likely to presume that the product quality has deteriorated and the sales may suffer.

The perception of price in the minds of the customers may affect the fortunes of a product in another way. If sufficiently large cross-section of the market believes, rightly or wrongly, that the price of a particular product is likely to be quite high, they may not even think of finding out facts, to the detriment of the market success of that product. In this regard, the experience of an American telephone company belonging to the Bell group, makes an interesting point. According to the offer of the company which was carried in its directories, the monthly rental for an additional parallel line was 75 cents. Since the demand for this facility was far below the estimates prepared by the company, it was considering reduction of the rental to 50 cents per month. In trying to find out the likely increase in demand at this reduced rental, the company came to the conclusion that the impression of an average housewife was that the monthly rental for the additional hike was likely to be $2 per month. When the company undertook a communication campaign to educate the customer that the rental was only 75 cents per month, it had the effect as if the company has actually reduced the rental from say, $ 2 to 75 cents and the demand picked up. An advertising campaign recently issued by New India, a subsidiary of GIC, brought out the fact that the premium for its Householder's Comprehensive Policy worked out to less than Re. 1 per day. This campaign served that purpose of removing any misconceptions in the market about the cost of this package plan.

Prices are generally stable when raw materials are freely available to more or less stable prices, other factors contributing to the production process are not subject to wild fluctuations or variations and demand for the products manufactured by the organisation is stable. During, however, times of stagnant demand, continuous inflation or recession, etc., there is a tendency on the part of prices to be flexible and elastic. Under inflationary conditions, companies often resort to such tactics as charging for services separately instead of including them as a part of the basic package, including price escalation clauses in long-term contracts or frequent revision of prices without prior notice either to the customers or distributors. In extreme cases, they may even resort to reducing the compensation payable to the trade channel or stipulate that orders may not be accepted for less than a given quantity. The stipulation of minimum sum assured at a level higher than for other plans can be construed as an attempt on the part of an insurance organisation to keep price competitiveness by specifying a minimum size of each transaction. Another method of coping with inflationary pressures is to discontinue some products which are unprofitable as was done by Life Insurance Corporation of India in withdrawing its Anticipated Endowment Policy and replacing it by an economically better viable plan, viz., Money Back Policy, which incorporates most of the important features of the former plan. Building up the brand image is also an important method of reducing price resistance and preparing ground in advance, for the contingency of having to rise prices in future for reasons beyond control.

Even though pricing is one of the important decisions facing an organisation and calls for great care and thought, it is quite often found that in practice, pricing decisions are taken in an *ad hoc* rule of the thumb manner, at a considerable cost in terms of lost opportunities or clientele and growth potential, paid by an organisation over the long run. About the quality of pricing decisions, Kotler observes as under:

> "In spite of the importance of setting the right price, most companies do not handle pricing well. The most common mistakes are the following:
>
> Pricing is too cost-oriented in those companies fail to take sufficient account of demand intensity and customer psychology; price is not revised often enough to capitalise on the changed conditions in the marketplace; price is to often set independently of the rest of the marketing mix rather than as an instrinsic element of market-positioning strategy; and price is not varied enough for different product items and market segments."

Pricing Objectives

A prerequisite for taking proper pricing decisions is to define pricing objectives. The pricing objectives of any organisation are an integral part of its marketing strategy and must, therefore, take due cognisance of the overall marketing strategy in defining the pricing objectives. The pricing objectives of a soap which is to be marketed as a utility product to be used by as large a cross-section of the population as possible will be quite different from those of a soap which is to be promoted as a beauty aid meant for the younger age group belonging to the higher income bracket. Likewise the pricing objectives of, say, cattle insurance will be quite different from those of the All Risk

Policy for jewellery and valuables. Similarly, the pricing objectives of an organisation whose basic marketing strategy is profit maximisation will be essentially different from those of another whose aim may either be to achieve maximum market penetration or to get the maximum possible gross revenue from sales. The following table will help to understand the marketing and pricing strategy which will be followed by three organisations having different priorities:

Name of Organisation	Selling Price per Unit	Profit per Unit	The Impact of Production & Pricing Policies on		
			Market Share	Revenue (1x2)	Profit (1x3)
1	2	3	4	5	6
A	Rs. 38	Rs. 20	1,000 Units	Rs. 38,000	Rs. 20,000
B	Rs. 31	Rs. 13	1,500 Units	Rs. 46,500	Rs. 19,500
C	Rs. 23	Rs. 8	2,000 Units	Rs. 46,000	Rs. 16,000

From the above table, it will be seen that an organisation which would like to plan for maximum market penetration with a view to maximise profits in the long run and gain the long-term benefits derived from economies of scale, will prefer the third option, whereas another organisation which would like to maximise its profits would follow the first course of action. The second course would, similarly, be adopted by an organisation which would like to have the maximum possible generation of revenue.

Even within the group of organisations which would like to maximise their profits, they can approach this objective from one of two alternate methods of pricing, viz., skimming pricing or penetration pricing. Each has its own advantages and drawbacks, as can be seen from the discussion which follows a little later.

While every organisation would like to enjoy the maximum possible freedom to decide and implement its pricing objectives, such freedom is, in actual practice, circumscribed by the actions and activities of several external forces over which it has no control. Thus, it has to take into account the prevailing pattern and expectations of its agents, salesmen and distributors in respect of commissions, discounts and other payments, the likely actions of its competitors including the possibility of attracting new-comers, its suppliers' likely demands for additional prices or, alternatively, reluctance to make the supplies regularly and systematically, if the price offered is below their expectations. The possibility of government intervention and consumer resistance are other factors, which merit careful consideration in formulating the price objectives and strategies. Last, but not the least, the demands of its labour force and even the approach to and expectations of the manufacturing, sales and financial control departments from the fixing of pricing may very widely.

Methods of Pricing

After deciding the pricing objective, an organisation must decide whether the pricing will be based primarily on cost, demand or with reference to the prevailing prices of competitors' products of the same or similar nature.

Cost-based Pricing

Cost-based pricing remains the most popular and most widely practised method of pricing primarily because it is the simplest and easiest to calculate, gives the seller a sense of equity and confidence and can remain fairly stable in normal times. To fix prices on the basis of costs, a careful calculation is made of all the costs to be incurred by the seller at a given level of production and these costs are distributed over the entire production to arrive at the unit cost. After a suitable mark-up for profits, the final price of the product is decided.

Costs are of three types. *Fixed costs* are those, like the rent, interests, administrative staff and officers' salaries, taxes on property, etc., which have to be incurred irrespective of whether any production is made or not. They do not vary according to the number of units produced, but if, at any stage, the full capacity of any means of production like, say, machinery is reached, they will rise to the extent of the increase in expenses attributable to the purchase of the new facility.

In addition to the fixed costs, *variable costs* are incurred which, as the title suggests, vary according to the number of units produced. These include cost of raw materials, electricity, power and other process, intermediaries, and so on. They depend upon the quantum of production but do not vary in direct proportion to the number of units produced. They will go down on per unit basis up to a point and may, thereafter, tend to increase progressively.

On the basis of the fixed costs and variable costs, the total costs can be found by adding both these costs. Average total costs are arrived at by dividing the total costs by the number of units produced. Cost-based prices can be marked up suitably by adding reasonable margins for distribution, advertisement, publicity and sales promotion and other post-production costs and profit margins.

Modern marketing concept also takes into account the marginal costs in taking decisions about pricing. Marginal costs are those which are needed to produce one additional unit with existing facilities. Thus, in the manufacture of, say, power generators by a heavy engineering concern, if the fixed cost component at a given level of production is Rs. X per unit and variable cost component Rs. Y per unit, it can be seen that one additional unit can be produced at an additional cost of Rs. Y only. If, for strategic reasons, the concern decided to accept the order for one unit at a price greater than Rs. Y but less than Rs. X plus Rs. Y, the difference between the price quoted and the marginal cost of producing that additional unit which, in this case is Rs. Y, will be the contribution made by the marginal unit towards the profit for that year and is, to the extent, welcome irrespective of the fact that it is less than the average total cost consisting of fixed costs and variable costs.

Skimming versus Penetration Pricing

In cost-based pricing, the cost of manufacture is arrived at in the above manner and is used in deciding the selling price. The final price will be decided according to whether the concern would like to resort to a skimming pricing or penetration pricing policy. Normally, skimming pricing policy can be followed in respect of new products based on improved technology or, because of the very favourable image an organisation has in the market in respect of its existing product portfolio, there is likely to be a substantial demand for its new product. Examples of the first type are the electronic goods like computers, calculators, watches, etc., or the photographic colour films introduced during the last decade for the amateur photographers' market segment. It may be recalled that these products were introduced at fairly high prices and, as competition developed and manufacturing process improved, the prices were progressively brought down. The second type of product for which skimming pricing may be successfully adopted is, say, the introduction of a new beauty aid or fashion fabric by that concern, which is the market leader for such products.

The advantages of following a skimming policy are that it brings accelerated return on the concern's investment or technological breakthrough and that the promotional efforts can be concentrated on the selected market segment avoiding waste of expenditure or effort. The drawback of such a policy is that it encourages more competition in the hope of lucrative gains. In the early stages of a product's life cycle, skimming pricing can help an organisation to keep the demand within manageable limits, encash on the initial enthusiasm or curiosity and progressively expand its marketing in a phased manner.

In penetration pricing, the initial price is kept as low as possible with a view to capture the maximum possible market share, discourage competitors and establish a favourable image of the organisation in the relevant market segments. Many products which have entered in the decline stage of their life cycle have been revamped or their life cycle extended substantially by the manufacturing organisation switching over from skimming pricing to penetration pricing. In penetration pricing technique, an initially low price is kept and may be, if necessary, progressively increased so as to strike a good balance between market share and profitability. It also helps in distributing the promotional expenses on a broader base. It is well-suited to products, the demand for which is subject to price elasticity, i.e., they can be sold more easily and in significantly larger quantities, if the price is lower. It also lends itself well to introducing a product in a new geographical market. However, in following this pricing policy, the organisation may be paying what are called 'opportunity costs,' i.e., the loss of possible income suffered by them which could have been earned, had the price been kept higher, without adversely affecting the demand.

In cost-based pricing, an organisation may decide to keep the price of one of their products from a line or related products, deliberately low so as to attract customers to its other products, which may more than make up the lost margin on that particular products. Thus, Gillette keeps the price of its razors as low as possible, hoping to make up the notional loss from the sale of this one-time product, through the sale of its razor blades, which is a repeat-sale product. Some departmental stores and other retailers deliberately sell some low-to-moderate priced products of common usage at or below cost, in the hope of attracting customers to their place of business and hoping that, once they have entered the stores, they will buy other profitably priced products. Such products are called 'loss leaders.' The same technique is also used in announcing 'clearance sale' or 'festival sale', etc.

Penetration pricing technique can be used in selling general insurance by offering low premium covers of any type which will open doors for the salesmen to that large section of population, which can be persuaded to buy other non-traditional covers with higher premium either in combination with the low-premium cover or separately. For example, a comprehensive cover offering liberal protection to the pillion rider of a two wheeler can be offered on all 'comprehensive' policies, thus, widening the scope for the sale of comprehensive policies. Or, all risks cover can be offered to a group of tenement owners in a building for jewellery and valuables at modified rates, provided at these apartment owners in the given building are insured against fire, theft, burglary, etc. The grant of supplementary benefits at very modest rates under the multipurpose policy of Life Insurance Corporation of India can also be construed as an incentive to ensure a basic sum assured of Rs. 5,000 per policy, thus, securing some economies of scale, comparatively speaking.

Cost-based pricing becomes very important in times of inflation, when the prices of raw materials, labour and other production process costs are rising and exert considerable upward pressure upon the final price of the finished goods offered for sale. However, most costing processes have some inherent limitations in properly assessing costs at any given point of time. "Most companies use a standard cost system to determine product cost. The 'standard' cost of materials and labour is determined and then employed for a fixed period of time (usually one year) to determine the 'cost' of the product. Obviously, the real cost of the product at any given time is not necessarily its standard cost. Manufacturing variances, raw materials' cost changes, increased indirect expenses and a host of other factors, acting singly or in combination, are responsible for the difference."

Demand-based Pricing

While cost-based pricing may, to some extent, help the seller to solve the problem of pricing, it also suffers from one major drawback in so far as the price changed may not be 'accepted' by the market and may, as a result, affect the sale potential of the product. No price can be deemed to be satisfactory unless it is perceived by at least a sizeable section of the market as fair and reasonable. If sales are adversely affected because the price is felt to be either too high or too low or if some potential sales revenue is lost because a product is sold below what the market construes as a reasonable price, such a state of affairs cannot be called satisfactory from a marketing point of view. To avoid such a possibility to the extent possible, demand-based pricing may become advisable.

Demand-based pricing may take several forms. The first and foremost is what Kotler describes as 'perceived value' pricing according to which, the price is based on what special features or advantages are offered to a customer. An interesting example of such pricing is given by Kotler in the following words:

> "Caterpillar uses perceived value to set prices on its construction equipment. It might price a tractor at Rs. 24,000 although a competitor's similar tractor is priced at Rs. 20,000. And Caterpillar will get more sales than its competitor. When prospective customers ask a Caterpillar dealer why they should pay Rs. 4,000 more for the Caterpillar tractor, the dealer answers:
>
> Rs. 20,000 is what the tractor's price would be if it were equivalent to competitor's tractor.
> Rs. 3,000 is the price premium for superior durability.
> Rs. 2,000 is the price premium for superior reliability.
> Rs. 2,000 is the price premium for superior service.
> Rs. 1,000 is the price premium for the longer warranty on parts.
> Rs. 28,000 is the price to cover the value package.
> \- Rs. 4,000 discount
> Rs. 24,000 final price."

Demand-based pricing can also be worked out after obtaining from a cross section of the consumers, their estimate about what they think should be the price of the product concerned. Alternatively, some product attributes like utility, service, durability, reliability, quality, etc., could be prescribed and consumer's estimation about how far, in their opinion, a given product measures up in respect of these attributes can be assessed as a prelude to deciding the price at which the product should be sold. Accurate estimate of the value of the product as the basis of pricing helps avoid either the over-pricing or under-pricing, both of which are against the selling organisation's own long-term interests.

Competition-based Pricing

In a pricing policy based on considerations of competition, the chief base of pricing is what may be popularly called the 'going-rate.' In products of similar nature or use, if one is priced far above others, it will have difficulty in reaching its proper sales potential and if, on the other hand, if it is priced far below the others, it may result either in price war at the one end to consumers' preception of inferior quality at the other. Of course, adjustments to account for quality differentials, brand image, etc., are not ruled out.

One example of completion-based pricing is the bidding by sealed tenders. In deciding the price in this manner, the primary consideration of any organisation is the likely bid by the competitors. However, in addition to this consideration, the organisation must also carefully weigh such other considerations as the other jobs on hand and spare capacity, transportation and other logistic problems, etc.

Price Changes

While, by and large, every organisation would like to keep the prices of its products stable both with a view to gain market confidence and to avoid the inevitable consequences of frequent price changes such as performance of various additional jobs connected with such revision of prices, issuing of revised price lists, incorporating the changes on the packaging and so on, it becomes necessary for any organisation, more especially in the context of the present-day inflation, to have a proper strategy and machinery to initiate price changes. Initiation of price changes may also be necessitated by the desire of the organisation to make optimum use of its existing or new machinery or production technology, to prolong the life-cycle of its product, to extend its market share and so on. The reduction of premiums by an insurance organisation may become necessary due to the increase in the yield of other comparable investments in case of life insurance or improvements in construction, safety provision or such other factors having a bearing on the risk to be covered in case of general insurance.

In taking decisions about initiating price changes, an organisation must consider the likely consequences of such price changes on the demand for its product as well as the likely response to the intended price change on the part of the buyers, the competition as well as the distribution channels, including its own sales force. In the final analysis, the short-term and long-term consequences of the proposed price changes on the fortunes of the organisation should influence the decision to change prices. It must be remembered that none of the above factors is quantifiable with any exactitude, but all the same, must be carefully taken into consideration and properly computed in taking decisions about the proposed price changes.

Just as an organisation may have to initiate price changes, it may have to respond to price changes initiated by its competitors. It has one of the several options available from maintaining its present price in the hope that the change is either temporary or inconsequential as far as its product is concerned, responding with a counter-attack on other than price considerations, temporarily reducing the price through special discount or similar offers, permanently reducing price, or even increasing the price to give the product a superior quality image. While it is not difficult to understand the logic of other steps enumerated above, the last step, viz., increasing the price, may need some clarifications. Depending upon the type of need a product satisfies, sometimes an increase in price with appropriate communication campaign may take the product to a superior class, which is not affected by the reduction in price by the competitor. For example, when a leading brand of *vodka* in the American market was threatened by the introduction of a competitive brand at lesser price, the manufacturer responded by increasing the price, using the expected increased revenue to further promote the brand and introducing another brand of inexpensive *vodka* to compete with the competitor's brand on price considerations. In deciding about proposed price changes, more especially price reduction, it is worth remembering that "the essential fact is that buyers choose the seller on the basis of a multiplicity of considerations: service, quality, reliability and other factors. These factors desensitise many buyers to minor price differences."

Value-added Margins

One more aspect of pricing decisions to be borne in mind is to provide adequate margins for the services provided by the distribution intermediaries. These intermediaries are adding some substantial value to the product in the eyes of the buyer through such considerations as availability, services, advisory assistance and so on, and should be adequately compensated for this. However, the margins cannot and need not be expressed as a fixed percentage of the final price but must also provide for the quick or slow turnover. In products like, say, cigarettes, matches, provisions, smaller margins coupled with quicker turnover may adequately compensate the retailer, whereas in the case of perishable, goods like fruits, vegetable, etc., the margins will have to provide for the loss suffered through the unsold stocks. An equitable way of providing margins for intermediaries would be to consider the periodical (say, annual) rate of return on the investment of capital and personal time and labour of the concerned retailer or his staff involved in the sale or distribution of the product. These margins must be equitably distributed amongst the different levels of marketing intermediaries in such a way that they provide the maximum impetus to each of these intermediaries to perform its part in the overall team effort well. Any lop-sided distribution between the different intermediaries *inter se,* will have the effect of demoralising the other intermediaries or of making them indifferent to their respective roles.

❑❑❑

5

Salesman and Salesmanship

Introduction

Production in modern era is in anticipation of demand. Large varieties of goods are produced on mass scale to be sold to consumers. Moreover, modern economy is highly competitive. Hence, every producer and dealer will have to try to capture the market by appealing to the tastes, preferences and general desires of buyers. For quick sale of goods is the test of business efficiency and prosperity. The need to increase the turnover of goods in a competitive market has given rise to the art of salesmanship and publicity. Salesmanship is personal convincing of goods, among consumers with a view to induce them to buy the goods. Publicity implies giving of information to consumers through press, posters, radio, exhibitions, etc., about merits of the goods in order to persuade them to buy. Both salesmanship and publicity aim at creating demand for goods and increasing their sales through appeal, persuasion and service.

The principles of salesmanship will be studied in this chapter and methods of publicity will be discussed in the next chapter.

Meaning of Salesmanship

Salesmanship is the art of convincing the customers about the given goods or services. It is rightly described as the art of persuasion. We give below two definitions of the term 'Salesmanship':

(1) **National Association of Marketing Teachers of America:** "It is the ability to persuade people to buy goods or service for a profit to the seller and with benefit to the buyer."

(2) **Garfiel Blake:** "Salesmanship consists of winning the buyer's confidence for

the seller's house and goods, thereby winning a regular and permanent customer."

Definitions given above indicate that the purpose of salesmanship is to create the demand, preserve it and further expand it so that the sale of a product will be maximised. It implies unique efforts on the part of the salesmen to stir up the desires of people to possess certain products. Utility, suitability and relative superiority of a product should be proved by salesmen in an effort to persuade the customer to buy it and derive benefit from its use.

Importance of Salesmanship

The importance of salesmanship is universally recognised today. It is considered as an effective process of understanding the needs and tastes of consumers, imparting full information to them about the utility of products and including them to buy. Its real importance lies in its attempts to bring a potential buyer into business contact with a seller.

It is persuasive in its methods and educative in its approach to consumers and hence it develops as a constructive factor in increasing the volume of sales. Following points underline its importance:

(1) Creation of demand for different goods by respective salesmen leads to increase in total production and allied business activities.

(2) It aims at increasing the tempo of turnover. Hence, accumulation of unsold stocks is avoided.

(3) Expansion of sales by salesmen's efforts results in larger profits.

(4) Increased business activity, induced by effective salesmanship, leads to increase in the level of employment and higher income for the community.

(5) Sales talks of different salesmen will give the customers the opportunity of wide choice in their purchase of different articles. Salesmen enlighten the consumers about the merits of different goods and hence help them to make a right choice.

(6) Salesmen act as useful links between the sellers and the customers. Sellers' products are brought to the notice of customers and customers' complaints, impressions and suggestions are brought to the notice of sellers. Adjustments

in selling policy and improvements in products can, thus, be made by sellers in order to satisfy the customers.

(7) Since salesmen try to create demand for articles of luxury and comfort the standard of living of the community would be raised.

(8) Salesmanship is a lucrative career for promising young people. It is a profession that gives a lot of experience in the working of human motivations.

Types of Salesmen

Having realised the importance of salesmen, let us briefly study the types of salesmen.

There are mainly four types of Salesmen:

(1) Manufacturer's Salesman.

(2) Wholesaler's Salesman.

(3) Retail Salesman.

(4) Speciality Salesman.

(1) Manufacturer's Salesman: The manufacturer's salesman sell either to dealers or middlemen or to the ultimate consumers. The manufacturer's salesmen selling to dealers are of three types: (1) Pioneer type, (2) Dealer-servicing type, and (3) Merchandising type.

The pioneer-type salesman has the tough job or creating market for new goods. His main task is to persuade wholesalers and other dealers to take up a business in new line of products. They should convince them of the speciality of the new products and create reasonable hope in them that ultimate users would like those goods. Then only the dealer may decide to stock those goods for re-sale. The pioneer type salesman, therefore, should be aggressive in his sales talk. He should be well-informed in the use of such goods and be lifted with high skill of persuasion.

Dealer-servicing salesman is one, who sells to the dealers those goods which have an established market. He visits the dealers periodically and books new orders from them. His main job is to maintain and extend the demand for the goods which are already known to the dealers. He is expected to render all possible help to the dealers in marketing the product to subsequent buyers. This type of salesman need not be much aggressive but should certainly possess a lot of energy and perseverance. "He needs persistence and enthusiasm and he should have a warm friendly personality."

Merchandising salesman is just required to tender advice and collect information. "Merchandising salesman are mere promoters of sales for their companies than they are creators of direct orders." Their main job consists not in booking actual orders but in collecting the information from the dealers and in giving advice to them about the various problems of selling the goods. They visit the dealers, inquire of their stock position, discuss their difficulties, and advice them on sales promotion activities. The guidance given by merchandising salesmen will be helpful to the dealers in giving push to the product. They also obtain the views of the dealers about the product and accordingly advise the manufacturers to improve the product or alter the terms of sale so as to increase the sales. Thus, they strengthen the reputation of the firm.

(2) The Wholesaler's Salesman: The wholesaler, who is an important link in the chain of distribution may appoint his own salesmen to sell his stock of goods to retailers. The wholesaler's salesman calls on retail dealers at regular intervals and book their orders. It is his essential task to ensure constant flow of orders from the retailers. He should be punctual and prompt in rendering services to retailers. He should be well informed about the goods. He should create goodwill and develop sales so that wholesaler's stocks are quickly cleared.

(3) The Retail Salesman: The salesman at the retail level is expected to push the sales direct to the ultimate consumers. Retail salesman are of two types: (1) Counter Salesman, (2) Outdoor Salesman. Counter salesman works in the retail store and attends to customers who call at the store. He has ample opportunities to sell suitable items to various customers visiting the shop. He has to exercise imagination and ingenuity to find out precisely the needs of customers and to persuade them go to in for the proper product which meets their needs. He should, therefore, possess adequate knowledge about stocks, prices and other selling points. He should be alert, accurate, patient, polite and considerate in his behaviour and talk with the customers.

The outdoor salesman is one, who is required to carry sample of goods and visit the prospective consumers and book orders. Large retail stores can employ outdoor salesman. He must be able to create interest and desire for the goods in the customers he visits.

(4) Speciality Salesman: Goods are broadly classified into staple goods and speciality goods. Staple goods are the goods which are known to dealers and consumers. They are in common use and have usually well established market, i.e., food, clothing, paper and other articles of necessity. Salesman selling such products are not required to create a new market for the line of such goods, though they should seek to maintain and expand their sales.

Speciality goods are those goods which are of relatively higher price and which are not regularly bought. Moreover, the purchase of such goods involves the exercise of personal selection by the buyers, i.e., automobiles, refrigerators, washing-machines, radio and television sets, cameras, household electrical appliances, sport goods, etc. Special efforts are to be put in by manufacturers of speciality goods to sell them. Hence, they employ salesmen to get into direct contact with customers so as to familiarise the use of such goods. Speciality salesmen have to create a want afresh for popularising the speciality goods. They should strive to locate the likely customers and employ maximum measure of persuasive skill in finalising a sale transaction of such goods. They are, therefore, called creative salesmen. They have to be highly intelligent, shrewd, impressive and effective in their sales talk.

Qualities of a Good Salesman

It is difficult to define an ideal salesman. The qualities and qualifications of a salesman depend upon the particular selling position he is seeking for. Different selling jobs require different types of salesmen. Broadly speaking, however, an aspirant for any sales job must grasp the fundamentals of salesmanship, viz., knowledge of one's self, knowledge of customers and knowledge of the product. A good salesman is he who has a charming personality, has the aptitude and skill required for a selling job, has the thorough knowledge of the goods he is to represent and who can study the different motives of numerous customers to be approached in the course of his sales efforts.

Following is the list of qualities of an ideal salesman:

(1) He should have attractive, cheerful and smart appearance which creates a favourable impression on prospective customers.

(2) He should be a man of excellent health as sound health is a key to efficiency.

(3) He should be well-dressed. Appropriate dressing improves the grace of his appearance.

(4) He should have a well-pitched voice. His tone should be pleasing, appealing and free from any artificial accents so as to create receptivity in the listening customer.

(5) He should master the art of conversation so as to inspire response in the customer concerned.

(6) He should have good manners revealing his sense of refinement and delicacy. Repulsive mannerisms should be avoided as they weaken his sales talk with the customer.

(7) He should have keen imagination and foresight so that he can develop 'new angles of approach' to the sales problem.

(8) He should have strong will and abiding self-confidence. Self-confidence is very essential for a salesman to create desire and press a point in his sales talk.

(9) He should have strong memory.

(10) He should be a man of tact. Tact means saving and doing the right thing at the right time, in the right way. It is this quality which infuses 'sales sense' in him.

(11) He should be courteous. Politeness and considerate attitude are assets of a salesman.

(12) He should be a man of calm and cool nature since short-temper comes in the way of successful selling.

(13) He should be honest, sincere, industrious and co-operative.

(14) He should be loyal to his firm.

(15) He should be social and a good mixer with the people since shy and reserved individuals can never become good salesmen.

(16) He should have sound general education. If necessary, he should possess specialised degree or diploma. Good education gives intellectual edge to his sales talk.

(17) He should know his products thoroughly. He should have complete knowledge of selling points pertaining to his product so as to convince the customers of its utility.

(18) He should learn to 'size up' the customers and understand their buying motives so that he can present his selling points to match with the buying motives.

Types of Customers

The selling efforts call for close study of human nature in its diversity. Salesman has to deal with different types of customers with varied leanings, likings, dislikings and misgivings. Different customers, therefore, require different approaches and appeals. The salesman has to adjust his sales talk according to the type of customer he is tackling at a particular time. Before beginning his sales talk he has to diagnose the nature of his customer, spot out his buying motives and grasp his peculiarites. 'Sizing up the customer' is, thus, his primary duty.

Customers are classified into many types on the basis of their personality traits. We can, however, discuss here only a few types of customers that need to be usually encountered by a salesman in the course of his duty. These are: (1) Time Waster, (2) Silent Customer, (3) Shy Customer, (4) Talkative Customer, (5) Impatient Customer, (6) Suspicious and Argumentative Customer, (7) Rude and Ill-mannered Customer, and (8) Conceited Customer.

(1) Time Waster: He is a person who has entered a shop just to while away the time. He might be idle, off from duty or otherwise worried. To feel relaxed, to forget his worries or spend the time, he may drop into a shop and just move around. He has no specific motive or impulse to buy. Such casual customers should not be ignored; nor should they be unduly pestered with questions. It is better to leave them alone except when they make an inquiry. Discourtesy to such customers should be avoided at all costs. For, in his normal mood he may visit the shop again and book his sales.

(2) Silent Type of Customer: Silent type of customer is a typical case for a salesman. He makes it a point only to listen to the sales talk without any question or comment. He keeps mum and thinks that silence shields him from any commitment to the salesman. He, therefore, does not let the salesman know his reaction. Silent type of customers are few in number. The salesman, however, should not get bored or upset with the customer's tight lips. He should plan his sales talk without expecting the participation of the customer in the business conversation. He should present the selling points with patience and tact. He may now and then pose question to the customer like "Do you agree, Sir? Shall I presume that the product suits your purpose? Can I write the order, Sir?" In this way silent customers should be induced to talk out their minds or place an order.

(3) Shy Type of Customer: Shy customer is polite and unassuming but he is not bold to express his views about the product. He feels hesitant even to ask for more varieties with a view not to trouble the salesman. He feels too much nervous to express his comment or commitment regarding the product. Such customers should be wisely handled and should not be cleverly trapped by the salesman. The salesman should befriend such customer, talk to him delicately, show all designs and explain all the relevant facts in detail. He should, thus, help the customer to overcome his shyness.

(4) Talkative Customer: A number of customers belong to this type. A talkative customer hardly allows the salesman to participate in conversation. He goes on talking unceasingly on various points which may not be relevant to the product under sale. The salesman should not attempt immediately to cut him short but should listen to him patiently. He may flatter the customer and nod his agreement with the latter's views. After letting him speak for a long time the salesman should try to bring the customer to the product and invite his attention to the main subject, i.e., buying the product.

(5) Impatient Customer: He desires to be promptly attended to by the salesmen. He does not like long arguments and is not disposed towards minute bargaining. A slight delay on the part of salesman to attend to him suddenly irritates him and may even make him shout and leave the shop abruptly. The salesman should ensure quick attention and prompt service to such customers.

(6) Suspicious and Argumentative Customer: Suspicious customer is temperamentally a fault-finder. He doubts every word of the salesmen. He refuses to believe in the suitability of the product or in the bonafides of the salesman. He always taunts, ridicules, and laughs at the salesman because he presumes that he is being duped by the salesman. The salesman, however, should not try to challenge the customer with heated arguments. He should pertinently strive to show concrete proof of firm's sincerity reputation and readiness for satisfactory service to customers. In this way, suspicion should be dispelled.

Argumentative customers like the suspicious type do not allow any statement of the salesman go unchallenged. The argumentative customer is found or raising some issue or the other for argument and tries to show that he is better informed. Salesman should not, however, lose his temper and should not try run down the arguing customer by sarcastic remarks. He should pick up logical arguments of the customer and answer them courteously to the satisfaction of the customer. The argumentative and suspicious customers also may be brought round by a skilful salesman, exercising tact, patience and courtesy.

(7) Rude and Ill-mannered Customer: Rude customer does not follow the normal code of good behaviour in society. He has no graceful manner. He talks curtly, shouts indiscreetly laugh unnecessarily, criticises wantonly, uses objectionable language, mishandles the products shown to him, etc. Salesman should not insult even such customers. He should take a liberal view of the lax manners of the customer and attend promptly and properly to the latter's needs with patience and without prejudice.

(8) Conceited Customer: He thinks too much of himself. He desires to be given special honour and respect. He suffers from superiority complex. He feels that he knows everything and is not in need of any enlightenment. Salesman should not hurt his sense of vanity but try to convince him of the suitability of the product in satisfying his vain glorious view. He should stress on the sophisticated nature of the goods and appeal to the customer sense of pride and prestige.

Buying Motives

Human behaviour is induced by various motives. Motive is an 'urge' which impels a person to act in a particular way. Buying motives are such 'urges' as would induce interest and awaken desire for a particular product. A study of such motives enables the salesman to present his product in such a way as would satisfy the particular motive of the customers concerned.

Motives can be classified under three categories:

(1) Primary, (2) Selective, (3) Patronage.

(1) Primary Motives: Primary motives are elemental urges common in all people.

Hunger, health, sex, fear, safety are some basic drives underlying human behaviour. Good food, nourishing fruits, drinks, medicines, clothes, etc., are bought under the stimulus of primary motives.

(2) Selective Motives: The nature of a product, the surrounding circumstances, the social status, the financial capacity and the personal habits all stir up a number of secondary motives in a person. Such motives include cupidity, variety, fashion, romance, affection, comfort, hobbies, etc. In addition to his minimum needs, man buys a number of other articles because of the above secondary urges, e.g., motive of affection induces a person to buy toys for children.

(3) Patronage Motives: Patronage motives spring from a buyer's to support and patronise a particular seller. Patronage motives may be induced by the most suitable or superior quality of a product available only with that seller. Or, convenient location of his shop, his fair requatation, reliability, attractive display at his shop, home delivery services, credit facilities offered by him, etc., may spur up patronage motives in the buyer.

An ideal salesman should take into account these types of motives while planning his sales talk.

Selling Points

Selling points refer to important features of a product that go to influence the decision of people to duty it. They indicate the advantages accruing to those who decide to buy the product. The unique methods of production, novel design, varied colours suitable sizes, special merits, attractive packing, liberal discounts, competitive prices, etc., constitute the selling points of an article.

Selling points differ from product to product. Necessary goods are sold on the points of utility, durability and price; speciality goods are sold on the basis of unique utility, convenience, economy, comforts, e.g., typewriters, bicycles, books, insurance policies, etc. Luxury goods are saleable on the score of the points which underline fashion, prestige, vanit, etc., radios, cars, costly clothes, etc. Selling points can be grouped under the following headings:

(1) Points Concerning the Manufacture of Goods: (a) Name and reputation of manufacturers are strong selling points of a given article, e.g., Godrej Products, Tatamake, Tagore's Books. Similarly, specific trade names and trade marks also increase the saleability of articles, e.g., 7 O'Clock blades, Ovaltine, Swastik Hari Oil, etc. (b) Normal tangible features of the product constitute its basic selling points such as size, colour, durability economy, etc. For example, in case of motor car: speed, petrol consumption, seating capacity, engineering design quality of tyres, etc., are the selling points.

(2) Points Concerning the Special or Novel Characteristics of the Product: Such points relate to unique features of a product not found in similar articles and are intended to satisfy buyer's sense of refinement or sophistication, e.g., noiseless stoves, silent typewriters, watch with automatic windability, magic eye in the radio set, etc.

(3) Points Concerning Terms of Sale: Cheaper price, higher discounts, credit facilities, instalment payment.

(4) Additional Attractions: After-sale Service, Prize and Gift Schemes, Home Delivery, etc.

Importance

Knowledge of selling points is highly important for a salesman. He can cite the correct selling points to suit the buying motives of the prospects. Selling points properly presented by the salesman will arouse genuine interest and strong desire among the prospective buyers. Salesman, therefore, has to make a complete list of all selling points relating to his articles before planning his sales talk. Alignment of selling points with buying motives proves his success as a salesman.

The Process of Selling

The process of selling is largely a psychological process. It involves intellectual efforts on the part of a salesman to induce the prospective customers to buy his products. The art of selling as noted earlier tactful persuasion. Hence, a salesman should know how to plan his sales talk in order to covert the prospective customers into actual buyers. He should learn what to say, when to say and how to say it, effectively.

The selling process consists of the following steps: (1) Prospecting, (2) Pre-approach, (3) Approach, (4) Presentation and Demonstration, (5) Meeting the objections, (6) Finalising the sale transition.

(1) Prospecting: Prospecting means search for valuable prospects. A prospect is he who is likely to take interest in the use of the product and can be expected to buy it. A salesman, therefore, should first find out such persons by personal observation, inquiry, casual visits, or from different directories. He should have in his mind a number of products to be approached. A salesman who is good 'prospector' can achieve better sales results. Prospecting, thus, is a stepping-stone to successful selling. Retail salesman need not do prospecting as the prospects themselves come to him.

(2) Pre-approach: Pre-approach means 'sizing up' the prospects with regard to their probable buying motives. This is a second step in selling process in which the salesman has to collect information about his different prospects with reference to their age, education, special status, usual habits, financial standing, buying practices, etc. This will help to his plan his 'sales talk' when he actually approaches the prospects. In case of retail salesmen, pre-approach has a different meaning. It impels suitable arrangement of the retail store in such a way as to attract the prospects to enter the shop. Its location, layout, lighting and display should be fascinating.

Pre-approach is an important step to get access to prospects. It presupposes thorough knowledge, on the part of the salesman, of buyer's psychology.

(3) Approach: Approach means coming into direct touch with the prospect, through telephone, visiting cards, personal letters, etc. Contact may be established and the actual date of sales interview may be fixed up. On the appointed day the salesman shall call on the prospect in time. He should begin his sales talk with confidence, skill and tact. He should, however, be graceful in his manners, courteous in his expression and well-balanced in his arguments.

In case of retail salesman, he should treat the visiting customer as his guest. He should suitably greet him, encourage him to reveal his needs, show him samples and gently persuade him to buy. Approaching, therefore, is a constructive step in selling.

(4) Presentation and Demonstration: After the usual exchange of courtesies, the salesman shall commence his talk with the prospect to make him buy to goods. In his talk he shall present the 'selling points' of his goods and prove their utility. Effective presentation is the crucial step in the process of selling since it seeks to condition the prospect's mind to buy the goods. "A sale is made not in the mind of the salesman, not over the counter or desk, but in the mind of the buyer."

While presenting the features of his goods, the salesman has to take the prospective buyer's mind through five stages : (i) Attention, (ii) Interest, (iii) Desire, (iv) Conviction, and (v) Action.

(i) **Attention:** It means the effort of salesman to bring to the notice of the prospect his goods and make him willing to bear the further sales talk. The sales talk may be inaugurated by showing the samples of goods, illustrated catalogue of descriptive brochures.

(ii) **Interest:** After inviting the attention of the 'prospect' the salesman should endeavour or create interest in him for the goods. The salesman has to emphasise are selling point of his goods in order to captivate the fancy of the prospect and make him think about buying the goods. The utility and speciality of the articles should be stressed so as to catch the attention of the prospect and arouse interest in their use.

(iii) **Desire:** Interest aroused has to be converted into desire. The salesman's real skill consists in creating an impulsive urge in the prospect to buy the product and test its suitability. The salesman can create this burning desire by proving how the goods would go to satisfy the buying motives of the prospect. Sometimes, by actual demonstration salesman seeks to prove the utility of the goods, i.e., ride in a car, working of a machine, etc. Reconciliation of selling points of the goods and the buying motives of the prospect is an important part of salesman's talk with his prospect.

(5) Meeting the Objection (conviction): It is not enough for the salesman to only create desire. He has to show that his product is relatively superior to other such products and is sold on comparatively more competitive terms. This will breathe 'conviction' in the prospect about the desirability of possessing the product. At this stage the salesman should anticipate or find out any doubts or objections that the prospect may have about the product and clarify them satisfactorily. Objection in an 'adverse reason or argument'. Behind each objection there lies a sense of fear, an element of mental reservation or some hesitation on the part of the prospect. "Objections are guide posts to prospects' reactions." It is the salesman's ask to meet their objections and turn the reactions into favourable response. He can infuse 'conviction' in the prospect by offering guarantees, more discounts, instalment payment facilities, etc.

(6) Finalising the Transaction (action): The final stage is 'Clinching the Sale.' By effective summarisation of selling points the salesman should try to stimulate final decision on the part of the prospect regarding the purchase of the product. He should tactfully request the prospect to book an order. He should thank him for his decision and assure that his firm would be always ready to provide service facilities to him. He should take down the order and assure early delivery. In case of retail salesman the goods selected by the buyer should be properly packed and handed over to him. The 'sale' thus would be finalised with exchange of courtesies and hopes for further business contacts.

Sales Organisation

Successful selling of goods or service is the main purpose of any business enterprise. A series of activities will have to be organised to sell the goods promptly. Organisation means systematic coordination of functions essential to achieve the desired objective. The desired objective of a commercial establishment is to sell at profit. Sales organisation, therefore, is a logical arrangement of various activities necessary to promote sales.

The functions of a sales organisation can be classified as given under:

(I) Planning Functions:

- (1) Market Research.
- (2) Sales Forecasting and Budgeting.
- (3) Selling Policy.

(II) Administrative Functions:

- (1) Selection of Salesmen.
- (2) Training of Salesmen.
- (3) Control of Salesmen.
- (4) Remuneration of Salesmen.

(III) Executive Functions:

- (1) Advertising.
- (2) Sales Promotion.
- (3) Selling Routine-Execution of Customers' Orders.

I. Planning Functions

(1) Market Research: The entire commercial activity of today is based on anticipation of demand. Market Research gives an idea about the extent of the expected demand for a given product. It means an analytical study of trends in the market and a scientific survey of the needs, tastes and preferences of consumers in order to discover the sales possibilities of a given line of product. The information revealed by market research facilities planning of sales campaigns. Bolling rightly sums up the significance of market research as follows: "Market research .... is a means of discovering who are the buyers, who are the potential buyers, where the buyers are to be found, when they will buy and what are the best methods of making it easy for them to buy."

(2) Sales Forecasting and Sales Budgeting: Sales forecasting and sales budgeting are the part of planning functions of a sales organisation. Sales forecasting means estimation of the aggregate volume of sales expected during a particular period - usually a year. This estimate made by the sales organisation on the basis of findings of market research and current sales experience. The main purpose of sales forecasting is to anticipate the probable volume of sales during the ensuing period and to treat it as a 'target' to be achieved by the sales organisation.

Sales budgeting implies estimation of the probable gross revenues and selling expenses. The budget is usually prepared for the coming year. Sales budgeting helps in ascertaining the approximate margin of profit in the ensuing year. It also helps in regulation of selling expenses.

(3) Selling Policy: It is the duty of sales manager as the head of sales organisation to formulate a suitable sales policy of the firm. The object of a selling policy is to place the right type of goods in the hands of consumers on competitive terms. It should be based on sound date and flexible approach according the changes in the market. It should aim at attraction of customers and rendering them satisfactory services.

Selling policy implies the laying down of a concrete line of action regarding the following matters:

(i) Method of Distribution (sale)

(ii) Terms of Sale

(iii) Guarantee and Service.

(i) **Methods of Distribution:** The method of selling the product should be decided earlier. The usual method of distribution are: (a) Sale direct to consumers, (b) Sale through retailers to consumers, (c) Sale through wholesalers and retailers to the consumers, (d) Sale through mercantile agents.

The selection of any of the above methods depends upon the type of the product, the customs in trade, extent of market, the nature of demand, the margin of profit, etc.

(ii) **Terms of Sale:** Fixation of the terms of sale is the most important function of sale organisation. Terms of sale include price, discounts, manner and time of payment, credit-arrangements, collection of dues, etc.

(iii) **Guarantee and Service (After-sale Service):** Sellers usually make it a policy to give a guarantee for a specified period about the suitability and durability of the product even after its sale. The object is to ensure that the article sold gives a satisfactory use or service to the buyer for a reasonable length of time. Guarantees are given particularly in case of costly articles like watches, radio sets, typewriters, etc. Articles found defective or without use are taken back or reconditioned or replaced on the loss suffered by the users may be made good.

In case of articles involving complicated mechanism, the seller renders what is called after-sale service. Technicians are sent to the user's place for repairing the machines free of cost or at a nominal charge. Usually free services are rendered during the 'Guarantee Period.'

After-sale service policy is a strong selling point to push the sales of heavy machines and other costly articles. It inspires confidence in the buyers about the fitness of the product and impresses them with the seller's concern for customer's convenience and goodwill. It will help in building up a higher rate of turnover. It is, however, necessary that the after-sale services should be rendered in time and at reasonable charges, which should not be prohibitive.

II. Administrative Functions

(1) Selection and Appointment of Salesmen: Selection of salesman is one of the important administrative functions of sales organisation. Success of any sales policy depends largely on the efficient sales staff. Hence, selection of the right type of salesmen is essential for popularising the products of any firm in modern competitive market. The sales manager responsible for selection has to adopt a scientific approach so that only competent persons are recruited for the job of salesmanship.

Before setting out to recruit the salesmen, the sales manager should lay down the requirements of the job and the characteristics of candidates who can fit into that job. He has to undertake job-analysis. Job analysis implies the analysis of duties implied in canvassing the sales, viz., planning of sales talk, prospecting, approaching the prospects, sales interviews with the prospects, adjustments of customer's complaints, providing after-sale services, miscellaneous duties like correspondence, reporting, credit investigation, collection of dues, etc. The selling duties differ according to the policy pursued by the firm. They also differ according to the nature of the articles to be sold, i.e., necessities, novelties, luxuries, service, etc. They also depend on the types of salesmen proposed to be recruited, viz., wholesaler's salesman, retailer's salesman, counter salesman, travelling salesman, sales supervisor, etc.

After analysing the job, the sales manager has to lay down the qualities and qualifications to be possessed by candidates who seek the job. In other words, he has to specify educational qualifications, length of experience, personality traits like health, appearance, etc. Social characteristics like tact, courtesy, amiability, mental traits like intelligence, aptitude, etc. Sales manager should, therefore, select only those who answer these specifications so that they can fit into the job defined already.

The sales manager has then to decide about the sources of recruiting salesmen. There are many sources open for the sales manager to find out his sales personnel. He can pick out suitable candidates from the existing staff. Persons already in the service of the firm working in different departments may be drafted for selling jobs in case they fulfil the criteria of selection. Other things being equal, the inside employee is sure to prove a better candidate for the selling job because he is already familiar with the product of the firm, its customers and its selling policies.

Salesmen may also be recruited from among the customers or their employees. Since they are quite acquainted with the uses of the product they may be able to boost up the sales. They should be appointed only if they possess the required qualifications and aptitude.

Salesmen, who are already working in other firms engaged in the same line of business may be attracted to join the service of the firm. Such persons already possess the experience of selling same goods and, hence, will prove to be great asset to the firm. But their services can be obtained by offering relatively higher remuneration. Salesmen already working in different lines of trade may also be selected if they are found suitable in other respects. Since they are already familiar with the general technique of selling they may prove to be worthy candidates.

Educational institutions also can provide good number of aspirants for jobs of salesmanship. Salesmanship as a specialised course of study is included in the curricula of commercial high schools and colleges. Students who have studied the course of salesmanship and other allied subjects will develop as more competent salesman provided they have the aptitude. The sales manager may visit educational institutions and find out suitable candidates.

Salesmen may also be recruited from among the candidates recommended by customers, existing salesman or by other influential persons. Of course, recommended candidates should be selected only if they are qualified and fit.

Advertising the posts of salesman is the most common method of recruitment. Advertisements are published in standard newspapers and journals offering jobs to those who possess specified qualifications. The scope for selection is wider in this source.

After deciding on the source from which candidates are to be recruited the sales manager should proceed with judging the suitability of the candidates aspiring for the job of salesmanship.

Candidates are usually required to put in applications giving full information relating to their physical traits, educational qualifications, experience, etc. Application forms contain a number of questions to be answered by the candidate. The questions are framed in such a way that the answers to them by the applicant would reveal the full particulars of his candidature. The application forms usually require information on the following points, viz., name, address, date of birth, native place, single or married, educational qualifications, previous experience, if any, salary expected, height, weight and other personal details, special talents, hobbies, etc. The applications are normally accompanied by testimonials and certificates to support the above facts.

After the completed applications forms are received those of suitable candidates are sorted out for follow-up.

The applicants, then, are called for personal interview. Interview is an important step in the process of selection. During the course of interview appearance, intelligence, aptitude, knowledge, mannerisms of candidates are judged with reference to the job to be filled up. Simple and searching questions are asked by the panel of interviewers to test the alterness, tact and intellectual abilities of the candidate. The impressions of personal interview with different candidates are recorded and tabulated on merit basis.

In addition to general interview, many business firm should psychological tests to discover the attitudes, aptitudes, abilities and character of the candidates. Aptitude and intelligence tests are nowadays commonly held by big firms to assess the intrinsic worth of the candidates for selling jobs. The sales temperament, reasoning powers, qualities of leadership, virtues of patience, hardwork, regularity, reliability, etc., are all found out by well-arranged tests that probe the candidates mind and reveal their calibre.

The candidates found fit as per the results of interviews and tests are then sent for medical examination. The medical examination is intended to confirm the physical fitness of the candidate for the job.

The selected candidates are thereafter called for the final round of interview, during which the terms of service and the nature of duties are ultimately settled. A written order is issued by the sales manager indicating their selection as salesmen. It is customary nowadays to execute agreements with the selected candidates. The appointment agreement takes the form of a legal contract which covers the following points: (i) duties of the salesman; (ii) authority of the salesman; (iii) territory allocated to him; (iv) quota of sales assigned to him; (v) remuneration payable to him; (vi) matters regarding leave, resignation and retirement.

Such a contract safeguards the interest of both the firm and the salesman. It will help the firm in the effective control of the work of the salesman.

(2) Training of Salesman: Selected salesmen have to be given suitable training in the technique of selling. It is the special responsibility of the sales manager to see that only trained salesmen are sent out on selling goods. Otherwise, the raw and inexperienced salesmen may find it difficult to pick up the clause of the job and ultimately fail in impressing the customers. Hence, it is an essential function of the sales organisation to devise an appropriate scheme of training for the sales personnel. Selected candidates should be immediately put on training for a specified period. During the course of training they will be taught the fundamentals of salesmanship and marketing by a panel of experts. The skill imparted to the salesmen during training will enable them to enter the market and the world of consumers with confidence and determination. Even highly qualified and gifted salesmen need training to develop their sales career on successful lines.

(i) Objects of Training: The objects of giving training to salesmen can be summarised as under:

(a) To teach the theory and techniques of marketing.

(b) To impart knowledge about the art of convincing the consumers and increasing the sales.

(c) To explain to the salesmen the features and speciality of the goods of the firm.

(d) To make the salesmen familiar with the firm's policies.

(e) To acquaint the salesmen with the dealers and users of the firm's products.

(f) To give them a complete idea about the competition in the market and the ways to be followed for increasing the sales of the firm's products.

(g) To provide them with a working knowledge of the laws and regulations affecting marketing of goods.

(h) To maintain a ready batch of salesmen to replace the retired, resigned or absent sales personnel so that the continuity of the selling work is not disturbed.

(i) To find out inefficient or unsuitable persons and remove them from sales department.

(ii) Methods of Training: There are manifold methods of imparting training to salesmen. Any of them can be adopted to suit the nature of the product and the temper of the market and can also be varied according to the calibre of the candidates put on training. The main methods of training are: (a) Lectures, (b) Sales Conferences, (c) Sales Manuals and Bulletins, (d) Field Training, (e) Postal Training (Correspondence Training), (f) Visual Training.

(a) Lectures: Lectures are given at appointed hours on the various aspects of selling and the salesmen are expected to take notes of the lectures and learn skills of salesmanship. The quality of the lectures and the attention and receptivity of the trainees determine the effectiveness of this method. Lectures should be interesting, intelligible and appealing to the salesmen. Otherwise they go waste. Lectures are to be followed-up by other methods like group discussions, seminars and written tests.

(b) Sales Conferences: Salesmen may be called to attend the sales conference at periodical intervals, say, once a week or fortnightly or monthly. Officers-in-charge of the sales of the firm may address such conferences on selling techniques. Subject like selling policies of the firm, complaints received from customers, improvements in the product, competition faced by the firm's product, proposed advertising programme, etc., are discussed in such conferences. Merits of this method of training are as follows:

(1) It develops logical thought.

(2) It trains salesmen in taking balanced decisions.

(3) Participants get broader views of the subject discussed at such conferences by exchanging ideas and experience.

(4) Combined thinking of the group of participants helps in finding solutions of problems defying solution by individual salesman.

Its limitations are that it is slow and costly and there is shortage of such persons who can preside over such conferences to guide the discussions on right lines.

(c) Sales Manuals: Salesmen are provided with hand-books, bulletins, catalogues, brochures, etc., for their reference. Sales Manual is a handbook containing a brief history of the firm, the particulars pertaining to the product dealt with the firm, its selling policies, advertising and sales promotion activities. It also contains detailed instructions to be followed by salesmen under different circumstances. It is a sort of ready guide or a tool of self-study for the salesmen so as to plan their sales efforts appropriately. Sales bulletins are published by some firms at periodic intervals (weekly or monthly) to give latest information to the salesmen.

(d) Field Training: After the salesmen have completed their basic training they may be given practical experience of the sales job by taking them to the prospects. The salesmen and the trainer approach the prospects. The trainer begins his sales talk. The trainer is expected to observe the whole process and bear the different crucial points in his mind. The trainer afterwards explains the different steps and points of his sales talk. Then, the trainee is asked to handle the sales job. This is an expensive method of training.

(e) Correspondence Training: Salesmen working in different territories are supplied, from time to time, with lessons bearing upon the technique of selling and giving other useful information. Instructions are also despatched to the salesmen through post. The salesmen are expected to go through the lessons and other literature and make use of the hints and information contained therein to reinforce the effectiveness of their sales efforts. The salesmen also may correspond with the training office seeking guidance on matters relating to their duties. This method of training is suitable only to the experienced salesmen and is meant mainly to provide extra information to them.

(f) Visual Training: Selling process is actually demonstrated through visual aids. By means of motion pictures of films, television, etc., the steps involved in selling process are picturised and exhibited at specified hours daily, weekly or bi-weekly. These pictures create permanent impression on the salesmen. Sometimes short plays, skits and dialogues are staged to educate the salesmen. This method of training is very costly. Besides, its effectiveness depends on the quality of the pictures, the theme and its presentation.

(3) Control of Salesmen: One of the important administrative tasks of sales organisation is to devise suitable methods and procedures for controlling the work of sales personnel. It is the duty of the sales manager to secure efficient work from his sales staff. His responsibility will not be over with the selection of salesmen and sending them for training. He has to see that the trained salesmen are put on work in different sales fields. He has to control and direct the efforts of the salesmen in such a way as to promote the ultimate interests of the firm.

The objects of control should be supervision, guidance, maintenance of discipline and evaluation of the work. Sales manager should wield effective purposeful control over sales, sales staff so as to secure productive performance from them. If there is no arrangement for watching and controlling the work of salesmen, then intensity of sales efforts will always be uncertain and the salesmen are likely to develop complacency. Hence, there is need for control.

(i) Methods of Control: Following are the important methods employed to control and evaluate the work of salesmen:

(a) Sales Territories: A certain territory is assigned to each salesman for the purpose of selling the goods. The entire sales field is divided into different geographical areas or zones and each such zone may be allotted to a particular salesman. The usual political boundaries may be adopted as the basis for allocation of territories or the sales manager may form his own sales districts for assignment to different salesmen. The size of sales territories are determined by various factors like the strength of demand, the extent of competition, transport facilities, climate, types of customers, capacity and calibre of salesmen, etc. The modern tendency is to assign smaller territories and asking the salesmen to develop the areas intensively in respect of sales. Compact territories make for quick and frequent contact with the prospects and customers. If the territories are large, the salesmen have to be provided with modes of conveyance to make frequent calls on dealers and users in the area.

The object of assigning sales territories is to tap fully the potentialities of marketing the products in different area and to control the activities of salesmen and evaluate their relative efficiency. The assignment of territories also facilitates planning of sales efforts and avoids duplication of efforts by many salesmen in one and the same area. The territorial allocation of duties provides incentive to salesmen to cultivate more sales in the areas under their jurisdiction.

(b) Sales Quotas: Quota "is the amount of business the sales manager has planned to achieve." It is used to define the work expected from each salesmen. Quota is laid down territory-wise. This territorial quota represents the selling task assigned to the concerned salesman. The quota may be fixed for the entire year or for shorter periods, say, a quarter or a month. It shows the target of sales to be achieved by a salesmen in his area within a given period. Quota is not to be fixed after taking into account several reacting factors in the market. Market research provides clues for setting the precise quotas. Quotas should be fixed at reasonable level so that salesmen can work up to it with their skill, ability and hard work. They cannot be pitched at such a high level which will dishearten the salesmen.

Quota system enables proper evaluation of the work of the salesmen. These facilities effectively control over the sales personnel. Remuneration to salesmen may also be based on quota system by providing commission to those who reach the target and granting a special bonus to those who surpass the target. Thus, the quota system subserves the two objects of control and stimulation.

(c) Salesmen's Authority: The scope of salesmen's authority should be clearly defined by the sales manager. In the course of business it would be necessary to give some measure of authority of salesmen regarding important matters of sales routine, viz., prices, granting of credit to new customers, guarantees, services to customers, special concessions, discounts, settlement of claims, etc. But in practice the policy in respect of above matters is more or less precisely standardised. Hence, there is nothing left to the discretion of salesmen. In some concerns salesmen are given limited discretionary authority in settlement of prices, rate of discount and granting of credit. This, it is argued, would stimulate the salesmen to display more initiative. But the modern trend of thinking is to define the extent of salesmen's authority and watching that the salesmen act within the limits of authority in their bargaining with prospective customers. Catalogues and price lists limit the authority of salesmen in settlement of terms of sale. The salesmen may, however, be given confidential instructions to offer any reasonable discounts and concessions so as not to miss any profitable business opportunity. Such special concessions are to be subject to sanction of sales manager. In other words, if salesmen think that more sales can be offering more liberal terms, they should contact the sales manager and obtain his approval.

Salesmen should be instructed not to give any high and unrealistic guarantees to customers regarding the quality, durability and repairability of the products. They should be guided by the normal sales policy of the firm. Likewise salesmen should not be allowed to transact credit sales without concurrence of the Credit Department. Otherwise they may be tempted to grant credit to all the sundry simply to inflate their quota of sales.

In an case salesmen should be directed to work strictly within the limits of authority laid down by the selling policy of the firm.

(d) Salesmen's Reports: Salesmen are required to submit periodical reports to the sales manager on their sales efforts in their respective territories. Salesmen's reports provide valuable information to the sales manager to watch, direct and evaluate the sales efforts of each salesman. "These reports," says Bolling, "will enable the sales office to follow the salesmen's progress, to criticise or advise them when necessary and to write letters to the prospective customers confirming any undertaking given, or enlarging upon any point made during the interviews." The sales reports are, thus, effective devices of exercising control over the salesmen. Sales manager will be able to keep in regular touch with his sales staff working in different areas and to send them suggestions, directive (and warning, if necessary, to such of the salesmen as are lacking in their duties). The series of sales reports by cash salesman will facilitate the objective evaluation of his abilities. Such evaluation will help in fixation of his remuneration and in determining the chances of his promotion to higher cadres.

Salesmen's reports also give good information about the trends in the market, impressions of customers about the product their complaints, the need for adjustments in the quality of the products or in the policy of the firm, etc. Thus, appropriate adjustments may be made by the firm on the basis of the information revealed by these reports. To the salesmen themselves, their own reports serve as important records of their achievements and failures and provide a clear opportunity for self-analysis.

(4) Remuneration of Salesmen: Payment of adequate remuneration is necessary to attract gifted and competent persons to the sales career. Remuneration is the material compensation paid to the salesmen for their efforts in promoting the sales. It should be adequate to enable them to maintain themselves on reasonable standard of living. It should also be such as to stimulate them to show keen initiative and better trading results. Fair remuneration and satisfactory service conditions of sales personnel ensure higher sales efficiency. It is the duty of sales organisation to devise suitable methods of remuneration in order to keep the salesmen contended and motivate them with higher sense of initiative and efficiency.

Remuneration to salesmen is in the form of salary, commission, bonus and profit-sharing: Salary is a fixed remuneration paid at specified intervals of time - usually every month. Commission is a remuneration paid on the basis of sales booked by the salesman during a particular period. Bonus is an extra remuneration paid to the salesman in recognition of his special service or any meritorious achievement. Profit-sharing obviously means giving a share in the annual profits of the firm.

Following are the methods of remuneration: (i) Straight Salary Method, (ii) Straight Commission Method, (iii) Salary and Commission Method, (iv) Salary, Commission, Bonus and Profit-Sharing Method.

(i) Straight Salary Method: Under this method a fixed amount is paid every month to the salesman irrespective of his sales efforts. Salesmen are put into different grades or cadres. Each grade carries a graduated scale of pay with provision of annual increments upto a maximum amount fixed for the grade. Salary is paid to the salesmen according to the scales applicable to their respective cadres. Experienced and meritorious salesmen are promoted to higher grades. Under this method remuneration of a salesman (i.e., salary) does not depend directly on the sales booked by him but on the length of the service and the cadre to which he belongs.

This method is simple and easily intelligible. It ensures a steady income for the salesmen. It is particularly advantageous for amateur salesmen. Even the experienced salesmen would like to have a part of their income in the form of a straight salary so that they are sure of a fixed source of earning. The main disadvantage of this method is that it does not differentiate between an ordinary salesman and an ambitious hard-working and more competent salesman. The competent salesman will find his special merits not being given the recognition. This method, therefore, fails to offer suitable incentive to sell.

(ii) Straight Commission Method: Under this method, salesman's remuneration depends on the actual sales booked by him. If no sales are made by the salesman during a particular period, he will not get any remuneration at all. Remuneration under this method takes the form of a commission calculated at a specified rate on the volume of sales transacted by different salesmen. The rate of commission may be flat rate or variable according to a sliding scale.

This method is also simple and it offers a strong incentive to sell. It is very advantageous for the firm since no remuneration is payable to the salesmen unless sales transactions are finalised by them. The capable salesmen will have full opportunity to show their abilities and book larger sales in order to earn more remuneration in the form of commission. But, inexperienced salesmen will find it difficult to earn even a modest income in the beginning. The drawback to this method is utter uncertainty of the income from the standpoint of the salesmen.

(iii) Salary and Commission Method: Straight salary method ensures a steady income and straight commission method offers high incentive. But both the methods have their own limitations as indicated above. Hence, most of the firms today adopt a combination of the two methods.

Under the salary and commission method a fixed salary is paid to each salesman irrespective of the sales affected by him. In addition to this salary, a commission is paid on the sales turned out by each salesman in his territory. Generally, sales quotas are fixed for each salesman to be fulfilled within a particular period. If the salesman surpasses his quota, he is given additional remuneration in the form of commission. If he does not reach the quota he gets only his salary. A highly competent salesman gets both the salary and the commission. This method ensures a minimum income to all the salesmen and at the same time provides adequate incentive to stimulate them for greater efforts to boost the sales.

(iv) Salary, Commission, Bonus and Profit-sharing Method: This scope of salary and commission method may be widened so as to include bonus and profit-sharing.

Bonus is a reward for special services rendered by a salesman. It is granted for marking collections of sales dues, selling special items setting up window display, booking record sales beyond the quotas, offering any valuable suggestion regarding improving the quality of the product, or introducing better method of selling, display or advertising. Payment of bonus in recognition of meritorious services will certainly invoke greater initiative on the part of salesmen and reinforce their efficiency.

Profit-sharing is giving a share in the profits made by the firm during the year. Some portion of the divisible profits of the firm is set aside for disbursement as a general bonus to all salesmen. This may be based on the total profits of the entire firm or on the profits shown by separate sales territories. Payment of a share in the profits to the salesmen takes into account the fact that they are also instrumental in raising the profits of the firm. Thus, profit-sharing method combined with the salary and commission methods is sure to stimulate the salesmen for better sales efforts.

III. Executive Functions

(1) Advertising: The objects and media of advertising will be discussed in next chapter.

(2) Sales Promotion: The meaning and the importance of sales promotion is dealt below.

(3) Selling Routine: The routine followed in executing the orders received from the customers.

Sales Promotion

Every effort put in by the Sales Department is in effect intended to promote the sales. Salesmen are appointed to canvass the sales and advertising media are used so push up the sales. Sales promotion, however, is a wider function performed by the sales manager. In large undertakings, sales promotion activities are organised under a separate department, whereas in smaller enterprises sales promotion is undertaken by the advertising department.

In manufacturing enterprises sales promotion becomes an important specialised function. The task of manufacturers is not complete until the products produced are sold out at profitable prices. Hence, they have to devise efficient and effective sales services to ensure quick turnover of their goods.

We have seen in the previous chapter that a suitable selling policy is essential for prompt marketing of goods. The executive steps taken to realise the ideals of sales policy can be characterised as sales promotion. The scope of sales promotion differs from firm to firm. The main purpose of sales promotion is to educate the dealers in the art of salesmanship and publicity and also to help the firm's own salesmen in their selling activities.

Sales promotion activities can be summarised as follows:

(1) Supplying information to dealers like wholesalers, retailers, mercantile agents so as to make them interested in the line of goods offered for sale.

(2) Equipping the dealers with materials of display and sales literature and to acquaint them with the necessary sales-technique. This would enable the dealers to arouse interest in their customers for the goods.

(3) Adjustment of the design and quality of the product and changes in terms of selling in accordance with the current trends in the market.

(4) Aiding the salesmen in their efforts of selling the goods by providing them with sales manuals, catalogues, brochures, etc.

(5) Handling complaints from customers and making due adjustments so as to satisfy them and create goodwill.

(6) Providing 'after-sale-service' to customers.

(7) Offer of special price-concessions and gifts to buyers on special occasions. Lotteries, lucky-dips and similar contests help to bring together large number of consumers and attractive prizes are awarded to the winning consumers. This would create further interest in the consumers for the goods and establish fair reputation.

Sales promotion materials include booklets, catalogues, calendars, etc. These have been explained in the next chapter. Sales promotion activities mainly aim at promoting goodwill for the firm among dealers and consumers.

Sales Manager

Sales manager is an important executive officer in a business enterprise. He is entrusted with the task of administering the sales organisation. The volume of sales, the extent of profit and the future prospects of a firm largely depend upon the influential personality and executive efficiency of its sales manager.

Sales manager should possess the qualities of effective leadership. He should have a commanding personality and organising capacity. He should be highly educated and thoroughly specialised in the science and art of management. He should be man of keen-initiative and push and imbued with high sense of duty, responsibility and loyalty. He should have strong determination and self-confidence. Patience, foresight, sociability and optimistic outlook are some other qualities to be possessed by an ideal sales manager.

Duties of Sales Manager

(1) He should plan periodical surveys of market conditions and formulate a suitable sales policy to keep up the tempo of sales.

(2) He should advice his proprietors on matters of location and layout of sales offices and branch organisations at different places.

(3) He should always be in search of new markets for creating increasing demand for the goods of the firm.

(4) He should suggest any improvements in the products and adjustments in the terms of their sale to accord with the trends in the market.

(5) He should devise a smooth sales routine to ensure prompt execution of orders placed by the customers.

(6) He should collect information from different areas of the market and prepare sales budget by scientific system of sales forecasting.

(7) He should study the need of advertising and display and advise the Advertisement and Sales Promotion Departments about the appeal and medium of advertising the goods.

(8) He should evolve economical methods of marketing. He should also keep a close watch on selling costs to minimise the overhead expenses.

(9) He should select the right type of salesmen and impart adequate training to them in the technique of selling the particular line of goods.

(10) He should exercise effective control over his sales staff to extract sincere, loyal and efficient work from them.

(11) He should stimulate sales efforts of his salesmen by recognising and rewarding the meritorious among them.

(12) He should call meetings of salesmen at stated intervals to discuss their problems and try to solve them with sympathy and understanding.

(13) He should coordinate his selling efforts with buying, credit, advertisement and financial policies of the firm.

(14) He should make a comparative study of competitors products and policies with a view to improve his sales efforts.

(15) He should keep in personal touch as many customers and dealers as is possible and seek to build goodwill for the firm.

In short, sales manager should prove to be a friend, philosopher and guide to the salesmen and as a loyal and competent employee of the firm.

❑❑❑

6

Advertising and Trade Associations

Publicity and Advertising

Publicity means spreading of information relating to a particular product. The purpose of publicity is to acquaint the customers with the utility of the product. In view of the modern structure of large-scale production and competitive marketing, the producers and dealers have to arrange for supplying necessary information about their goods to consumers situated far and wide. Publicity is a wider term and it includes advertising. Advertising also means publishing the product. While publicity merely implies supply of information, advertising means presentation of the information in such a way as to create interest and arouse desire among the consumers for the product by appealing to their buying instincts. Thus, it is a specialised technique of popularising the products. It is, therefore, described as salesmanship-in-writing or non-personal salesmanship.

Objects of Advertising

Advertising, which is an important step in modern marketing, performs following functions:

(1) creating demand for a new product by skilfully invoking interest for it among consumers;

(2) extending the market for an established product by repeated stress on its selling points;

(3) educating the public in the use of the product;

(4) creating goodwill by ensuring guaranteed standards of quality and providing quick, honest services to the customers;

(5) overcoming present and potential competition by tactfully underlining the relative superiority of the products in question;

(6) assisting the salesman in his personal efforts to persuade the prospective customers to buy the product; and

(7) warning the public against imitation of the particular product by other producers through precise description of the special features of the product to distinguish its identity.

Advantages of Advertising

(1) Advertising Stimulates Production: Since its object is to create demand and expand the market for different goods, it tends to encourage their production on larger scale.

(2) Quickens the Tempo of Turnover of Goods: Advertisements seek to induce the customers to buy the goods and hence the stocks of goods cleared quickly. Advertising is basically sales-oriented.

(3) Gives Wide Choice to Consumers: Advertisements of different varieties of products enable the consumers to make comparative assessment of various products and to select any variety that suits them.

(4) Ensures Better Quality of the Products: Every competitor seeks to advertise his product as one of standard quality. The various advertisements describe in writing the salient features of the goods and hence act as sure guarantors of quality.

(5) Leads to Increased Employment Opportunities: Larger productive activities induced by advertising imply creation of larger avenues of employment. Advertising has given rise to a new professional class of commercial artists.

(6) Lowers the Price of Goods: Expansion of sales through advertising results in reduction of costs per unit of the products. The price of goods, therefore, can be proportionately lowered.

(7) Helps the Salesmen in their Efforts of Promoting Sales: The consumers would be more favourably respective to salesmen's persuasion because of the preliminary background already created by appeals of advertisements.

(8) Adoption of Inventions to Evolve New Line of Product: This is made possible by effective advertising. New products can find market only through advertisement.

(9) Advertising has also Educative Value: Facts, figures, stories, tables, poems, etc., used as illustrations in the advertisements to increase the knowledge of the consumers.

(10) Creates Goodwill: It makes the name of the manufacturer and his products a household name everywhere. This reputation is very significant in successful business.

Objections against Advertising

(1) Advertising does not Necessarily Lead to Lower Prices: It is a quite likely that the final price is inflated because of addition of advertising expenses incurred by producer, dealers and retailers.

(2) It is a Waste: Since a number of advertisements either escape the attention of the consumers or are ignored by them. Moreover, most of the advertisements instead of creating additional demand only shift the demand from one variety of produce to another. This will have no effect on total demand and economic activity. It will manipulate and confuse the motives of the buyers and thus prove to be sheer waste.

(3) Becomes the Nursery of Monopoly: Only few firms which can afford to incur heavy advertisement expenses remain in the field of competition. Each advertiser tries to create an artificial ring of monopoly around his own variety and may be tempted to exploit the consumers through unjustified increases in price.

(4) Many Advertisements are Deceptive and Misleading: Wrong emphasis, perverse appearance and exaggerated claims confuse the consumers. There is, thus, the possibility of inferior goods getting underserved publicity.

(5) Advertisements Induce People to Spend on Goods which are not absolutely essential and which may be beyond their resources. Thus, it encourages extravagance and indebtedness among the people.

Advertising Media

There are different media of advertising. The media to be selected depend upon the area to be covered, the nature of the product, the types of buyers to be approached and the selling policy followed by the business firm. The costs of advertising also should be taken into consideration while adopting any particular medium. The medium selected should enable the message to be carried to the large number of consumers likely to take interest in the product advertised. It should also be such as to provide enough scope to present the sales message in a suitable style so as to awaken interest in that product.

The following are the main media of advertising:

(1) Press Advertising.

(2) Outdoor Advertising.

(3) Radio Advertising.

(4) Television Advertising.

(5) Film Advertising.

(6) Direct Advertising by Mail.

(7) Window Display.

Press Advertising

Advertising through press is the most common method in modern marketing. Petty shops as well as big commercial undertakings adopt the press as the medium of approaching and appealing to numerous customers situated in different areas. It is considered as the most economical effective and elastic method of advertising the goods among the prospective buyers in the literate community.

By press advertising we mean publication of particulars relating to certain goods in newspapers, magazines and journals which are read by a number of people.

(1) Newspapers: Newspapers having good circulation are highly useful media for advertising all types of goods. Newspapers reach even far-flung villages and are read by all sections or classes of the community. Advertisements may be given in daily, weekly or bi-weekly newspapers. In selecting the newspapers, the advertisers have to take into account the strength of their circulation, the class of readers they serve, and the cost of space. Goods advertised in popular and largely circulated newspapers are brought to the attention of larger number of people and carry easy conviction with them. When it is intended to appeal to a particular locality, it is more economical to select a local or provincial newspapers, preferably in the language predominantly spoken there. National newspapers are suitable in case of products needing market support from all over the country.

The advantages of newspaper advertising can be summed up as follows:

(i) larger circulation of newspapers widens the appeal of advertisements;

(ii) continuous publicity is possible since newspapers are published daily or weekly;

(iii) advertising messages can be changed promptly whenever necessary;

(iv) appeal can be concentrated on particular localities by selecting the local press;

(v) newspapers are suitable for brief or lengthily or illustrated appeals; and

(vi) results of advertising can be tested accurately and quickly.

The limitations of newspapers advertising are that, the life of newspapers is short and all the people may not be regular readers and even the readers may ignore the advertisements.

(2) Magazines: Magazines are specialised publications brought out weekly, fortnightly, monthly or quarterly. They may be exclusively devoted to literature, art, politics, economics or similar specialised branches of knowledge. Many of the magazines are, however, general being mixture of different topics and news-coverings and comments. Magazines have a longer life and their readers are enlightened. The paper used, the design and get-up of the cover and the methods of printing are relatively superior and hence the advertisements too can be presented in an attractive manner. Magazine advertising is, however, not flexible. The copy of the advertisements has to be sent to the publishers some weeks in advance of their publication. By the time they reach the subscribers, the theme of advertisements may go out of date. Sudden changes in the price of the product or the policy of the firm cannot be quickly announced in the magazines since they are published only periodically.

(3) Other Forms of Press Advertising: Advertisements are also given in trade journals which are meant for a selected section of the community. There are quite a few journals published for the professional use of doctors, engineers, agriculturists, business community, bankers, investors, etc. The products likely to be used by these specialised classes can be advertised in the related technical and trade journals. Advertisements in these journals are expected to yield quick and more or less sure results and are also economical. Advertisements, however, should be informative and intellectually convincing. Besides trade journals, advertisements also appear in General and Trade Directories, Almanacs, Annual Numbers, Special Issues of Magazines, etc.

Outdoor Advertising

Outdoor advertising means exhibition of advertisements at street corners, railway stations, bus-stands, on moving vehicles, etc. It is intended to attract the ready attention of the passers-by. The appeal of such advertisements certainly takes a mass form. This method is relatively more effective because outdoor advertisements are seen by a large number of persons. After seeing the advertisements in a street corner a person may make up his mind to purchase the articles advertised and may sometimes even walk immediately into a nearby shop where it is available. Hence immediate suggestibility and possibility of prompt response are the main merits of outdoor publicity.

The main forms of outdoor advertising are: (1) Posters and Painted Displays, (2) Electric Signs, (3) Car-cards and Travelling Displays, (4) Sandwichmen, (5) Sky-writing.

(1) Posters and Painted Displays: Posters or playcards pasted or otherwise exposed to view on walls, roadsides, street-corners, bus-terminus, railway-stations, tower fencings, etc. The message may be printed on sheets of paper or may be painted on wooden panel or a metal plate. With a pleasing colour background the posters and paintings should be boldly displayed at conspicuous places so as to produce intimate visual effect on passers-by. The message, however, should be brief so that it can be read within a couple of minutes.

(2) Electric Signs: Electric and neon signs are the most spectacular media of advertising. Advertising messages consisting of letters, figures or pictures are illuminated by electric bulbs or neon tubes. Lights of various colours and shades are used to attract the attention and grip the response of passers-by. The message so illuminated should, however, be brief and pointed. This method of advertising certainly strengthens the reputation or prestige of the advertising firm and brightens its business prospects. But since it involves heavy costs it can be adopted only by the firms having regular and well-established business.

(3) Car-cards and Travelling Displays: Car-cards are posters placed inside railway carriages, buses, taxis, tramcars, and other vehicles. Thousands of persons who travel daily by different vehicles read the messages contained in the advertisements. Passengers have adequate time to go through the messages while travelling. The advertisements placed in the vehicles catch their eyes many a times during their journey and hence they produce steadfast impression on the passengers.

Advertisements displayed outside the moving vehicles are called Travelling Displays. The posters or painted panel containing the message to be advertised are pasted or fixed on the different sides of the exterior of the vehicle. These messages are read by passengers while boarding the vehicles or while getting down. They are also read by passers-by. The messages, however, should be brief, clear and suggestive so that they can be read and grasped with case by the onlookers who are in a hurry.

Advertisements displayed on the vehicles or inside the vehicles thus carry message to large number of people and also to remote areas.

(4) Sandwichmen: Sandwichmen carry poster or playcards containing the messages to be advertised and move about in different streets. They are dressed in fancy attires and walk about in an orderly batch carrying on their person the posters. They sometimes raise slogans hailing the product they represent. Sandwichmen, thus, attract the attention of the passers-by the transit the message to be advertised.

(5) Sky-writing: Sky-writing is the most modern method of advertising. Balloons fitted with illustrative pictures and suggestive messages are flown in the sky. The aeroplanes are also used to display the illuminated banners containing the message in the open sky particularly during evenings. This method makes the appeal of advertisement more catching.

Radio Advertising

Radio is a newcomer in the field of advertising media. It has, however, been already developed as one of the effective methods of placing the sales messages before the public. The messages can be carried right upto the home of the listeners of radio. The advertisements can be broadcasted from all stations to be heard by listeners in different areas or they may be beamed to select areas for advertising the product intensively in a particular region.

Radio advertisements are normally accompanied by light music to ensure regular response from the listeners, e.g., Binaca Geetmala. Otherwise the listeners may not choose to tune the station broadcasting bare advertisements. The common feature of radio broadcasting is the 'Listeners' Request'– programme of music, songs, dialogues, interviews, etc. Along with these popular programmes, the commercial announcements are broadcasted. In the USA sponsored commercial programmes are very popular among the radio audience.

It can be concluded that radio advertisements carries an effective appeal and can cover numerous listeners of different tastes and views. The programmes should not be such as would debase public taste. Radio advertisements should have entertaining, informative and educative value.

Commercial Broadcasting in India

Broadcasting in India is owned and controlled by the Central Government. So far, it was government policy not to allow commercial announcements to go on the air. Moreover, it was felt that radio was a luxury in India and hence could not be adopted as the medium of mass-communication unlike in other advanced countries. But the situation has changed in the present times.

As per the recommendations of the Chanda Committees on Broadcasting, the Government of India reversed the earlier policy and decided to introduce commercial messages on the AIR.

Commercial advertising on the radio was introduced on 1st November, 1967 from Bombay, Nagpur on an experimental basis. It was gradually extended to Calcutta (1968); Chandigarh-Jullundur, Bangalor, Dharwar, Ahmedabad, Rajkot, Kanpur, Lucknow, Allahabad, (1970); Hyderabad-Vijaywada (1971) and Bhopal, Indore, Cuttack, Jaipur, Jodhpur, Patna, Ranchi and Trivendrum (1975).

Since May, 1970 'Sponsored Programmes' have been introduced in the commercial broadcasting. The total time available for sale on the commercial channels is between 75 to 85 minutes per day (10% of the total daily Vividh Bharati Broadcasting time). The advertisements are accepted in any language as tape-recorded 'Spots' of 15 seconds and 30 seconds duration. No 'Spot' exceeds one minute. 'Sponsored Programmes' have a longer duration ranging from 10 to 15 minutes.

Time on the air is sold through accredited recognised advertising agencies as well as through convassers and also to individuals directly. The category of the time is determined by the Audience Research Unit of All India Radio. The rates are determined on the basis of area covered by the transmitters, the buying capacity of the customers, the economic conditions prevailing in the region and the number of licences obtaining there.

It is hoped that this would accelerate more industrial growth expansion of markets.

The revenue yielded by commercial broadcasts can be utilised for greater extension of broadcasting facilities in the country. It will also lead to higher scope for technicians and talented artists. Recent launch of F.M. Radio has further boosted the field of commercial advertising.

Television Advertising

This is the most recent medium of advertising. Television is a device combining spoken word and visual presentation of facts. The particulars of products, their benefits, the method of using them etc. are featured in television programmes and transmitted to different areas for reception by numerous television sets. The message to be advertised in the form of both pictures, scenes, dialogues, speech, etc., can be carried out right to the home of the televiewers. Thus, it would be more effective. This is, however, a costly method and can be adopted by well-established firms only.

Film Advertising

Film also have become the prominent media of advertising. A short motion picture is prepared and distributed to different theatres for displaying the picture before the commencement of their regular shows. The picture runs for about five minutes and its theme is cleverly designed to underline the ability and superiority of the product in question. Large industrial and trading undertakings take out special full-length industrial films for their exhibition in selected areas. The films are accompanied by running commentary to explain the different features shown in the films. Only well-established firms can adopt this medium since it entails high cost. Instead of motion pictures, screen slides are prepared and displayed on the screen of the cinema houses before the beginning of the regular show and also after the interval. Film advertisements screened through countrywide cinema houses carry the sales message to big audience.

Direct Advertising by Mail

Direct mail advertising means despatch of advertising literature direct to the prospective customers with a view to awaken their interest in the products concerned. The advertising firm maintains a 'Mailing List' for sending the literature. Mailing List contains the names and addresses of regular customers who can be expected to take conscious interest in the products to be advertised. The list is prepared on the basis of information collected through salesmen by reference to trade directories, telephone directories, statistical publications of the government or trade associations, etc. The list is periodically revised to being up-to-date. Advertising appeal is, thus, made direct to the firms and individuals mentioned in the list.

Advertising messages that are sent by direct mail may be in the following forms:

(1) Sales Letters, (2) Circular Letters, (3) Leaflets, folders, calendars, booklets and catalogues.

(1) Sales Letters: Sales letters are written to a selected number of firms, dealers and consumers with a view to approach them directly with the sales messages. Sales letters are personal messages containing a graphic analysis of salient features of the products and setting forth the terms of their sale. The letters are drafted in such a way as to catch the attention of readers (prospective buyers) and get their support for the product under reference. They seek to underline the quality, utility and suitability of the product in a convincing style supported by evidence in the form of testimonials and samples.

(2) Circular Letters: Circular letters are sales letters containing the same matters addressed to numerous prospective customers. Sales letters are addressed to different persons and each letter may contain a different message. Sales circulars, however, convey a common message and are, therefore, printed or cyclostyled on large-scale. Circular letters are expected to achieve the object of sales appeal through wider but direct approach. Effectiveness on both sales and circular letters depends upon the forceful and convincing style in which their messages are casted.

Both these types of letters are to be nicely-printed on highly quality paper and sent in attractive covers. Advantages of sales and circular letters are:

(i) They are relatively cheaper media of advertisement.

(ii) The sales messages conveyed by them are not mixed up with other advertisements unlike in press advertising. Hence the messages carry their own exclusive appeal to the readers.

(iii) They are personal appeals and hence are more effective.

(iv) Since there is no restriction of space they can be more informative and more persuasive.

(3) (i) Leaflets: It is a single sheet of paper printed either on one side or on both sides. Leaflet gives a brief account of the features and uses of the product. It also contains directions for using it. Leaflets are distributed, displayed and are also sent along with sales and circular letters. Very often leaflets are placed in packages or cartons containing the article.

(ii) Folders: When the leaflet is folded it is called folder. Folders give a neat appearance. They are usually sent along with circular letters.

(iii) Calendars: Calendars are today one of the most popular media of advertisement Calendars are a guide to dates, and main holidays during a given year. They are attractively designed with impressive pictures of leading personalities, sceneries, factory products, etc. With such background, the name of the firm, the products dealt in etc. are specified on the calenders. They are indicative of the product and seek to underline the reputation of the firm. The calendars are sent to select number of customers and dealers.

(iv) Booklets: Information relating to the utility, speciality and other particulars of a product is sometimes printed in the form of small books instead of loose leaflets. Booklets are useful for giving a clearer and more detailed description of the product. The style should be simple, precise and intelligible. Illustrations increase the effectiveness of booklets. They can be sent by post to a limited number of potential customers or distributed free to create mass appeal.

(v) Catalogues: A catalogue is a booklet showing the list of goods and the prices chargeable for each article specified in the list. Diagrammatic illustrations of goods enhance the value of catalogue as the advertising medium. Catalogues are used often by mail order business houses. Catalogues are sent to the regular and potential customers so as to keep them in touch with changes in the availability of goods and in their prices. Sales or circular letters are also accompanied by catalogues to be restored to by their readers for detailed reference.

Window Display

Window display is another specialised form of modern advertising. The object of window display is obviously to draw attention of the public and arouse their interest in the products displayed. It is arranged particularly by retail stores.

Window display means exhibition of goods in artistically laid out windows at the shop fronts, or at important busy centres like railway stations, bus-stands, market place, etc. Large showrooms are organised by manufacturers and wholesalers at main centres in order to publicise their products and lead the prospective buyers to the retailers. The retailers also organise attractive display of their goods in the windows in or near their shops. The visual effect of showrooms and windows with neatly arranged goods brightened by glamorous multi-coloured lights will be so strong as to create desire among the passers-by and persuade them to visit the shop for buying the goods.

Window display is a significant factor in effective selling appeal. The display of select specimens in the show-windows enables the public to compare their needs or requirements with the variety of goods exhibited. Attractive windows raise the reputation of the firm and leave an unforgettable impression with the onlookers who readily remember the firm-whenever they feel the need for the goods (displayed). Well laid-out show-windows reduce the sales resistance on the part of the prospective buyers. It is, therefore, looked upon a silent salesmanship, window display is, thus, a highly important medium of advertisement from the standpoints of suggestibility, sales and goodwill.

Planning for Advertising

A firm which wants to advertise its products has to develop an advertising campaign. Advertising campaign is "a planned, coordinated series of advertisements built around a central theme and designed to achieve a specific objective."

First, the goals to be achieved are established. Then the central theme of the advertisements is decided.

Appeals to be stressed are thought of in the light of the buying motives of consumers to be covered. Then media are selected. Finally, individual advertisements are created and produced.

Selection of the media is usually based on the following:

(1) Objective of the advertisement.

(2) Circulation of the medium, i.e., whether it reaches the market to be covered or not.

(3) Requirements of the message, i.e., the medium should be suitable for the presentation of the message to the market.

(4) The cost of the medium.

(5) Cooperation and promotion aids offered by the medium. For example, the firm will prefer a magazine offering 'reprints' for use in counter or window displays.

Methods of Organising Advertising Campaign

There are four alternative methods for organising an advertising campaign. These are as follows:

(1) The firm may have its separate advertising department.

(2) The work may be done by the sales department of the firm.

(3) The firm may decide to use an advertising agency.

(4) Combination of the own advertising department of the firm and advertising agency.

Relatively small firm uses its sales department to organise its advertising campaign. Large retailing and manufacturing firms prefer to have separate advertising department for the purpose.

Many manufacturers combine the efforts of their own advertising department and advertising agency. In such a case advertising department acts as liaison between the advertising agency and the firm. The advertising department is responsible for the preparation and administration of the advertising budget. It also approves the plans and advertisements prepared by the advertising agency for the firm. The advertising department is also responsible for undertaking direct mail advertising, dealer displays and other activities not undertaken by the advertising agency.

Preparation of Advertisements

Advertisements are the heart of the entire advertising campaign, therefore, preparation of an advertisement is very important. Preparation of advertisement involves the following:

(1) Writing the copy.

(2) Selecting illustration to be used.

(3) Preparation of layout.

(4) Reproduction of advertisement for the selected media.

Copy of an advertisement consists of the written or spoken material which includes headline, coupons, name and address of the advertiser and the main body of the message.

Headline should be capable of catching the attention of the prospect. It should also suggest the central idea of the main body of the copy.

Other methods of attraction attention are: (i) the use of illustration, (ii) use of distinct colour or sound, (iii) distinct arrangement of different materials of the advertisements.

Illustration may be in the form of a photograph, drawing, reproduction of a painting or cartoon. It is a powerful feature of an advertisement.

Layout refers to the physical arrangement of all the elements in an advertisement. A good layout attracts the attention and holds the interest of readers who are persuaded to read the whole advertisement with interest. Layout is concerned with placing the headline, copy, illustrations of the advertisement most attractively within the allotted space of time.

Advertising Agency

Meaning

An advertiser firm may organise the advertising campaign through its own advertising department or may entrust the work to an advertising agent.

An advertising agent or an advertising agency is "an independent company rendering specialised services in advertising in particular and marketing in general."

Advantages

Advertising agencies induce manufacturers to advertise. They help them in selecting and obtaining the means of advertising and in planning and writing advertisements.

Many large modern advertising agencies maintain staff composed of experts in various fields related to advertising such as copy writing, layout, photography, display, printing, typography, radio and film publicity, marketing, etc. Actual composition of the staff varies according to the clients of the advertising agency. But services of other experts, such as engineers, dietitians, bio-chemists, etc., are obtained when required. Therefore, even manufacturing firms having their own advertisement departments find the services of advertising agencies useful for following reasons:

(1) Individual firm cannot maintain such a large force of experts as an advertising agency. By using advertising agency's services it can have the advantage of these experts.

(2) An advertising agency possesses the experience of the problems faced by its clients, i.e., firms organising their advertising campaign through the agency. Benefit of such experience naturally goes to any firm faced with similar problems.

(3) It is easier to know the number and class of listeners of radio programmes or readers of newspapers, periodicals, etc.

(4) Use of the advertising agency brings to the client firm benefits of economical rates for buying space or time from various media.

(5) The advertising agency has close contacts and contractual relations with the site owners, block makers, poster contractors, etc. Therefore, their services can be secured at lower rates and without loss of time.

(6) The firm using the services of an advertising agency gets the benefits of the wide knowledge and experience of the agency regarding the various media and their relative effectiveness.

(7) Advertising agency can help the firm in choosing the most suitable medium of advertising.

(8) The manager of the advertisement department is relieved of the details like preparation of the advertisements, etc., and can concentrate his time and energy in evaluating the effects of advertising campaign and consulting various departments on the matter.

How does the Advertising Agency Work?

The representative of an advertising agency contacts the manager of the advertisement department or sales manager of the client's firm. After the order for advertising is procured, services of various experts of the agency are called for in the process of executing this order. The whole process involves following functions which are performed by the advertising agency:

(1) The marketing or research department of the agency studies the characteristics of the product and its marketing considerations.

(2) On the basis of this study, advertising policy for the firm is determined and the media to be used are decided upon.

(3) Then, the media to be used are approached to buy the 'space' or 'time' required.

(4) The copy writer prepares the appeal and layout-man designs the form in which it is to be presented. Necessary photographs, drawings, or charts to be inserted in the advertisements are procured. The typists or printers produce the copy of advertisement.

(5) After the copy of advertisement is ready, space and position in case of press advertising or time in case of radio and television is negotiated for.

(6) Proper checks are kept to see that advertisements are inserted correctly and reproduced satisfactorily. Similar checks are kept in the case of media like radios, films, posters, etc.

How is the Advertising Agency Remunerated?

The advertising agency relies for its income on the commission it receives from the owners of the advertising media and publishers. It is clear from the description above that the advertising agency brings business to the owners of the advertising media. In recognition of this fact the advertising agency is paid certain commission, usually 15 per cent of the total amount of the bill, by the owners of the media. As such the advertising agency frequently makes no charge to its clients – the firm advertising through it – for handling their advertising. In effect it means that the large firms pay nothing for the service rendered by the agency in preparing and placing their advertisements.

However, the advertising agency has to charge a fee for its services to smaller firm. Also, it charges the client firms for extra services rendered such as undertaking market research, arranging shop display, etc.

Institutions for Furtherance of Trade

Trade flourishes under conditions in which increasing opportunities are provided for constant and continuous contact between prospective buyers and sellers. Efforts have to be made to bring the products to the notice of consumers and create interest among them in the use of the products. Arrangements have to be made for coming together of suppliers and buyers so as to bring about business transactions involving the exchange of goods between them. The arrangements by which trade prospects become brighter constitute the functions of institutions for furtherance of trade.

Objectives of these Institutions

Following are the objectives of these institutions:

(1) Arranging for the display of goods.

(2) Providing a common meeting place for buyers and sellers.

(3) Ensuring a steady supply of goods.

(4) Assisting the seller and the buyer in concluding a commercial bargain.

(5) Collecting and disseminating the information relating to different aspects of trade such as source of supply, trends in tastes or fashions, price-movements, credit dealings, government regulations, taxation laws, etc.

In short, promotion of trade through guidance, publicity, localisation of supply, etc., is the main objective of such institutions.

Forms of these Institutions

In the words of Stephenson "The chief institutions through which trade is directly furthered are markets, fairs and exchanges while those through which it is only indirectly influenced are chambers of commerce, trade organisations, etc."

Now, we will discuss briefly the following institutions for furtherance of trade:

(1) Marketing Institutions.

(2) Produce Exchange.

(3) Fairs and Exhibitions.

(4) Trade Organisations.

Marketing Institutions

Marketing institutions are places where buyers and sellers meet to exchange goods or services. Commercial dealings are systematically conducted through organised meeting of buyers and sellers at a certain place and at certain time. Markets grow into permanent institutions to equate demand and supply. Traders dealing in different merchandise gather at a place and consumers, by conventions, are habituated to visit such places for purchasing their requirements. In towns there are specific places where particular products are available and are identified as markets; for example, vegetable market, fish market, cloth market, grain market, etc.

There are also regulated markets with their notified trading areas constituted under the law to help in the marketing of agricultural produce.

Marketing institutions consists of the following:

(1) Wholesale Markets.

(2) Retail Markets.

(1) Wholesale Markets: These markets are located in big towns and cities. It is through these markets that most manufactured products are released for sale. Wholesale markets provide adequate storage facilities for stocking the goods to meet the recurring demand. Retailers will find it convenient to inspect the goods, compare their quality and select those goods which suit their customers' (consumers) needs and tastes as Stephenson said, "wholesale markets make steady and economic distribution."

(2) Retail Markets: These are the big and small shops located in villages, towns and cities almost in every street to sell goods to the ultimate users or consumers. Retail markets are continuous markets, that is, they are confined to define days and time. They provide the public with shopping facilities in respect of a large number of products of daily use. Easy accessibility, convenient timings, adjustable size of purchases, varieties of articles for choice, personal touch with the customers are some of the features of retail markets which promote trade.

Produce Exchanges

A produce exchange is an organised market which functions under a set of rules and regulations. It furnishes marketing facilities for transacting business on a large scale in commodities of specific grades. It provides a market place where its members meet at definite times and transact business under the rules laid down by the organisation.

The produce exchange does not enter into any dealing on its own or in its own name. It only provides facilities for the promotion of business and regulate the business dealings of its members.

(1) Commodities Transacted: The commodities usually traded on produce exchanges are: wheat, cotton, tea, oilseeds, jute, sugar, cotton piece goods, gold bullion, metals, etc. The commodities to be traded on these exchanges should be such as can be described by grades. Also, there must be steady demand for them and trading in them should be on sufficiently large scale. Their price should be subject to changes so that dealers are induced to enter into contracts for purchase or sale of these goods.

(2) Transactions: Transactions on these exchanges are mainly of two types: (i) Spot or cash contracts, and (ii) Future contracts.

Spot contracts are transactions concluded for actual delivery of goods, immediately or in a few days time. They are affected for the purpose of merchandising.

Future contracts refer to transactions to be settled at a future date. These contracts are entered into either for the purpose of speculation or for protection against the risks arising out of likely changes in prices. Thus, futures contract is an agreement to buy or sell as per rules and regulations of the produce exchange a specified quality of commodity at an agreed price during a specified future month.

Speculators are those dealers on the produce exchange who seek to earn profit out of the differences in anticipated prices of commodities over a specified period. There are mainly two types of speculators: bulls and bears.

Bulls buy long, i.e., they expect rise in prices in near future and, hence, they enter into buying contracts at an agreed price with a view to settle the deal in future by selling at the higher prices if their forecasts come off true.

Bears expect a fall in prices and hence sell short. They agree to sell at an agreed price but promise to give delivery at specified time in future. They would give delivery on the settlement dates by buying the goods at lower prices as per their expectations.

Futures contracts have to be made in the market ring of the exchange.

(3) Importance: Produce exchange provides convenient place for its members to carry on their transactions, both spot and future.

Produce exchanges collect and disseminate market information for the benefit of its members. They lay down standards and grades according to quality and, thus, facilitate trading without physical inspection of goods. They help in stabilising prices of goods at different places and at different times.

Fairs

Fairs and Exhibitions are important media of communication between the prospective purchasers and supplies of goods.

Fairs mean improvised market for goods. They are held on a fixed day or days in a year on some social or religious occasions. During the days of the fairs, commodities are displayed for sale. The intending buyers visit the fairs and select the goods of their choice.

Fairs bring buyers and sellers together and facilitate exchange of goods. Fairs are conducted and organised in such a way as to attract large number of visitors and fascinate them to buy the products. Fairs provide opportunities for direct or face-to-face negotiations between the dealers and users for the sale of merchandise. Since different producers or manufacturers come to the fairs with their varieties of products, prospective buyers get an opportunity to see the varied types of goods displayed there, compare the standards and prices of these goods and then enter into trade agreements.

Fairs were significant in ancient times when means of communications and transport had not developed. In the social organisation based on self-sufficient village units, scope for trade was widened through occasional fairs. Special facilities like protection to goods and traders during their journey and duration of fairs were given by the royal officials. Important bargains were concluded in the presence of royal officials and witnesses. In course of time arrangements were made for prompt settlement of disputes and payments of debts.

In the seventeenth and eighteenth centuries also most European countries had fairs of national importance. The famous fair was the Leipzing Fair. At Leipzing (now in East Germany) the main highways of Central Europe converged and hence fair was held at that place. Traders from Hungary, Russia and Poland visited the fair to bargain with the traders from Italy, Holland and Greece.

During the nineteenth century the importance of fairs diminished due to growth of quicker modes of transport and communication and the change in the economic structure. However, still international fairs are held at Vienna, Frankfurt and Leipzing. British Industries Fair, Motor Show, etc., in England attract large number of buyers from home and foreign countries.

Exhibitions

(1) Meaning: In modern times, exhibitions on national and international scales are held to facilitate trade through display and publicity. Local exhibitions are also organised by trade associations to demonstrate mainly the local products and find out new buyers.

Exhibitions are defined as 'long period show' of goods accompanied by entertainments. In earlier days exhibitions were looked upon just as a medium of conveying informations to the public. But in course of time, they have developed into medium of advertisement in order to induce the visitors to place orders for the goods displaced therein. A trade exhibitions is, in fact, a large fair. Large number of producers and traders gather together at a chosen place to display their goods. This provides an opportunity to the visitors to select the goods of their liking and purchase them. In the words of Stephenson, "Exhibition is the means by which exhibitors' goods are brought to the notice of visitors and he hopes that new business relations will be opened up during the period of the exhibition."

Exhibitions play an important part in marketing and consumer education. The visual effects of exhibition create wholesome impact on the minds of visitors and widen their knowledge. The information and impression imparted by the exhibitions eventually lead to the persuasion of the visitors to buy the products. Psychological stimulation through attractive display of goods in the exhibitions lead to successful marketing.

(2) Objectives: Following are the objectives of exhibitions:

(i) to attract the attention of the visitors to different types of goods of different manufacturers;

(ii) to provide information about the availability of goods, their sources of supply, terms of sale, their utility and speciality with particular reference to the customers' needs and tastes;

(iii) to educate the visitors on the use of the products exhibited;

(iv) to advertise the products by effective emphasis on their selling-points so as to convince the visitors about the benefits of the products and make them to buy on the spot or place orders for delivery in due course; and

(v) to project new ideas and demonstrate new methods of production.

(3) How to Organise Exhibitions?: Exhibitions are to be designed suitably to fulfil the objectives mentioned above. The area complex of many stall and stands where goods of different manufacturers are displayed. Exhibition pandals should be inviting and impressive. Stalls and stands also should be artistically and elegantly designed and laid out in order to attract the huge crowd of visitors to drop in at the stalls. The personnel in the stall should be experts in fascinating the people and creating interest among them for the products displayed. There should be arrangements for the distribution of folders, handbills, illustrated catalogues and other forms of informative and persuasive literature. In case of products of technical nature, demonstration by well informed technicians should be held to educate and impress the visitors. For example, working of pump-sets and electric appliances should be demonstrated.

Exhibitions are also regarded as a form of entertainment. Therefore, programmes like musical concerts, folk songs, dramas, humorous dialogues, magic shows, etc., should be arranged inside the exhibition pandals.

In shorts, exhibitions should be informative, instructive and interesting to the visitors in whom an impelling feeling has to be roused to go in for the products on their liking.

(4) Importance: Nowadays, exhibitions perform many functions. These range from the documentary publicity sponsored by the government, prestige shows arranged by commercial organisations and firms to the dissemination of technical knowledge and processes concerning complicated, bulky and delicate industrial products.

Exhibitions of local character help in tapping and publicising the commercial talents in the area and familiarising the people with products available in the region.

Exhibitions at national level facilitate expansion of trade between different regions specialising in particular products. They are useful in strengthening the commercial and cultural contracts among traders, consumers and artists coming from different areas of the country.

Similarly, international exhibitions are held on massive scale to promote contact and communication among the nations of the world and facilitate trade on wider scale. International exhibitions serve to publicise the products for export and industrial potential of the country. They also help the domestic traders and industrialists to get or learn new ideas from produce exhibited by traders and producers of foreign countries which they can use for improvement of their products or trading methods and for setting up new lines of business in their own country. The first international exhibition was held in 1851 in London. It was named–the Great Exhibition.

Promotion of trade, both bilateral and multilateral is the objective of these fairs. Hence high power business delegations, both official and non-official, from different countries visit these fairs to negotiate business dealings.

Trade Organisations

Trade organisations are voluntary associations formed by industrialists, traders, employers, etc., for the purpose of safeguarding their interests. These organisations are conducted through voluntary subscriptions of their members who are benefited by the services rendered by these organisations.

These organisations "are of great service to the markets they control in standardising the forms of contacts and grades of produce, in settling the disputes swiftly and in guarding the interests of their members and at times interest of public."

These organisations promote the prospects of trade by increasing opportunities of commercial intercourse and providing useful information.

A review of the working of the various forms of trade organisations reveals that the organisations facilitate trade by rendering following services to their members:

(1) Scientific research.

(2) Collection of trade statistics.

(3) Communication of research and other business data to the members.

(4) Legal advice to the members.

(5) Formulation of standard forms of contract.

(6) Collective advertising of the products.

(7) Joint marketing of products.

(8) Common price policy and prevention of unfair competition ruinous to trade.

(9) Promotion of goodwill and reputation of the business community among the public.

Following are the main forms of trade organisations:

(1) Trade Associations.

(2) Chambers of Commerce.

(3) Trade Protection Societies.

Trade Association and Chambers of Commerce are discussed in the next section. Here we discuss Trade Protection Societies.

Trade Protection Societies are the associations formed to safeguard the financial interest of the merchants by giving to them the needed information in trade deals. Information relating to the credit worthiness of persons desirous of securing credit is provided to these sellers who are members of the Trade Protection Society. These societies prepare confidential reports on the credit-standing of new and old customers and forward these reports to the members making inquiries. Trade Protection Societies are also known as Mercantile Agencies. The well-known agencies are 'stubs,' 'duns' and 'streets.' They have valuable information about the business of numerous customers, their credit-rating, bills of exchange honoured or dishonoured, bankruptcies, financial crisis facing the firms, legal suits pending against the firms for defaulted debts, etc.

Trade Associations and Chambers of Commerce

Trade Associations and Chambers of Commerce are necessarily the outcome of development in the field of trade, commerce and industry after the Industrial Revolution. With the widening of the market and large-scale production, competition among the rival units became intense, acute and wasteful. Unrestricted formation of undertakings led to the over-crowdings of industry which worsened the situation. The result was that smaller and relatively less efficient undertakings were forced to close their shops. Only big concerns were left out to fight the struggle for survival. Even big undertakings competing against one another found that they were fighting a losing battle. They realised that competition was meaningless and inconsistent with the changed circumstances under which they were operating. They felt the need of co-operation, consultation and some form of concerted action of their part to protect and further their common and individual interests.

This feeling was further strengthened by the rise and growth of the labour movement and socialist ideas. Firstly, there was the need of collective stand in regard to collective bargaining for wages and other working conditions. Secondly, under pressure of the organised section of the working class, government had to interfere more and more to protect the interests of the workers in particular and the society in general. Therefore, producers had to think in terms of cooperative action on their part to secure favourable legislation and other privileges from the government. Thus, "the evils of wasteful and cut-throat competition led to the recognition of the common interest of the independent entrepreneurs." They began to realise that they had common problems and that the best way to solve them was to get together and help each other. This led to the formation of Trade Associations and Chambers of Commerce. These were "associations for mutual protection and advancement of the interests of the entrepreneurs."

Trade Associations

(1) Definition: "Trade Association may be defined as voluntary organisation for mutual protection or advantage of independent enterprises producing or distributing similar goods and services." It is an organisation formed to promote the mutual interests of individuals or companies engaged in the same kind of business. Members of a trade association are usually competitors. It is a non-profit organisation which attempts to promote the interests of its members. It does not enter into any business transactions on its own account. The name of the association is usually after the nature of business conducted by its members. It tries to enrol as members all those engaged in the same line of business in a particular region. It does not involve loss of independence of its members who are free to conduct their business as they please. No member can interfere with the working of other members or member-units. It is essentially 'educational in character.' Thus, it may be defined as a non-profit voluntary organisation of business competitors operating in the same line of business for the promotion of their common economic interests.

(2) Functions: Functions of the trade associations are usually determined by their constitution embodied in the Articles and Memorandum of Associations. They vary from country to country. They may be listed as follows:

(i) Provision of market information to its members.

(ii) Supply of legal advice to its members in matters like customs, regulations and factory legislation.

(iii) Safeguarding of credit and strengthening the hands of their members of collective bargaining.

(iv) Maintaining technical staff who are constantly engaged in research, testing and standardising the various processes of production.

(v) **Maintaining Trade Missions:** These trade missions explore the possibilities of new markets and study the causes of the loss or relative decline of old markets in different parts of the world.

(vi) Most of these associations form special committees to study the employment situation. These committees scrutinise demands put forth by the trade unions, enforce the agreements reached between employers and employees and undertake survey of 'labour efficiency throughout the industry.'

(vii) They collect, compile, analyse and disseminate business and technical information.

(viii) They engage themselves in legislative lobbying and try to influence legislation by educating public opinion in various ways.

(ix) Some of the large associations maintain their research sections. The work of the Ahmedabad Textiles Research Association (ATRA) deserves special mention.

(x) They supply legal, economic and technical information to their members.

(xi) They send their representatives to serve on various statutory boards and committees.

(xii) **Self-governing Agency for the Trade or Industry Concerned:** Trade associations try to serve as an instrument by which abusive, unfair and unethical practices in the trade can be eliminated. For this purpose many associations adopt codes of ethics to be followed by their members. They also provide facilities of commercial arbitrations. Arbitration may be voluntary or compulsory. The purpose is to help the members to settle their disputes without taking report to the courts. For arbitration to be successful rules and regulations governing the rights and duties of the parties are clearly laid down.

(xiii) They try to bring uniformity into the system of cost accounting.

(xiv) **Exchange of Credit Information:** It is always advantageous to exchange information about the creditworthiness of customers served by various undertakings. A large number of associations undertake this work.

(xv) **Activities Connected with Market Research and Advertising:** It is necessary for the manufacturers, wholesalers and retailers to know the changes in the tastes, fashions or buying habits of the consumers. This necessitates market research. Many trade associations undertake this work on behalf of their members. Similarly, for the sake of economy and effectiveness, advertising is carried on by members through their trade associations.

(xvi) **Miscellaneous:** Many trade associations set up central selling agencies and debt collection department for the benefit of their members.

(3) Organisation and Working: Trade associations may be registered under the Companies Act or the Trade Union Act. They may be formed with or without shares. Usually they are formed on the principles of liability limited by guarantee. In case of an association without shares, payment of entrance and subscription fees is necessary to become a member. If it is formed with share capital, persons intending to become members have to purchase its shares. For the regulation of its working Memorandum and Articles of Association or the Bye-laws lay down the powers and duties of the office-bearers of the Association.

The administrative set-up of a trade association is similar to that of an ordinary company form of business organisation. The members of the association elect a Board of Directors to supervise the management of the association. The board appoints officers to execute the policies adopted by the association. Usually, these office-bearers include a president, a vice-president, secretary, and treasurer. The president and vice-president retire at the annual general meeting, but are eligible for re-election. The president usually presides over the meetings. Secretary is the most important executive officer. Generally, he is a full-time salaried official.

Chambers of Commerce

(1) Meaning: A Chambers of Commerce is an association of merchants, financiers, manufacturers and other engaged in business in a particular locality or region for promoting the general commercial interest, of all the members. Chambers of Commerce work to protect the interests of their members and foster the growth and development of commerce and industry of the respective regions in which they operate. They are formed to promote and protect general trade interests of all the members irrespective of the kind or class of trade they are engaged in.

(2) Organisation: In regard to the formation of a chamber of commerce, there is some difference between some of the European countries on the one hand and countries like India, England, the USA, etc., on the other. For example, in France, a chamber of commerce in established by law and is subject to government control. It is financed by a government subsidy or special tax payable by all traders of the district or the region covered by it. Contrary to this, in India, England, the USA, etc., it is a creation of private initiative and is "purely a private and voluntary institution." It has no financial resources other than collections through membership dues and small incidental earnings.

Voluntary chambers of commerce are formed in the same way as trade associations.

They elect a Board of Directors in the annual general body meeting of the members. The board elects them from among its members a president and a vice-president. The board also forms various sub-committees in-charge of different functions or to look after the interest of different traders.

Thus, the administrative set-up and working of the chambers follow more or less the same pattern as that of the trade association.

(3) Functions: Functions of chambers of commerce may be broadly divided into two groups:

(i) Technical and administrative services for the members and the commercial class in general.

(ii) Representation of the business community before the government.

(i) Technical and Administrative Services: It has been said above that in some of the European countries like France Chambers of Commerce are semi-official organisation whereas in our country and in England, the USA, etc., they are voluntary associations. This difference gives rise to some variation in the functions of the two kinds of chambers as well.

In France, chambers of commerce performs the following technical and administrative functions:

(a) They manage and own stock exchange, employment exchanges, docks, warehouses, commercial schools, museums and libraries.

(b) They prepare reports on the development of trade.

(c) They issue export certificates and certificates of origin.

(d) They appoint experts, inspectors, accountants and commercial arbitrators.

Functions of chambers in England, the USA, India, etc., are limited in nature. Their functions may be summarised as given below:

(a) They provide information on traffic routes and method of packing for foreign shipping.

(b) They collect and disseminate information on general trade conditions and the existing and potential markets.

(c) They help the members in exchanging notes on the creditworthiness of their customers.

(d) They try to secure for the trade improved transportation at lower freight rates.

(e) They act as centres for collecting claims.

(f) Many of them maintain research establishments.

(g) They make arrangements for labour supply.

(h) They try to introduce standardised methods of trade.

(i) They undertake general publicity work like advertising, etc.

(j) They provide for commercial arbitration.

(ii) Representation of Business Community before the Government: In France they have 'formal contacts' with the government. They send their representatives on the legislative council and other official committees. Government receives from the chambers reports, advice proposals for enacting any law.

In England, the USA, India, etc., chambers approach the government unofficially. They engage in lobbying, try to bring political pressure, send representations and give general publicity to their views on matters pertaining to the commercial interest. All those activities are directed to get a favourable budget, laws passed, etc., or to see that unfavourable legislation does not get the support of the legislature. Thus, they function outside the ordinary legislature to influence legislation.

Apart from lobbying and bringing political pressure on the government they perform the following functions:

(a) They act as spokesmen of the business community and express their views on such policies of the government as are likely to affect their interest.

(b) They make representation to the government against an existing piece of legislation or a proposed legislation and make suggestions for legislation necessary for the promotion and development of commerce and industry.

(c) They support candidates for election to the legislatures.

Special Features of Trade Associations and Chambers of Commerce

Trade Associations and Chambers of Commerce possess some distinct features of their own. These distinct features are:

(1) Their membership is voluntary.

(2) They are non-profit organisations.

(3) They do not run any business of their own.

(4) Their activities are financed mainly out of the entrance fees and annual subscription fees collected from members.

(5) They do not interfere with the internal administration or working of the members concerned.

Difference between Trade Associations and Chambers of Commerce

Much similarity is found in the function, aims and objects of the trade associations and chambers of commerce. In spite of this similarity they differ in many respects. Points of difference between them are given below:

Trade Association	Chamber of Commerce
1. A trade association is formed by those engaged in the same trade.	1. A chamber of commerce is an organisation of businessmen from a particular region belonging to different trades.
2. A trade association is concerned with the interest of a particular trade.	2. A chamber of commerce serve the interest of all businessmen engaged in different trades from the region it represents.
3. A trade association is named after the class of trade it	3. A chamber of commerce is named after the locality or area from which its members

represents. For example, Mumbai Mill-owners Association or East India Cotton Association.	come. For example, London Chamber of Commerce or Mumbai Chamber of Commerce.
4. Members of a trade association are competitors.	4. Members of a chamber of commerce may be both competitors and non-competitors.

Trade Associations and Chambers of Commerce in India

General

The growth of the trade associations and chambers of commerce has followed the expansion of commerce and industry. The history of such associations and chambers in India is not an exception to this fact.

Trade Associations

The growth of trade associations followed the growth of different trades in the country. After the advent of the East India Company's rule in our country, initiative in the development of trade and industry, at the early stage, has passed into the hands of Europeans. The first industry developed by them in India was the indigo industry. For the protection of the interest of the indigo factory owners, an Association of Indigo Planters was formed in 1801. In the beginning Europeans in India were mostly traders and merchants. European traders in Bengal formed the Calcutta Trader's Association in 1830. Their counterparts in Madras formed the Madras Trader's Association in 1856.

After the abolition of the monopoly right of the East India Company in 1833, Europeans started thinking in terms of exploiting India's potential resources. This tendency became more market after 1860. They began with the development of the plantations. Soon they came forward to develop the coal mines and jute industries as well. This development led to the formation of the following associations:

(1) Indian Tea Associations in 1881.

(2) Indian Mining Association in 1892.

(3) United Planters' Association of Southern India in 1893.

(4) Indian Jute Mills Association in 1894.

All these associations were formed by the Europeans for the promotion and protection of their interest.

The first, association with which Indian businessmen were also associated was the Bombay Mill Owner's Association formed as a result of the combined efforts of the Indian and European businessmen in 1875.

It was only after the Government of India adopted the policy of discriminating protection after 1921 that many industries came to be established by Indian interests. This was followed by a number of associations formed to meet collectively the problems and difficulties faced by each to them. More important of them are listed below:

(1) Indian Mining Federation formed in 1930.

(2) Indian Sugar Mill's Associations established in 1933.

(3) The Indian Collery Owners' Association in 1934.

(4) The Indian Soap Makers' Association in 1934.

(5) The Bengal Glass Manufacturers' Association in 1935.

(6) The Indian Paper Mills' Association in 1939.

Chamber of Commerce

As in the case of trade associations, initiative in the formation of chambers of commerce also was taken by the Europeans. The first chamber of commerce was established in 1834, one year after the abolition of the monopoly of trade of the East India Company in 1833. This was in Calcutta. The Calcutta Chamber of Commerce was followed in 1836 by the Bombay Chamber of Commerce and the Madras Chamber of Commerce. Both were formed by the European merchants. These chambers were organised on the pattern of Chambers of Commerce in England. They were named after the names of the cities in which their offices were situated. They were to promote exclusively European interests.

The first Chamber of Commerce of Indian businessmen was formed in Cocanada in 1885, the year in which the Indian National Congress was also founded. Two years later, in 1887, the Bengal National Chamber of Commerce was founded in Calcutta. Soon this, chamber became the mouthpiece of the national business community. Not only Indian merchants from Calcutta, but merchants from different parts of the country also came to be associated with this national chamber.

By this time in every state and in every important centre of trade and industry chambers of commerce have been established. In Kolkata alone there were five chambers of commerce - the Bengal Chamber of Commerce and Industries; the Indian Chamber of Commerce; the Bharat Chamber of Commerce; and the Oriental Chamber of Commerce.

Chambers of commerce have been organised on local, state or all India basis. The state chambers are interested in the promotion and protection of commerce and industry of the state.

There are 15 all-India chambers of commerce.

Also, there are two Federations of Chambers of Commerce in India. These are:

(1) The Associated Chambers of Commerce of Calcutta; and

(2) The Federation of India Chambers of Commerce, Delhi.

The Associated Chambers of Commerce was formed in 1920 in Calcutta, to represent European business interests in India. Fifteen local chambers are affiliated to it.

The Federation of Indian Chambers of Commerce and Industry (FICCI) was established by Indian businessmen in 1926. Its headquarter is in Delhi. It has been recognised by the Government of India as the premier representative organisation of the Indian business community. It has 123 ordinary members, 214 associate members and 9 overseas members. Ordinary members consist of trade associations and chambers of commerce operating in different parts of India. Overseas members are those chambers which are operating in foreign countries. Associate members are individuals, firms and companies which join the Federation in their individual capacity.

The FICCI renders useful services to the Indian business community and the government. It sends its representatives to various committees of the government, such as the Central Advisory Council of Industries, the Import Export Advisory Councils, the Capital Issue Advisory Committee, etc. The Indian Industries Fair organised in 1955 by the Federation was the biggest of its kind in our country and was much appreciated both in India and abroad.

Importance of Trade Associations and Chambers of Commerce

These associations and chambers can play very important role in the rapid economic progress of our country. All the functions performed by them, which have been discussed earlier, are of immense importance for the smooth progress of commerce and industry in the country. There is much need in our country for research in the field of production, marketing, etc. More of such institution like the Ahmedabad Textile Research Association are required to be established at the initiative and with the resources of the private enterprise. Industrial exhibitions, shows and fairs are needed to be organised to popularise our products in the home market as well as in foreign markets. Common understanding between employers and employees is necessary for unhampered industrial growth. Trade associations and chambers of commerce, as voluntary organisations of the business community, are ideally suited to be helpful in these directions.

Further, by taking reasonably sympathetic attitude towards the fiscal and other measures of the government, they can create favourable climate in the country and, thus, ensure speedy realisation of the long-cherished goal of industrialisation and social and economic justice and equality among people in our country.

International Chamber of Commerce

No discussion of the associations and chambers will be complete without a reference to the International Chamber of Commerce.

The International Chamber of Commerce was set up in 1920 at the initiative of some important businessmen from the USA, England, France, Belgium and Italy. It was established to replace the International Congress of Chambers of Commerce which used to be held from time to time before the First World War (1914-18) but never had any permanent organisation.

It may be called a federation of the national chambers of commerce of different countries. Its members are from more than 50 countries of the world. Its headquarter is located at Paris.

(1) Objects: The International Chamber of Commerce aims at "improving the conditions of business between nations and to encourage better international understanding." For this purpose it seeks to bring businessmen of different countries on a common platform for discussion of matters relating to common interests.

(2) Working: It has a permanent staff which function in Paris. Its General Congress meets once in two years in one of the affiliated countries. It has its National Committees in all the affiliated countries. The National Committees elect representatives of the Council which governs the chamber. The Council has its President and a small Executive Committee. The Secretary-General has the executive authority, though he has to work under the supervision of the President and the Executive Committee of the Council.

It maintains a Court of Commercial Arbitration for speedy settlement of commercial disputes between merchants of different countries. It mainly concerns itself "with the problems of double taxation, export credits, foreign exchange, customs regulation, port facilities, neutrality of seas, etc."

India is also a member of this chamber. The Indian National Committee was organised in 1928 with its head office in New Delhi.

❑❑❑

7

Recruitment and Selection of Marketing Personnel

Introduction

Marketing force management is a specialised version of personnel management. Yet, there are good reasons why the responsibility for marketing force management is assigned to marketing executives rather than to personnel executives. While the same set of basic human problems must be dealt with in personnel management of marketing, production, or office workers, each class of problem varies in nature and importance with the work field. In contrast to production and office workers, for example, marketing personnel most often work independently; therefore, close and constant supervision is usually impractical. In further contrast, marketing-people generally work at some distance from their immediate superiors and coworkers, so it is more difficult to develop a spirit of identity with and loyalty to the company and to weld them into a unified team.

Of necessity, then, marketing personnel are given freer rein than most other workers at the comparable organisational level. To a considerable degree they must be relied upon as individual to plan and control their own activities. Despite a growing trend for marketing-people and executives to travel more by air, a marketing-person's visits to the home office are still usually infrequent, and centralised direction of his or her activities continues to be mainly by letter, telegraph, or long-distance telephone. The nature of the marketing-person's job provides only limited opportunity for face-to-face contact and supervision. Indeed, because of this necessary independence, marketing personnel are often described as 'account administrators'.

Still other unique conditions surround the marketing-person's job, often requiring that he or she be away from home and family for extended periods. It involves great dependence upon human actions and reactions. Disheartening order turndowns and dealings with rude customers frequently require the marketing-person to repress natural responses and to suppress a natural tendency to become discouraged. The psychological effects of such condition accentuate the need for marketing management's continual attention to motivational factors.

Similarities with Conventional Personnel Management

Although there are distinctive features of marketing force management, there are similarities to conventional personnel management. People are still being managed, and substantially the same human relations concepts are applicable. Marketing personnel share feelings resembling those of other employees with respect to job tenure, old age security, guaranteed wages, and equality of opportunity.

The basic steps in general personnel management are equally basic to marketing force management. The starting point in all personnel work is job analysis, to determine the nature of each position in terms of its component tasks. Then, each job is evaluated to ascertain the necessary qualification of employees. Next, there is the recruiting of qualified applications, and the marketing executives must be well informed with respect to prospective source of employees. From the supply of application, it is necessary to select those who meet the job specifications and, through interviewing and testing techniques, to evaluate qualification of applicants. Once a person is hired, marketing force management focuses attention on training, which ranges from informal instruction to highly organised formal programmes: training may consume a few hours or several years, depending upon the complexity of the marketing job. An additional step is to develop compensation plans, and these range all the way from the straight salary to the straight commission.

Once a marketing-person is assigned to the field, other personnel problems are encountered. The marketing-person must be motivated and encouraged to plan and make productive use of working time. If a marketing-person is to maximise the effectiveness of marketing calls, counselling aimed at improving working habits methods is required. The final step in marketing force management relates to control, which involves analysis of marketing and other records with the objective of improving the planning and supervising of operations. For example, the marketing-person's work week may be analyse to determine the proportion of time spent in actual marketing. Such information is used to plan territory coverage and to evaluate marketing performance. Each of these aspects of marketing force management is discussed in greater detail in following pages.

Interrelations of Marketing Force Management Activities

The various activities performed in marketing force management mesh together and should be thought of as a system. Faulty execution of any part of the system results in complication for other parts. If a substandard job of recruiting and selecting is done, tasks involved in training are magnified, problems of supervision become greater, motivating and controlling marketing-persons is more difficult, and the marketing force turnover rate is accelerated. If training is inadequate or poorly administered, potentially good people fail to each high productivity, the compensation system does not work as planned, supervision is ineffective, and there is high personnel turnover. Similar difficulties arises in cases of ineffective performance of other activities in the marketing force management system.

Economies of Effective Marketing Force Management

Economies result from effective marketing force management. Assume that Company X has ten marketing-person, each making five calls per day, a total of 50 per day for the company. If, through better management and control of workday activities, each marketing-person increases the number of calls to six per day, the company's total calls per day become 60. This is equivalent to adding two new marketing-people at the old call rate. If marketing personnel are paid wholly, or partially, on a commission basis. Because some costs are related directly to the number of marketing-people, the company's average cost per call is also reduced.

The expenses of maintaining marketing people may be divided into fixed items identical for all marketing personnel regardless of efficiency; and into variable items costing proportionately more for the last effective marketing-people. Fixed expenses include those for transportation and travelling, equipment (automobiles, marketing folios, marketing manuals, and so forth), and advertising used to assist the marketing force. These expensed are essentially the same for every marketing-person. Variable items are those for which the most efficient marketing-people spend less than inefficient marketing-people, and they include expenses for training, motivating, supervising, controlling, and evaluating. For these items a company usually receives it highest return from its best marketing-people.

Fixed and incentive pay are classified separately. From the fixed portion of compensation, the poor marketing-person usually receives more than he or she deserves and the good marketing-person is underpaid. Because the incentive portion of compensation varies with productivity, it is generally true that individuals are paid amounts proportionate to their efficiency. A useful generalisation, which should be kept in mind by marketing executives, is that expenses per unit of product sold tend to vary inversely with effectiveness of the marketing-person.

Reducing the Rate of Personnel Turnover

One measure of the quality marketing force management is the rate of turnover of the marketing personnel. This is calculated as the ratio of separations per 100 marketing-people. For example, a company employing a marketing force with an average strength of 250 persons and having 20 separations during the year has a rate of turnover of 8 per cent.

The marketing executive should keep the turnover rate at a reasonable figure, because costs of marketing force management are strongly affected by the turnover rate. Costs of recruiting, advertising, fees to employment agencies, and so forth, often cost in excess of Rs. 10,000 per recruit. Interviewing costs are also high, because most companies interview several applicants for each selection. If an interview by an executive takes two hours, and executive time is worth Rs. 400 per hour, total interviewing costs amount of Rs. 24,000 per person hired if 30 people are considered for each vacancy. The costs of travel and time used for preparatory and follow-up training run as high as Rs. 20,000 per person.

Some costs are not so readily calculated. For example, new recruits do not usually produce as much as experienced marketing personnel, and the ratio of marketing expenses to marketing for a new person is likely to be excessive for at least the first year. A conservative estimate of these excess costs is at least Rs. 1,50,000 per new marketing-person during the first year, and in some companies this cost will be higher because it takes even longer for a marketing-person to get fully into stride.

When costs of breaking in a new marketing-person are totalled, a sizable sum is seen to be at stake. In a survey of member companies, the American Management Association several years ago found that the average cost for replacing a marketing-person was Rs. 2,67,500. Almost one-fourth of the respondents said their costs of turnover were Rs. 4,00,000 or more per marketing-person. A few placed the cost at over Rs. 8,00,000. No recent study is available, but a conservative estimate is that the current average cost of marketing-person replacement exceeds Rs. 4,00,000.

The costs of personnel turnover can account for a significant drain on profits. For example, in a company with a force of 400 and an annual turnover of 25 per cent, if the costs of replacing a single marketing-person come to Rs. 4,00,000, the annual costs of turnover total Rs. 40 million– and this relates only to out-of-pocket costs. Other important costs are increased expenses for supervision and motivation, lost business, decline in customer goodwill from mistakes of unexperienced marketing-persons, and miscellaneous expenses associated with taking on people who do not succeed. Few companies have accounting systems that permit quantitative measurement of the impact on profit of excessive personnel turnover. But it cannot be denied that profits are lower because inexperienced marketing-people are assigned where turnover has occurred. Profits are not realised from marketing never consummated.

Little comparative information is available on average turnover rates for marketing personnel in various industries. However, the annual turnover of marketing personnel in companies marketing staples and industrial products is usually less than 5 per cent. Companies marketing intangibles, such as insurance, securities, and specialty or luxury items have a higher rate, sometimes 50 per cent per year. Marketing forces of manufacturers generally show a lower rate than those of wholesalers; and firms whose marketing-people call on middlemen and industrial users commonly experiences less turnover than those engaged in door-to-door marketing.

All turnover is not bad, even though it may seem expensive at the time. Many marketing executive report that most marketing-people who leave a company have less than three years of service. In other words, turnover is largely accounted for by relatively new personnel. If a person is providing unsuccessful, and it is likely that he or she will leave eventually, it is desirable that he or she do so immediately. The earlier the unsuccessful person leaves, the better for the marketing-person and the company, both in terms of dollar costs and in terms of effect upon attitudes of other marketing-people. Too low a rate of turnover may indicate that the marketing force is overloaded with veterans who do not produce as much as new personnel might. Where this situation exists, it may be assumed that the entire system of marketing force management needs re-examining and possible overhauling. Some turnover is desirable. A marketing force with no turnover may be growing stale; prospective new marketing-people are not attracted, and older persons may linger on because of management laxity and the comparatively security of established positions.

The age distribution among marketing personnel should be analysed for its impact on marketing force turnover. It is usually desirable to have marketing-person's ages spread over a wide range. Otherwise, the productivity curves for all may rise together, with all reaching their peaks and decline together, and all reaching retirement at the same time. Under these circumstances, it is necessary eventually to recruit an entire marketing force almost at once, at considerable loss in market coverage and customer relations. Companies should establish an average length of service, which management considers desirable for marketing personnel, before evaluating the turnover rate. If management decides that the average length of service should be 20 years, then, assuming no errors in selection, the personnel turnover rate should be 5 per cent–one-twentieth of the marketing force should be replaced each year. Because even the best selection procedure is far from perfect, the actual turnover rate would run higher than 5 per cent. In addition, many people do not take marketing jobs with the intention of keeping them forever. A marketing job is often the springboard to higher positions, and a company using its marketing force as a source of managerial talent should anticipate higher turnover.

Awareness of the current turnover rate is also necessary for planning the operation of service function. The personnel turnover rate is an important factor in planning recruiting, selection, and training programmes. For example, a company with a turnover rate of 25 per cent is replacing its marketing force every four years. It must organise its service functions to handle an annual volume of new recruits equivalent to one-fourth of its marketing force. The costs and extent of the recruitment selection and training programmes largely depend upon the magnitude of turnover.

The personnel turnover rate should be analysed periodically to determine the causes. Analysis often uncovers areas where improvement is needed. A useful information source is a terminal interview between the departing marketing-person and either a line executive or a personnel consultant. This exit interview provides the marketing executive with an opportunity to identify conditions contributing to personnel turnover. Identification enables management to modify or correct conditions that lie within its control.

Causes of personnel turnover can be separated into two main groupings, as shown in Table-1. Management should take appropriate corrective action when the causes are largely concentrated on the controllable list, particularly when turnover is caused by reasons 1 through 7. Turnover resulting from reason 8 sometimes is unavoidable, and that resulting from 9 and 10 is usually desirable. Managerial action may be called for, even in the cases of some reasons appearing on the 'non-controllable' list, in fact, only reasons 2, 3 and 6 may be regarded as completely unavoidable.

Table-1

Causes to Turnover of Marketing Personnel

Caused by Action Controllable by Company	Caused by Actions Not Controllable by Company
(1) Poor recruiting	(1) Retirement
(2) Improper relation and assignment	(2) Death
(3) Training deficiencies	(3) Illness of physical disability
(4) Inadequate supervision and motivation	(4) Personal and marital difficulties
(5) Breakdown in communications	(5) Dislike for the job-travel, type or work, working conditions, etc.
(6) Unsatisfactory performance customer complaints, etc.	(6) Military duty
(7) Discharged for cause, e.g., alcoholism, conviction of a felony, dishonesty, etc.	(7) Better position elsewhere
(8) Cutback in personnel	
(9) Transfer to another department	
(10) Promotion to a higher position	

Marketing Executive as Leader

Competent marketing executives are leaders, rather than drivers, of people. They earn and retain the voluntary cooperation of their followers, inspiring them to strive willingly toward mutual goals. They coordinate their follower's activities so that efficiency of the group is maintained at a high level; they find ways to overcome difficulties in the application of marketing plans and policies; and they devise methods for dealing with other problems. Development of leadership ability is a matter of great importance.

Contrary to popular belief, leadership ability can be developed. Although some executives may be 'born leaders,' most acquire leadership ability through education, training and experience. It is not possible, of course, for everyone to become a leader; not everyone possesses, or can acquire, the necessary qualifications. As to the exact nature of these qualifications, management writers are divided. Several have constructed lists of leadership traits. Among the items included in such lists are:

(1) The true leader possesses a high degree of self-control and has stable emotions. An executive, who is moody and inconsistent misleads subordinates. If they are unable to judge their superior's reactions, they cease to function as a team.

(2) A leader has a through understanding of how people think and react. By absorbing many points of view—those of superiors, associates, subordinates, competitors, and others—a leader can anticipate their reaction to particular situations.

(3) A leader is decisive—both willing and able to make decisions. The poor administrator makes decisions by default, delaying and hoping that someone else will bring for the solution or that the problem will solve itself. The effective leader decides and then acts. Because the decision is reached after a careful review of the facts, the leader acts with confidence.

(4) The leader readily accepts responsibility. Although the capable executive delegates authority to subordinates according to their abilities, he or she willingly accepts final responsibility for their actions and never shirks responsibilities.

(5) The leader's mental ability is superior to the majority of the followers yet the leader is not surrounded exclusively with less able people. The leader secures capable subordinates to whom authority can be delegated, and develops the most capable of these as possible successors.

(6) The leader is technically competent, skilled in the discharge of particular administrative tasks. The leader also has some competence in tasks assigned to subordinates; this is a prerequisite to effective training and supervision.

(7) The leader possesses the ability to communicate ideas and thoughts clearly. Subordinates carry out the programme more fully because they understand what is expected. Top management regards the leader more highly because the leader succeeds in communicating plan and needs effectively.

(8) The leader has the ability to teach and to motivate other. The good leader knows people's motivations, desires, and ambitions, and used this knowledge to lead them into the necessary activity—whether it is learning or performing.

(9) The leader enjoys above-average health and energy, and sets the pace for the followers, and physical stamina enables the leader to do his or her own job alertly and enthusiastically.

Beyond possessing leadership traits, the executive leader must use tested management procedures. First, as many problems as possible should be made subjects of group-thinking. People cooperate more willingly in carrying out policies they have helped to make. Subordinates should feel that some plans are their plans, not directives imposed from above; but this does not mean that the administrator should abdicate executive responsibilities. The final decision is still the executive's. After problems have been discussed with subordinates, it is up to the executives to face the issues and decide.

Second, a leader is courteous to subordinates. Courtesy goes beyond mere politeness; it reflects sincere consideration for the ideas and feelings of others, politeness is an outward manifestation of good manners. Courtesy and consideration arise from a genuine interest in others. Subordinates are quick to recognise the difference.

Third, a leader gives credit where it is due. When a subordinate's idea proves successful, recognition should be given. Some executives are too easily tempted to accept credit for subordinates' ideas in order to build personal prestige. In the long run, this discourages the submission of ideas and destroys the executive's effectiveness.

Finally, the leader sets a good example. The "do as I say, not as I do" approach is not effective in motivating people. The executive works with the same diligence he or she expects of the staff, and the executive leads his or her life as he or she expects them to lead theirs. It is natural for subordinates to emulate the superior. The superior is, or should be, a symbol of success.

Unionisation of Marketing Personnel

The marketing-person has been the target of organising drives by various unions since the Great Depression of the 1930s. Despite such efforts, unions have made only slight inroads in organising marketing personnel as compared with their success elsewhere. There are several reasons. First, in most marketing departments it is difficult to develop strong group identification because each person works alone and sees his or her peers on the marketing force only infrequently. Little opportunity exists for mutual exchange of grievances, and organising is difficult because marketing-people are generally isolated from one another. Second, in contrast to most employee groups, marketing-persons usually think of themselves as independent operators rather than as cogs in large industrial machine. Third, managements' working-hour problem is less significant with marketing personnel than with other workers, because most people on the marketing force have some control over their workday and work week. If they work excessive hours, it is often to add to their compensation; but they may occasionally take an afternoon off or start a working day later than usual. There are no time clocks to provide checks on their actions. And finally, higher wages have never served as a string organising incentive for marketing personnel. Rightly or wrongly, marketing personnel have been made to feel that low earnings are the results of personnel ineffectiveness, not of the employer's niggardliness.

It is estimated that only one of ten marketing-persons belongs to a union. When unionisation has occurred, it has usually been because of management failure. Some grievances of marketing personnel are: too many reports, competition of house accounts, inadequate expense allowances, unequal territories, too many people on the marketing force (which results in inadequate territories), and too many non-marketing duties.

Unionisation has made the most headway in industries where marketing-people are paid largely on a straight-salary basis, where they work together on the same premises (retail marketing), and where the marketing job is combined with that of delivery, as in the distribution of beer and soft drink. Unions have made little progress in organising marketing-people who sell directly to industrial users or those who make calls on middlemen. Marketing personnel in these classifications, generally paid in whole or in part on the basis of productivity, almost all oppose union affiliation.

Many marketing executives oppose unionisation of their marketing forces. Their opposition is based chiefly upon the effect that unionisation may have on the control of individual marketing-persons and upon the limitations that union contracts place on aggressive management. Managerial action in important areas be circumscribed by rules laid down in the collective-bargaining agreement, and uses of incentive system of compensation are restricted. Commonly, unions object of marketing contests and other devices for motivating the marketing force; sometimes they insist that all additions to the marketing force be recruited through the union; they discourage the use of quotas and other standard of performance; and a strict systems of seniority is almost always among their demands. Furthermore, marketing executives generally maintain that the organisational structure of existing unions does not harmonise well with the demands of the marketing job, since marketing and marketing management require more flexibility than running a plant or an office. They argue that in the nature of things all marketing-people are called upon at times of extra effort, this being the price a marketing-person pays for comparative freedom from day-to-day supervision.

Federal law prohibits marketing executives from active discouragement of unionisation, and it is wise to take a positive approach. Progressive marketing management has come more and more to recognise that the interests of the marketing force are usually not in conflict with those of the company. Normally, marketing personnel are reasonable people, and usually they regard themselves as members of the management team. The wise marketing executive utilises every opportunity to hammer home the mutuality of interests.

Marketing Manager's Creed

Sales and Marketing Executive-International (SME-I), a professional association with members throughout the world, has long concerned itself with the improvement of relations among marketing personnel and marketing executives. In an effort to apply its members' knowledge of special employee conditions affecting the marketing-person's job to the general problem of employer-employee relations, SME-I has published, and revised from time to time, a code of ethical conduct known as the Marketing Manager's Creed. The most recent revision is reproduced in Table-2. Although not every marketing executive subscribes fully to this creed, all are well advised to study its provision—most are directly or indirectly traceable to company practices and policies that have been frequent causes of unrest among marketing personnel.

Table-2

A Creed

I Subscribe to the Marketing Manager's Creed, Prepared by Marketing and Marketing Executives-International, which I Believe to be in the Best Interests of Business

All marketing-men shall receive fair compensation during their initial or subsequent training periods.	Marketing-men's expense reimbursement policies shall be uniform, after taking all variations of condition into consideration.
While recognising changes in compensation or territory to be functions of marketing management, marketing-men shall be consulted prior to establishing such changes and given reasonable notice of the effective date.	A sharp distinction shall be drawn between salesmen's earnings and expense allowance, and any systems that affords salesmen either a substantial profit or loss on expense accounts shall be corrected.
Earnings of commission or bonus of marketing-men shall be unlimited, unless otherwise specified at the time of their employment. Should basic changes in a business justify modifying this policy, all marketing-men affected shall be advised of the fact a reasonable time prior to establishing such ceilings as become necessary.	Marketing-men shall be given either a contract, agreement, or letter covering those conditions of his employment which might otherwise be the basis of later misunderstandings.
When evaluating the ability of marketing-men, conditions beyond their control, such as differences in the marketing potentials of their territories, shall be given full consideration.	If quotas are used– (a) Marketing-men should know how their figures have been determined, and (b) The quotas shall be based on reliable seasonal personal evaluation of accurate and adequate criteria.
Marketing-men shall be offered the same vacation, job or income security, and other employee benefits as are enjoyed by other employees in comparable positions in the same company.	A marketing-men whose health or well-being gives evidence of being prejudiced by the nervous tensions involved in his work, shall be given such relief as may be possible.

The only 'house' or 'no commission' accounts shall be those clearly defined in advance of solicitation.	Pressure to achieve results shall be of a constructive nature, avoiding the use of 'fear' psychology or threatened loss of employment.
The paper work required of marketing-men shall be held down to a minimum and its value clearly justified.	No matter where a marketing-men may be located, he shall be provided with a simple means of stating his grievances, which shall be promptly considered and answered.

Contracts with Marketing Personnel

A marketing employment contract is a formally executed agreement between the employer and the individual marketing-person, outlining condition of employment. Citing the possible avoidance of later misunderstanding as the justification, the Marketing Manager's Creed suggests the use of written agreements ('contract, agreement, or letter') covering employment conditions. Proponents of marketing-person's contracts argue also that some measure of legal protection is provided both parties—the marketing personnel against arbitrary company action, such as cuts in commission rates, and the company against unauthorised action by the marketing-person, such as marketing outside the assigned territory. Table–3 shows a marketing-person's contract of the sort used by insurance companies for their 'agents' (that is, independent marketing-persons) and by some firms manufacturing products sold on a straight-commission basis. The most extensive of contracts is made companies marketing such 'products' as insurance, securities, other intangibles, and real estate—in all of which marketing compensation is primarily by commission. Some use of contracts is made by firms in other fields where marketing-people are paid wholly or mostly by commission. Otherwise, contracts are little used, the main reason being that many marketing executives look upon written job descriptions (covering job objectives, duties and responsibilities, etc.) as a more effective means of avoiding later misunderstandings. Furthermore, unlike contracts, the written job description can be altered without necessarily obtaining the marketing-person's consent.

Several other reasons can be cited for nonuse of contracts. One is that many employers consider them unenforceable, since it is often impractical, unwise, or both, to take marketing personnel into court for non-performance. When court action is taken and the judgement is favourable to the company, it may be difficult, often impossible,

Table-3

Contract Form for Agents Used by the Travellers Insurance Company and the Travellers Indemnity Company

THE TRAVELLERS INSURANCE COMPANY

THE TRAVELLERS INSURANCE COMPANY

of Hartford, Connecticut, hereinafter called the Company, and

----

____

of ______________________ hereinafter called the Agent, pursuant to request that the underwriting facilities and other services of the Company be made available to the undersigns as Agent and for the considerations hereinafter expressed, agree together as follows:

1. This contract shall become effective on the .... day of .... 20.

2. The Agent has full power and authority to solicit applications or proposals for insurance, and to bind the Company and issue policies, for such classes of risks as the Company from time to time may authorised to countersign policies of insurance, renewal receipts, certificates, and endorsements pertaining it such classes of risks; and to collect, receive, and receipt for premiums on such insurance, except for premiums which the company bills directly.

The Agent shall promptly forward applications, proposals or daily reports to the Company's Office at ______________________

The Agent shall promptly pay over premiums to the Company's Office at __________

____

3. Commission shall be payable in accordance with the commission schedule adopted by the Company and supplied to the Agent. On business for which premium are collected by the Agent, commissions may be retained by the Agent out of premiums collected, as full compensation for such business. The Company at any time, by written notice to the Agent, may change the commission schedule as to premiums due on and after the date specified in the notice, provided such notice shall be given 60 days in advance of the effective date whenever a material change in commission is involved.

4. It is a condition of this contract that the Agent shall refund ratably to the Company,

on business heretofore of hereafter written, commissions on cancelled insurance and on reductions in premiums at the same rate at which such commissions were paid to the Agent.

5. If the Agent notifies the Company within his customary accounting period that an additional premium is uncollectible which was developed by audit or report or values on any account where coverage is no longer in force and the Agent has exhausted his normal collection efforts, the Agent shall be relieved of the responsibility for collection and shall have no commission interest in such premium. This provision shall also apply to uncollectible anniversary premiums on court, probate, licence, permit and other miscellaneous surety bonds.

6. Except as specifically authorised by the Company, the Agent has no authority to make, alter, vary, or discharge any policy contract. To extend the time for payment of premiums, to waive of extend any policy obligation or condition, to incur any liability on behalf of the Company, or to insert any advertisement respecting the Company in any publication.

7. The Company shall not be responsible for agency expenses such as rentals, transportation facilities, clerical help, solicitors' fees, postage, advertising, exchange, personal licence fees, or any other agency expenses whatsoever.

8. The Agent shall be responsible for all risks placed in the books of the Company through his agency by any sub-agents or brokers together with all premiums or moneys collected by them in connection with such risks the same as if they had been produced directly by the Agent.

9. Any Company supplies furnished to the Agent by the Company shall always remain the property of the Company and shall be returned to the Company or its representatives promptly upon demand.

10. The Company shall indemnify and hold the Agent harmless from and against all sums, including costs and expenses of suit defense and settlements, which the Agent shall become legally obligated to pay by reason of liability imposed on him by law for damages sustained by policyholders, caused solely and directly by error or omission of the Company in the preparation and handling of policies, including timely premium notice.

11. All moneys collected or received by the Agent for or on behalf of the Company shall be held in a fiduciary capacity and shall not be used by the Agent for any purpose

whatsoever except as specifically authorised by the Company and shall be paid over to the Company in accordance with the terms of this contract.

12. This contract cancels all previous contracts or agreements whether oral or written between any of The Travellers Companies and the Agent covering the classes of risks referred to herein, This contract may be terminated by either party at any time upon written notice to the other, provided any such notice by the Company shall be given 60 days in advance of the effective date if the Agent has paid all balances due the Company in accordance with the Company's customary arrangements with the Agent.

13. In the event of termination of this contract:

(a) The Agent's records, use and control of expirations, including direct billed business, shall remain his property and be left in his absolute possession.

(b) The Company shall furnish the Agent upon request a record of direct billed policyholders, expiration dates and details of the coverage provided, including the latest rating information recorded.

(c) Paragraphs 3 and 4 of this agreement shall continue to apply to additional or return premiums on policies written prior to the date of termination but expiring subsequent thereto.

The provisions of this paragraph shall apply so long as premiums are remitted in accordance with the Company's customary arrangements with the Agent. If at the time of termination the Agent has failed to pay balances due the Company, this paragraph shall apply only if the Agent shall thereafter pay all collected premiums to the Company immediately.

IN WITNESS WHEREOF, the Company has caused this contract to be signed at the Home office and the Agent has subscribed his name here to this_______________day of________200___

Sd/-
President

____

____

Agent

Second Vice-President Casually property Dept.

__________ Sd/- __________
Authorised Signature

to collect it; yet the company is tied to the contract terms when the marketing-person sues. It is seldom possible to foresee all contingencies at the time the contract is drafted, and changes in conditions may make certain stipulations unworkable. Still another reason for nonuse is that, since contracts generally set forth specific grounds on which marketing-persons can be discharged, the release of incompetents may be made more difficult. Although these problems do not destroy entirely the envisioned purpose of the marketing contract, they do point up the importance of careful preparation and use. If the main role of the marketing contract is that of reducing the seriousness of later misunderstandings on employment terms, its provisions must anticipate matters about which misunderstandings are most likely to arise, and on which it is especially critical to have a clear meeting of minds. The more common matters of this type are: work assignments, working hours, compensation arrangements, and requirements concerning reports and other written records.

Recruiting and Selecting Marketing Personnel

A prime concern of the marketing manager is to field sufficient marketing-people to service the needs of prospective customers for the company's products. Ultimately, marketing managers must concern themselves with achieving efficient marketing-performance, but they must first find the potential performers. The effectiveness of marketing performance depends both upon the calibre and the number of marketing people at the disposal of marketing management. Spatial problems make the task recruiting and selecting marketing-people more difficult than for other employees. Since a marketing force works over broad geographic areas rather than in restricted plant locations, it is often necessary to recruit marketing personnel in the markets they are to serve, a factor that makes the recruiter's task much more difficult.

From management's standpoint, there are four important steps in recruiting and selecting a marketing force. Step one is, to determine marketing personnel needs, and this requires job analysis and the establishment of job specifications. Step two is, to identify the sources from which marketing-people with good potential might be obtained. Step three is to locate and recruit prospective marketing-people from the identified sources. Step four is to select from among these prospects the ones who have the highest probability of success.

Organisation for Recruiting and Selection

Responsibility for recruitment and selection of marketing personnel is assigned to the marketing manager in some organisation, the personnel manager in others, and to the two executives jointly instill others. There is no one best place for assignment of this responsibility. Company size, executives' personalities, and departmental organisation all affect this decision. Where the marketing manager has a personnel staff assistant, recruiting and selection of a marketing staff usually is handled entirely within the department. In companies with small marketing forces, it sometimes is desirable to have these functions under the control of the personnel manager, but this is unusual. It is more common for the personnel department to handle recruiting and preliminary screening and for the marketing department to make final selections. In all companies, whatever the formal organisation, considerable exchange of information and cancellation takes place between the two departments.

Location of responsibility for recruitment and selection of marketing personnel in concerns with regional marketing offices is another organisational factor that varies from one company to another. These functions tend to be centralised at the home office when the firm requires high calibre marketing personnel. Other factors, for example, size of regional organisations and location of training programmes, make it difficult to draw further generalisations. However, decentralised recruitment and selection generally result in reduced interviewing and time and facilitates the hiring of local applications for marketing work.

Need for the Proper Setting

For recruiting and selection programmes to succeed, they must be installed in a favourable setting. Market exploration must have been carried to the point where management knows: the size of the potential business, identities and locations of customers and prospects, which individuals in customers' organisation influence buying decision, and the best methods for reaching them. Product used and applications must have been identified and the different marketing appeals evaluated as to relative effectiveness. With this foundation of market and product knowledge, management is prepared to determine its marketing-personnel requirements, draft appropriate recruiting and selection programmes, and install them in an environment conducive to success.

Marketing Job Analysis

No matter what position, a company is seeking to fill—marketing-person, file clerk, executive, factory hand, plant guard, or other—the task is approached, consciously or not, with some preliminary analysis of the job. Even though management may not have recognised this need for job analysis to the extent of marking a formal evaluation, it recognises instinctively the desire to fit the individual to the job. In companies where this need has been recognised, formal system of job analysis have developed. Experience indicates that the formal, systematic approach to job analysis results in a much higher proportion of people being placed in the right job.

Analysing a marketing job is basically a matter of developing the information needed for a job description. It involves asking question to determine the job's objectives and to uncover what the marketing-person does or should do in pursuit of them. The first question, for example, should be. What the purposes of this job? What is the title of the job–marketing-person, marketing representative, marketing counsellor, or what? These questions might be followed by: To whom does this person report? What products does this individual sell? To whom does this person sell? What information should this person gather, and what reports should this person make? The answers might elicit details concerning special skills required, planning responsibilities, relations with customers, service duties, and the like. Such question asking, together with formal arrangement and systematic grouping of the answers, provides the means of analysis and results in a marketing job description. Outlined below is a suggested nine-step procedure for marketing job analysis:

(1) Prepare a questionnaire for marketing personnel, asking them to list the main objectives of their job, together with the major functions and sub functions performed in doing the job effectively.

(2) Prior to receipt of the completed questionnaires, have all executives interested in marketing activities write down their conceptions of the marketing-person's job objectives and the functions they feel should and should not be performed in achieving them.

(3) Survey customers to find out, what they believe should and should not be the functions of a company marketing-person.

(4) Tabulate the information received.

(5) Reconcile differences revealed by the three viewpoints, write a concise statement of job objectives, and prepare a detailed list of activities that marketing personnel are to perform.

(6) Classify the activities into major functional groups, such as marketing, service, territory management, marketing promotion, executive, and goodwill duties.

(7) Determine, what a marketing-person needs to know, the qualifications necessary to perform designated activities, and the reasons that necessitate performance of each activity assemble this information into a written job description.

(8) Submit the written job description to marketing-persons for discussion and recommendations, and make alternations as required.

(9) Periodically revise the job description, following the preceding eight steps, when changes in products, competition, the economic climate, or customers' demands require a review of job objectives and the activities involved in reaching them.

An alternative approach to marketing job analysis to use checklist itemising the functions and sub-functions generally accepted as comprising the marketing-person's job. One such checklist, organically developed for the US Small Business Administration is shown in Table-4. The checklist approach is less reliable than the suggested nine-step procedure, as it fails to provide for definition of job objectives; does not focus on the viewpoints of marketing personnel, executives, or customers; and does not require 'reasons' in support of activities eventually written into the job description. However, this approach can be helpful in preparing tentative descriptions of a new marketing job when the time factor is important.

Job Specifications

The duties and responsibilities set forth in the job description should be converted into a set of qualifications that a person should possess in order to perform the job satisfactorily. This set of qualifications is called the 'job specification.' If the job description states, for example, that the marketing-person is to train dealers' marketing personnel, then the marketing-person must be qualified to conduct such training. What will the marketing-person have to know about the products and the dealers' customers? About the dealers' operating methods and problems? About training methods? Will this duty require the marketing-person to have a certain amount and kind of experience? Similar sets of questions must be answered with respect to each of duties and responsibilities contained in the job description.

Table-4

Checklist for Use in Analysing Marketing Jobs and Compiling Job Descriptions

Outline for Compiling a Marketing Job Description
Sales:
Make regular calls
Sell the line; demonstrate.
Handle questions and objections.
Check stock; discover possible product uses.
Interpret marketing points of the line to customer.
Estimate customer's potential needs.
Emphasise quality.
Explain company policy on price, delivery, and credit.
Get the order.
Service:
Install the product or display.
Report product weaknesses, complaints.
Handle adjustments, returns, and allowances.
Handle requests for credit.
Handle special orders.
Establish priorities, if any.
Analyse local conditions for customers.
Territory Management:
Arrange route for best coverage.
Balance effort with customer against the potential volume.
Maintain marketing portfolios, samples, kits, etc.
Marketing Promotion:
Develop new prospects and accounts.
Distribute home office literature, catalogues, etc.
Make calls with customer's marketing-people.
Train personnel of wholesalers, jobbers, etc.
Present survey reports, layouts, and proposals.

Contd. . . .

Executive:

Each night make a daily work plan for the next day.
Organise field activity for minimum travel and maximum calls.
Prepare and submit special reports on trends, competition.
Prepare and submit statistical data requested by home office.
Investigate lost marketing and reason for loss.
Prepare reports on developments, trends, new objectives met, and new ideas on meeting objections.
Attend marketing meetings.
Build a prospect list.
Collect overdue accounts; report on faulty accounts.
Collect credit information.

Goodwill:

Counsel customers on their problems.
Maintain loyalty and respect for the company.
Attend local marketing meetings held by customers.

There are, of course, differences among the qualifications that a new addition to the marketing force may be expected to bring to the job, those that an individual may acquire through training, and those that a person will gain through field marketing experience. It is marketing management's responsibility to decide which qualifications all new recruits should possess, and which should be provided through training. A company specifying somewhat higher entrance qualifications than another can expect, other things being equal, that its training programme will have to accomplish less. But the first company is likely to encounter greater difficulty in finding as many possible recruits as the second company, with its lower entrance qualifications. A trade-off must be made between (1) recruiting persons with many qualifications, which reduces the need for training; and (2) recruiting persons with few qualifications, which increases the need for training.

Marketing job specifications should set forth the personality characteristics required. These the marketing-person must bring to the job, since marketing, training programmes are seldom effective instruments for personality development. All marketing personnel should have certain traits: empathy and the ability to get along well with other; integrity and character; and maturity, in terms of a sensible self-perspective. Motivation is especially important—some marketing jobs require their holders to be routine order takers only, but others serve as proving grounds for future managers. There is a kind of optimum level of motivation for each job. If new marketing-persons are too strongly motivated, they may not be content for long with a routine job or one lacking in advancement opportunities.

Job specifications may stipulate minimum requirements with respect to education and product or technical knowledge, but *legally so only if* the company can prove that such requirements are significantly related to successful job performance. The importance of such requirements, as one would expect, varies widely. Some marketing jobs demand the detailed and highly technical training offered only by colleges of engineering; others require only average ability to read, write, and do simple arithmetic; and there are all gradations in between. Graduation from an educational institution is tangible evidence that the job candidate has a certain level of ability. If a specified amount of formal education is set as an absolute minimum requirement, however, a risk is taken that some otherwise highly qualified applications will be eliminated from consideration. In addition, setting a specified amount of formal education as an absolute minimum requirement is dangerous on legal grounds—EEOC guidelines, for instance, specify that the employer must prove that this requirement is significantly related to successful job performance and does not result in discrimination on the basis of race, colour, religion, sex, or national origin.

Flexibility in defining standards of age and physical appearance is usually desirable. A company that is putting new recruits through a long period of marketing training and internship may well want to recruit younger persons than a company with only a brief training period. Except for this consideration, however, age should be a selection factor only to the extent that it helps or handicaps marketing-persons in their work. The same applies to physical appearance. Short, fat, or ugly marketing-persons may be handicapped in some marketing situations, but they may have an advantage in situation where their appearance increase customer empathy.

Job specifications sometimes provide recruiters with an important device for the conservation of time and energy—the set of minimum requirements or standards to use in weeding out obviously unqualified applicants. This usually takes the form of a list of negative factors, the presence of any of which automatically disqualifies as applicant. Factors such as the following often were included in these lists prior to the passage of the Civil Rights Act of 1964: inability to express one's thoughts clearly;

unusually poor language usage; sloppy or dirty clothing or grooming job-hopping-more than a given number of previous jobs, or too frequent job changes, acne or other skin disease, or unusually unattractive teeth. Such a set of minimum requirements, or preliminary screenings standards, should be prepared only after a company analyses its dismissals and should reflect the main reasons why a company's marketing personnel fail. Since 1964, companies have become increasingly careful in setting such minimum requirements or standards because they now must be prepared to prove that each is significantly related to successful job performance and does not result in discrimination on the basis of race, colour, religion, sex, or national origin.

Analysis of the qualifications of a company's marketing personnel helps recruiters determine what they should look for in job applicants and assists in planning the marketing training programme. Guidance to recruiters is provided by studying the qualifications, which the company's successful marketing personnel had when hired, for instance, education, material status, previous experience, and size of savings. Guidance in planning marketing training is furnished by answering such question as: How specialised are the marketing people? How long does it take to become familiar with the line? What were these people doing immediately before they came to the company? After analysing company marketing-person's backgrounds, one marketing manager concluded that:

(1) Marketing personnel who preciously sold competing or related lines learned more rapidly, but not significantly so.

(2) The average marketing-person knew the product line sufficiently well to sell productively in four weeks time.

(3) The new marketing-person's awareness of specialised problem with respect to the product line equalled that of any veteran marketing-person within four months' time.

(4) All successful marketing personnel had previous marketing experience, although the range varied from house-to-house to industrial marketing. This indicated that the ability to sell was transferable to the company's products.

Because no two companies have exactly the same situations, each must construct its own specifications. Questionnaires are helpful in obtaining the necessary information. Marketing-persons, supervisors, and others of the marketing staff can be asked to express their opinions of the qualifications for success. Customers, as well as others, can provide similar information. From the returns of wisely designed questionnaires it should be possible to write a description of physical, mental, and skill requirements.

Source of Marketing Force Recruits

Thus, far we have examined certain factors that marketing management should consider in determining personnel requirements—job analysis comes first and results in job descriptions from which are derived job specifications. These are necessary preliminaries to the next step—the identification of sources of promising recruits.

Recruiting-source Identification

One approach to the identification of the best source of recruits is to analyse those used in the past. Each source is analysed to determine the total number of recruits produced, and 'successes' and 'failures.' Each source, in other words, is analysed quantitatively and qualitatively. One source may have provided numerous recruits but few successes; a second fewer recruits but a high proportion of successes. Consider the analysis given in Table-5 of 80 marketing-people recruited by one company over a period of five years.

Table-5

Source Analysis of Marketing Personnel Recruited by Electrical-Products Manufacturer

Source	Number of Recruits	Percentage of Total	Number of Successes	Ratio of Successes to Total
Recommendations by own marketing-people	22	27.50	10	0.455
Educational institutions	14	17.50	10	0.715
Marketing personnel for noncompeting firms	12	15.00	2	0.167
Employment agencies	10	12.50	3	0.300
Personnel acquaintances of executives	8	10.00	5	0.625
Customers' employees	6	7.50	1	0.167
Unsolicited applications	5	6.25	2	0.400
Competitors' marketing-people	3	3.75	3	20.670
	80	100.00	35	23.499
Ratio of success of total from all sources				0.437

In the figure, the source accounting for the largest number of recruits showed a success ratio only slightly more favourable than the ratio for all source—but is did account for ten of the 35 successes recruited and, for this reason, management might want to continue using it. Three sources had higher-than-average success ratios, and management should explore ways of increasing the number of recruits from them. Three other sources had very low success ratios, and management should use them sparingly in the future. A word of caution: These results indicate the experience of only company, and should not be considered typically of industry in general. Furthermore, the definition of 'success' adopted by a particular management affects this sort of analysis. In the example given, success was defined as "demonstrated ability to meet or exceed quotas in two years out of three." Other managements might well define success differently.

Another word of caution with regard to data of the above type: Its reliability depends upon the size of the group evaluated. More reliable conclusion could be drawn on the worth of a source producing 22 recruits than one producing only three recruits. However, even if, only a small number of cases is available, the data may still serve as a helpful, although necessarily less reliable, guide in identifying promising sources of new marketing-people.

Some frequently used sources of recruits are discussed below. The intent is to describe general source characteristics and to point up significant advantages, disadvantages, and other pertinent information concerning each source.

Source within the Company

(1) Company Marketing Personnel: Individuals apply for specific marketing jobs because they know company marketing personnel; and marketing-people's recommendations may constitute an excellent source. Often such applicants already know something about the job and about company policies; and the fact that they apply is an indication of favourable disposition toward the company. Marketing-people fairly typically have wide circles of acquaintances, since both on and off the job they continually meet new people and generally have many friends with similar interests. It is natural, then, that many of their contacts have good potential as marketing personnel-indeed, many now well for other firm. However, some marketing-people are not discriminating in their recommendations, and for this reason such recommendations need careful appraisal. One special recruiting situation in which marketing-people are a particularly useful source of recommendations is when jobs must be filled in remote territories; then marketing personnel in the same or adjacent areas may now considerably more about unique territorial requirements and local sources of personnel than home-office executives.

(2) Company Executives: Recommendations of the marketing manager, the president, and other company executives are another internal source of recruits. Marketing executives' personal contacts may yield top-calibre people because of their own involvement with the marketing field and understanding of the needed qualifications. Other executives' recommendations, by way of contrast, more often are based mainly upon personnel friendships and tend to represent less objective appraisals. Experience is almost the only way to evaluate each executive's worth as a source of new recruits, and the type of analysis shown in Table-5 adapts easily to this purpose.

(3) Internal Transfers: Two additional sources of personnel from within the company are other departments and the non-marketing section of the marketing department. Employees desiring transfer are already familiar with company policies, and the personnel department should have considerable detailed information about them. One factor that limits the recruitment of transfers is that the company usually knows little about their aptitude for marketing work; an offsetting factor is that they often possess excellent product knowledge. Aptitude for marketing, of course, can be tested formally or by 'trial' assignment to the field. Transfers are especially good prospects for marketing positions whenever product knowledge makes up a substantial portion of marketing training, since their background makes it possible to accelerate field assignments.

Sources Outside the Company

(1) Educational Institutions: The source includes colleges and universities, business college, high schools, and night schools. It is reasonable to expect that graduates have attained certain minimum educational levels, the amount depending upon the school. Moreover, many have had training in general business, marketing, and marketing techniques. Schools are a particularly fruitful source of new marketing personnel at graduation time, and some maintain year-round placement services for graduates seeking job changes. Most recent graduates represent net addition to the labour market and, consequently, need not be attracted away from other jobs.

Colleges and universities have become increasingly important sources of marketing and management trainees, and competition is keen for their graduates. Often the graduating senior is in a position to choose from among several attractive job offers. Companies not maintaining close relations with the colleges are at a disadvantage, frequently being unable to obtain appointments on overcrowded campus recruiting schedules, and finding it difficult to attract students away from companies better known to the college. Even better-known companies face stiff competition with each other in hiring the cream of the graduates. A few companies offer marketing-training programmes to outstanding juniors during vacations periods. Thus, the trainee and the company have an opportunity to evaluate each other, and trainees who prove satisfactory are offered jobs upon graduating.

(2) Competitors' Organisations: Marketing personnel recruited from competitor's organisation generally require minimal training because of experience in marketing similar products to similar markets. But this is often a costly source, because a premium must be paid to persuade marketing-persons to regions their present jobs. Some marketing manages are reluctant to hire competitor's ex- marketing-persons because they suspect their loyalty. An individual hired away from one organisation for higher pay may be similar tempted at a future time. An important question to answer is: Why is this person leaving his or her present positions? When the new job does not improve or status for the applicant, his or her desire to change may result from personality conflicts, or instability. Dissatisfaction with the present job is not necessarily the fault of the marketing-person. If good reasons exist for making the change, it may be possible to obtain in first-class person who is ready at once for productive work.

(3) Marketing-people for Noncompeting Companies: Marketing-people working for firms in related and no related industries constitute a source of recruits. Such recruits may not be fully acquainted with the product line, but they do have marketing-experience. This source provides a channel of advancement for marketing-people in 'dead-end' jobs to those seeking to upgrade their employment.

(4) Marketing-people Making Calls on the Company: The purchasing agent is in daily contact with marketing personnel from other companies and is in a strategic position to evaluate their on-the-job performances. It is not unusual for the purchasing agent to meet high-calibre marketing-people for whom jobs with the company would be attractive financially or in other respects. The purchasing agent should be encouraged to make the appropriate recommendations.

(5) Employees of Customers: Some companies regard their customers as a recruiting source. Customers are asked to recommend able persons in their own organisations who have reached the maximum potential of their existing jobs. Such transfers may have a favourable effect upon morale in customer's organisation. However, since customer goodwill is of prime importance, a customer's marketing-people should normally the recruited only with the prior approval and recommendation of the customer.

(6) Marketing Executives' Clubs: Many marketing executives' club operate placement services. Marketing-person's seeking new positions submit personal data sheets that are duplicated and forwarded to members. At regular club meetings, the marketing executive has additional opportunity for informal discussion and exchanges of placement information.

(7) Employment Agencies: Many marketing managers traditionally have regarded employment agencies as unpromising sources of recruits. Many use agencies only after other sources are exhausted. Many believe, usually with little evidence, that 'good' marketing-people neither need nor will use an agency's services. Experience, unfortunately, tends to reinforce such attitudes, because too often agency referrals fail to meet marketing job specifications. Sometimes this traceable to agency deficiencies (such as the overzealous desire to receive placement fees); but at least as often the fault is that of the prospective employer, who may be using unrealistically high job specifications, may not make the company's requirement clear, and so on. Unquestionably, an employer would be unwise – as well as unjustified – in generalising from unsatisfactory experiences with one or a few agencies, whether they be privately operated or local offices of state employment services. Experiences with individual agencies should be reviewed periodically, using the pattern of analysis illustrated in Table–5.

Whenever an agency is used, it should receive a clear statement of the job's objectives and a complete rundown of job specifications. If possible, the recruiter should meet with the agency counsellor to assure that pertinent information is furnished and fully understood. Also, agencies need time to learn about an employing firm and its unique requirements, thus, considerable gains accrue from continuing relationships with agencies that perform satisfactorily. Agencies have steadily improved and expanded their services (often they administer tests of various sorts, check references, and perform tasks otherwise done, if at all, by the employer). As the nature of these service becomes better understood by marketing executives, this source should grow in importance. One development of interest to marketing executives is the growing number of agencies that take the initiative in searching out promising job candidates, employed or not, instead of confining themselves to 'volunteer' applicants. Unfortunately, most such agencies recruit only executives and are, therefore, of no use as a source of marketing personnel.

(8) Direct Unsolicited Applications: Most companies receive some unsolicited 'walk-in' and 'write-in' applications of marketing positions. Some marketing managers favour immediate hiring of applicants who take the initiative in seeking marketing jobs, the reasoning being that this may indicate marketing aggressiveness. Others reject direct applications automatically because they believe the proportion of qualified applicants from this source is low. Probably the most logical policy is to treat all volunteer applications the same as solicited applications—applicants not meeting minimum requirements as set forth in job specifications should be eliminated at once; those meeting these requirements should be processed together with other applicants. The selection systems, if it works well, should result in hiring the best-qualified applicants regardless of the sources from which they come. It should be noted that direct unsolicited applications cannot to relied upon to provide a steady flow of applicants; the volume fluctuates markedly with changing business conditions.

(9) Older Persons: In the past many companies, as a matter of policy, refrained from actively recruiting individuals over 40 years of age. As noted earlier, the Age Discrimination in Employment Act prohibits discrimination in hiring decisions against persons 40 to 65 years of age. In spite of the fact that discriminations against persons in this age group is outlawed, such individuals frequently have a difficult time obtaining jobs, so companies willing to consider them many select from a group for which there is little competitive bidding. Many people in this age group have years of marketing experience and the maturity that is so valuable in most marketing situations. It is important, of course, to ascertain why an apparently good persons is unemployed, but the reasons are often beyond the control of the individual. When older persons are under consideration for marketing jobs, assuming that their qualification compare favourable with job specifications, hiring decisions may hinge upon the length of the training period needed to bring them up to full productivity.

The Recruiting Effort

The marketing-personnel recruiting effort differs in importance from firm to firm, the differences stemming in part from variations in the calibre of person desired. The higher the calibre desired, the more difficult it is to obtain. The calibre desired, of course, is influenced by the nature of the job, complexity of the product line, problems in serving customers, and so forth. If job specification call for a special talent, such as the ability to apply considerable imagination to the solution of customer's problems, then individuals of high calibre are needed. If job specifications require only order-taking ability, as in the case of many beer and soft drink marketing personnel, then persons of lower calibre will suffice. Similarly, a higher calibre is generally indicated for a product that is technical, complex, or that sells at a high unit price.

The importance-and the scope—of the recruiting effort are also influenced by the number of recruits that must be obtained. Recruiting rises in importance with the number of persons needed, and this, in turn, is affected by such factors as forecasted marketing, promotional and marketing strategy, and the marketing force turnover rate. Normally, a large business with a large marketing volume needs more marketing-people than does a small business. But two firms of comparable size in the same industry may have significantly different-sized marketing forces, often because one uses a different marketing channel or stresses advertising more in its promotional programme. As might be expected, firms with high marketing force turnover rates must do much more recruiting than those with lower rates.

It is wise to precede actual recruiting with and analysis of methods currently in use, an evaluation similar to that used in identifying sources of promising recruits. Success, failures, and terminations should be analysed to determine if they are related to specific recruiting methods. Such analysis should aid in choosing the most appropriate methods. There are two basic methods of recruiting—personal recruiting and indirect recruiting.

Personal Recruiting

Personal recruiting is chiefly used for recruiting graduates of schools and colleges. Campus interviewing is often planned as a company-wise affair, because this avoids much duplication of effort. Although representatives of different departments do the interviewing, the personnel department plans and coordinates the recruiting drive. In many efforts of this type, an assistant marketing manager shares with the regional or district marketing manager located nearest the campus responsibility for interviewing students. In other cases, home-offices marketing executives rotate campus interviewing responsibilities among themselves; sometimes each returns annually to the same campus, thus building long-term relationships with individual schools.

College recruiting requires planning well in advance of the campus visit. Statement of trainee requirements should be mailed to college placement officers early, preferably no later than January. The list of colleges, based primarily upon past interviewing experience, is updated, and letters are sent out requesting interview dates. The best months for recruiting graduates are February, March, and April; and March in the most demand. If the visit comes too late in the spring, interviews find that many of the best-qualified graduates have already taken jobs. After visiting dates have been confirmed, college are sent letters specifying such details as salary, desired marital status, and starting data of employment. Some recruiters also send copies of promotional materials, company histories, and applications blanks.

College placement officers schedule a 20 to 30 minutes interview for each student. All interested students are granted interviews—few companies prescreen college applicants. Generally, interviews are the only screening devices used. The most promising candidates are invited to company officers for follow-up interviews. However, many campus interviewers have authority to do hiring if it appears that promising candidates will be lost through delay.

Indirect Recruiting

Advertisements in classified and other sections of newspapers and trade journals have long been used for recruiting marketing personnel. Until recently, however, advertisements were considered useful only for hiring low-grade marketing personnel for routine jobs. Even for this grade of personnel, the proportion of qualified to unqualified respondents to a given advertisement was often small; and it was time consuming and costly to screen all applicants. Furthermore, most marketing executives believed that high calibre people would not seek employment offered in such an impersonal way. Nevertheless, a change in thinking has occurred. Today, city newspapers carry many advertisements publicising openings for marketing personnel and even for marketing executives.

So great is the number of prospective job candidates reached by a single advertisement that companies often must take steps to reduce the volume of applications. If the employer is willing to publish details about the company and job, fewer persons who obviously are not qualified will answer the advertisement. Specific details vary with the company and its situation, and should be in the ad if it is to attract good applicants. Some ads mention the salary range of successful company marketing personnel. Other explain that the person selected is to the replace a regular marketing-person in an established territory with active accounts. Still others specify that only professional marketing-people need apply. Information of this sort helps convince promising applicants that the opening represents a legitimate established job.

Most marketing managers favour 'open' over 'blind' advertisements, although mixed practice exists. The company name, especially if well known and respected, should be prominently featured so as to attract the best applicants. Location of the advertisement in the publication is also important. Newspaper advertisements on sports or financial pages are usually more productive but cost more per insertion than those in classified sections. Display ads on a sports page, for example, not only attract unemployed persons looking for work but employed individuals who are not in the job market but who can be attracted by the lure of better jobs.

Sometimes brochures outlining company's marketing-career opportunities are distributed to applicants answering advertisements as well as to those contacted by other methods. The most effective brochures are written from the viewpoint of the prospective marketing recruit.

Besides describing the company and its history, they make clear the qualifications required for marketing jobs, and the marketing-person's duties, responsibilities, and advancement opportunities. It is effective to include short, case histories of those who have been successful marketing-people with the company. Many brochures make liberal use of pictures, charts, diagrams, and other visual presentations.

Direct-to-consumer organisations have a particularly difficult time in recruiting marketing personnel. The type of marketing and the uncertainty of earnings result in high turnover rates among these marketing-people. Fortunately, these companies can rely upon recruiting methods that are satisfactory in obtaining the lower-grade marketing-people they require, although almost useless for recruiting high-grade marketing personnel. Their best source of recruits is recommendations from their own marketing-people, and they often offer bonuses for each new person recruited. When time method proves inadequate, direct-mail recruiting is used, the mailing list often consisting of the names of former marketing people the company hopes to re-employ. In addition, 'help wanted' ads are placed in local newspapers or in publications. As a last resort, direct-marketing companies, especially those with field supervisors use cold canvas recruiting in open territories.

The Selection System

Selection systems range from simple one-step systems consisting of nothing more than a single informal personnel interview, to complex multiple-step systems providing many devices and techniques designed to gather information. It is helpful to visualise a selection system as a set of successive 'screens,' at any of which the applicant may be removed from further consideration. Because some screens are more expensive to administer than others, the system should be designed to incorporate the most inexpensive screens early, thus eliminating unpromising candidates with minimum delay, and economising on money and effort invested. Applicants who survive all screenings are offered positions.

No selection system is infallible; all eliminate some who would have succeeded as a marketing-people and recommend hiring some who fail. A selection system fulfils its main mission if it improves management's ability to estimate success-and-failure probabilities of individual applicants. Every company should design its selection system to fit its own requirements. Each step should be included for a purpose, and each should be eliminated when it no longer makes a worthwhile contribution. The selection system should be well integrated, with each step contributing needed information for hiring decisions.

Pre-interview Screening

Many companies use an initial screening before the first formal interview to eliminate obviously unqualified applicants and save the time of both interviewers and applicants. This screening may be in two steps: (1) providing the applicant with a job profile and basic data on the company, and (2) gaining initial information about the applicant from an interview application form and perhaps a screening test. The interview application obtains information on the job candidate's basic qualifications. Before routine interviewing and testing are begin, predetermined minimum qualifications regarding such factors as educations, health, and experience must be met. The interview application form, which is at most two pages long, is completed in a few minutes. It should not be confused with the longer, more detailed application form used later in the selection system.

The Interview

The interview is the most widely used selection step, and in some companies, it comprises the entire selection system. Some personnel experts criticise the interview as an unreliable selection tool, but it is an effective way to obtain certain needed information. Not other method, for instance, is quite so satisfactory in judging an individual with respect of such matters as ability in oral communication, personal appearance and manners, attitude toward marketing and life in general, reaction to obstacles presented face to face, and personal impact others.

Importance over the years have operated to increase the reliability of interview results. Newer techniques, such as patterned and nondirective interviewing, are being used with apparent success. Many companies now provide training for all executives and staff members who interview, and scientifically designed rating scales and interview record form help interviewers to guide discussions along orderly lines. The net effect is more reliable interview results that yield more easily to analysis.

Because of the time involved, interviewing is costly. Consequently interviewers should avoid covering the same ground as other selection devices. The interviewer should review the completed application form before the interview in order to refrain form asking questions that have already been answered. Perusal of the completed application should indicate areas that require further questioning. Too often the interviewer appends for too much time in telling the applicant about the company and its policies. Although, it is important to sell the individual on the organisation, particularly when there is a scarcity of marketing personnel, there are more efficient ways of accomplishing this. One is by providing the applicant with a brochure relating important facts about the company and asking that it be read before the interview. Another may be used when several applicants are to be interviewed consecutively, as in college recruiting. The interviewer holds meetings preliminarily with the whole group, and describes general company policies. But even after such orientation, it is necessary to answer additional question during individual interviews. Nevertheless, most of the interview should be used for obtaining information about the applicant. A helpful rule is that, during an interview, the interviewer should do a minimum of the talking.

The job interview can be a trying experience for the applicant. Even for experienced marketing-persons accustomed to marketing themselves and their products daily to strangers, the great importance attached to a job change and the unfamiliarity if the situation may cause nervousness. The interviewer should put the applicant at ease. One way to relieve tension is for the interviewer to begin with questions on the person's family and educational background, subjects about which most people talk freely. The interviewer must remember that the applicant is not the only one marketing himself. It is the interviewer task to persuade the potential employee that the firm is a desirable employer. Far too often, the job interview impresses the applicant as an inquisition so that the applicant's nervousness makes the results less reliable. Throughout the interview, pleasant rapport between interviewer and job applicant should be maintained.

(1) How many Interviews? A single interview seldom provides sufficient information to evaluate an individual as a potential marketing-person. At the second interview, additional facts secured may cause a revision of the first impression. Many tensions present in the first interview are reduced, since the applicant no longer is a complete stranger in an unfamiliar situation. The applicant's behaviour should be more nearly normal.

Commonly, the first interview is short, perhaps no more than 20 minutes. Questions about the company and the job are answered while the interviewer determines whether the applicant meets minimum qualifications. If this hurdle is passed and the applicant expresses interest, he or she is asked to fill out a detailed application form, and an appointment is made for the second interview.

(2) Who shall Interview? In filling most marketing jobs, it is advisable to have several persons interview and evaluate all applicants considered worth hiring. In most large companies, first interviews are conducted by personnel department representatives. Next, promising applicants are invited to the home office or, in a decentralised company, to a regional office. These interviews vary in number and kind with the importance of the opening. One large steel company, which needs persons capable of highly specialised marketing to important accounts, brings applications to Pittsburgh for interviews by two assistant marketing managers, and the general marketing manager, and the marketing vice-president. All four executives must approve a decision to hire an applicant. A manufacturer of office machinery and supplied which required marketing personnel for more routine marketing work hires applicants after two interviews, one by a branch marketing manager and one by an assistant branch marketing manager.

(3) Interviewing the Spouse: Because of the necessity for frequent overnight travel, the majority of outside marketing-people are men. Some employers sound out the attitude of the male applicant's wife. If she objects, for instance, to having her husband out of town several days at a stretch, it is unlikely that he can succeed in a job requiring extended travel. This is the main reason that an interview with the wife is often part of the selection system. Frequently, however, the occasion amounts to nothing more than an import dinner with the applicant and wife, during which the wife's' attitudes can be ascertained.

(4) Interviewing Techniques: The informal, unplanned interview has been giving way in many companies to newer techniques, some of are described below:

(i) Patterned Interview: Here the interviewer uses a prepared outline of questions designed to elicit a basic core of information. The interviewer may work directly from the outline, recording answers as they are given; but this tends to make the conversation stilted and the applicant nervous. Greater spontaneity results when the outline is memorised and the answers recorded after the interview. Interviewers should avoid too many questions that can be answered with a simple 'yes' or 'no'. It is better to use more penetrating questions that reveal the attitudes and thinking of the prospective employee.

(ii) Nondirective Interview: Some personnel experts say that a nondirective technique yields maximum insight into an individual's attitudes and interests. In this technique the applicant is encouraged to speak freely about his or her experience, training, and future plans. The interviewer asks few direct questions and says only enough to keep the interviewee talking. The nondirective interview does not provide answers to standard questions, and much time is spent on outwardly irrelevant subjects. Export interpretation, however, reveals, much about the applicant—often including things of which the individual is not consciously aware. This technique's proponents claim that it is the best method for probing an individual's personality in depth. The main drawback to its use is that administering the interview and interpreting the results demand specialised instruction.

(iii) Interaction Interview: The interaction interview simulates the stresses the applicant would meet in actual marketing situations and provides the occasion for observing the applicant's reactions to them. This form of interview requires two interviewers. One uses psychological techniques to set up the simulated situations, and the other, who is present but not an active participant in the interview, observes and records the applicant's reactions. Because of their subtlety, the delicacy involved in application, and the need for exert interpretation interviews should be planned, administered, and interpreted by trained psychologists.

(iv) Rating Scales: One widely recognised defect of the personal interview is its tendency to lack objectivity, a defect that can be reduced through rating scales. These are so constructed that interviewer's ratings are channeled into a limited choices of responses. In evaluating an applicant's general appearance, for instance, one much-used form forces an interviewer to choose one of five descriptive phrases; very neat, nicely dressed, presentable, untidy, slovenly. Experience indicates that this results in more comparable ratings of the same individual by different interviews. One drawback of the rating scale is that its very objectivity restricts precise description of many personal qualities. It is good practice, therefore, to encourage interviewers to explain ratings in writing whenever they feel comments are needed. Companies using rating scales as a technique for accessing job suitability must keep in mind—in accordance with the guidelines issued by the EEOC and OFCC—that they also need empirical data to demonstrate that the technique is predictive of or significantly correlated with successful job performance and does not result in discrimination on the basis of race, colour, religion, sex, or national origin.

Formal Application Form

The formal application form serves as a central record for all pertinent information collected during the selection process. When completed, it becomes part of the permanent personnel record of the new employees. As a general rule, a formal application is filled out only after a preliminary interview indicates that a job candidate has promise as a company marketing-person. The application form may be filled out by the applicant personally or by interviewer who records the applicant's response. Practice varies in this respect, but in either case the completed formal application amounts to a standardised written interview, since most of the information that it contains could be obtained through one or more conventional and more personal interviews. Sometimes, sections are reserved for later recording of the results of such selection steps as psychological testing, reference checks, and physical examinations standardised application blank is prepared by Marketing Management magazine. One other standard forms are available, but ideally each company should prepare its own. No two companies have precisely the same requirements, and information significant for one may be useless for another. However, if a firm has only a small marketing force, and recruits relatively few people, the time and cost of preparing its own application form may warrant the choice of a standard form. Firms using standard forms simply ignore inappropriate items and obtain needed additional information during interviews.

Certain items of information are almost always needed for selection decisions, and these can be conveniently assembled on the application form. Among these are: present job, dependents, education, employment status, debts, time with last employer, membership in organisations, previous position, records of earning, reasons for leaving last job, networth, living expenses, and length of job hunting period.

Final decisions as to the specific items to include on the form should be based upon analysis of the existing marketing force. The names of marketing personnel should be arranged along a continuum, the best performer at one end and the worst performer at the other. This list is divided into three or more parts; for example, good, average, and poor; if the marketing force is large, finer subdivisions are justified. In measuring current qualification, data are collected from marketing records, supervisors' evaluations, and similar sources. The next step is to compare good and poor performers according to qualifications possessed by each at time of hiring. This should reveal any factors that differentiate the two groups, and these are the items that should be included on the application form. The validity of this basis of evaluation depends upon the size of the several groups studies, and for reliable results no group should be smaller than 30.

Objective Scoring of Personnel-History Items

It the total profile, rather than any single item, that determined the predictive value of personnel-history items. Considered singly, few items have value as selection factors, but individuals with all the personal-history requirements are those most likely to succeed. However, many potentially successful marketing-people do not possess all the requirements. One company, for instance, found that most of its best marketing-people were hired between the ages of 30 and 35 years, yet there were some as young as nineteen and as old as fifty-two. The significance of each personal factor is relative, not absolute. Although 30 to 35 may be the preferred age range, applicants outside this age range should still consideration (since other factors in their backgrounds may more than offset the fact that they are outside the desired age range).

Some firms with large marketing forces establish objective measures for personal-history items. A maximum possible score is assigned for each items, and the points given to a particular individual depend upon proximity to the ideal. In one firm 15 personal-history items are used as selection factors, at a maximum value of ten points each. The maximum score is 150 points, and the cut off score is 120. Successful marketing-persons in this company all scored over 100 when hired, and the company automatically disqualifies all applicants with scores under 100.

Objective personal-history scoring was pioneered by the life insurance companies. Their marketing forces were sufficiently large to permit establishment of reliable standards. It is doubtful practice to set such scoring standards when the marketing force is rather small (say, under 100 people), as the distortion of scores tends to increase in inverse proportion to the size of the marketing force used for setting the standards. Furthermore, with the passage of the Civil Rights Act and the Age Discrimination in Employment Act, a company using objective personal-history scoring must be prepare to prove empirically that the technique does not result in discrimination against applicants on the basis of race, colour, religion, sex, national origin, or age. Further, they must prove that the scores above the cutoff point are predictive of or significantly correlated with important elements of work behaviour which comprise or are relevant to the marketing position for which applicants are being evaluated. Therefore, marketing executive should use objective scoring or personal-history items with great caution, although they may safely use 'cut-off scores' to indicate the need for further investigation of an applicant's qualifications.

Reference and Opinions of Acquaintances

References provided by friends and former employers of the applicant are used to secure information not available from other sources. The value of references denied by some employers, who contend that writers of reference letters generally hesitate to criticise personal friends, or even ex-employees. But the experienced employer 'Reads between the lines' of letters of reference, where, for example, the weak candidate may be damned by faint praise. Personal contact is the best way to obtain information from references, since facial expression and voice intonations can reveal a great deal, and most people are more frank orally than in writing. When a reference is located at a distance, a telephone call may substitute for personal contact. Solicitation of written recommendations is the weakest approach and should be a last resort.

Applicants tend to name as references only those on whom they can rely to speak in their favour. In addition, there is a natural tendency for references to be biased in favour of an applicant. These limitations can be partially offset by contacting persons not listed as references but who know the applicant. Individuals, who know the applicant but who are not specifically listed as references often are excellent source for candid appraisals of the candidate. These acquaintances fall into four classifications:

(1) Present or Forms Employers: These persons have observed the applicant under actual work conditions. As a matter of practice, however, many marketing executives do not approach the present employer without the applicant's permissions.

(2) Former Customers: If applicants have marketing experience, their former customers are in a position to assess their marketing ability. It is advisable to contact these individuals without the applicant's assistance. This helps avoid those who are personal friends of applicants.

(3) Reputable Citizens: If references suggested by the applicant are used, it is best first to contact those who are reputable, well-know citizens. Such people do not stake their personal reputations on those in whom they have little confidence.

(4) Mutual Acquaintances: Those who know both the applicant and the employer may give frank evaluations. What is even more important is that the employer is better able to judge the reliability of such evaluations.

Physical Examinations

Since good health is important to marketing-person's success, most companies require physical examinations of all applicants seriously considered for marketing positions. Because of the relatively high cost of the physical examination, it generally is one of the last steps in the selection system. Even in companies requiring entrance physical examinations, poor health often accounts for separations; but when the examinations are not compulsory, the number is higher. It is advantageous to the applicant as well as to the company to identify physical ailments that may later prevent the attainment of full productivity.

Credit Information

Many companies run credit checks on applicants for marketing positions. Credit files are compiled on most people by local credit bureaus, and special credit reports are obtainable through such organisations as Dun and Bradstreet. When a heavy burden of personal debt is found, it may be indicative of financial worries interfering with productivity, or of a motivating factors serving to spur productivity—to determine which one of these may be true requires, and should be given, further investigation. In analysing the entire credit report the executive should look for the 'danger signals'—chronic lateness in marketing payments, large debts outstanding for long periods, or bankruptcy history—the presence of any of which should signal the need for additional probing of the underlying facts. Financial irresponsibility may or may not be indicative of irresponsibility in meeting job obligations; hence considerable data on all aspects of the applicant's behaviour, non-financial as well as financial, must be on hand to warrant whichever conclusion is drawn.

Psychological Tests

Physiological testing provides objective way to measure many traits or characteristics of applicants for marketing positions. Until the mid-1960s the trend was for more and more companies to make some use of psychological tests as one of the last steps in selection system (the tests come toward the end because of their relatively high cost). Since the passage of the Civil Rights Act in 1964 and with the issuance of guidelines by the EEOC and OFCC, there has been tendency for companies to either abandon or rely less upon psychological tests as an aid in making selection decision from among job candidates. Roughly 20 per cent of the complaints filed under Title VII of the Civil Rights Act change that tests have been used in way that result in unfair discrimination against members of minority groups. One reason fewer companies use psychological tests today then previously is the difficult in validating them and in securing the empirical data needed to prove that test results are predictive of or significantly related to successful job performance and—further—that test results are being used in ways that do not result in illegal discrimination.

The task of validating tests is complicated because many situations exist in which different sets of behaviours or attributes can lead to successful job performance. Because of this, separate validity studies should be performed for different ethnic groups. The different cultural experience and exposure of each group may affect the relationship of test scores to job-performance criteria. Results of certain tests may underestimate the true ability of disadvantaged applicants and cause tests that are valid for the advantages to be invalid for the disadvantaged. White marketing personnel, for instance, may make effective use of certain marketing techniques with white customers that are different from the technique black marketing personnel find effective with the same customers. Tests can predict aptitude for using these techniques; but such tests would be appropriate only for white applicants if the tests have not been validated for use with black applicants. In some situations differential avidity is found, in others not.

Actual research is required in each situation to determine whether or not differential validity exists, and both the EEOC and OFCC emphasise the need to validate test results separately for minority-group members.

(1) Validation of Tests: Because of the increasingly important need for proof that a test is related to job-performance criteria and because of the possibility that differential validity exists (for different groups of applicants), it is important to discuss the validation of tests. The illustrations used relate to validity studies conducted on separate ethnic groups, but the same general approach is used for validity studies conducted on other types of groups, for example, for different age groups or for males and females.

Using psychological tests for selection purposes, then, required considerable sophistication. Not only is there the possibility that certain tests possess differential validity, but the very objectivity of tests leads many users to expect more validity and reliability in predicting marketing success than the tests can offer. Furthermore, it can be said in all fairness that some widely used tests are almost worthless for selection purposes, simply because they were designed for entirely different purposes; others are of questionable value even for measuring what they were intended to measure. Psychological testing is still an experimental field, and every experiment does not succeed. Yet more than a few testing 'failures' are on the market, are even promoted and recommended by the producers, and used by executives unaware of the limitations. In addition, tests tend to favour conformity rather than individual dynamics—they tend to rule out creative thinkers and imaginative, aggressive individuals who might be ideal for the job being filled.

Nevertheless, there are some useful and reliable tests available, and certain basically weak tests can serve as screening devices as long as their limitations are recognised, but, as brought out earlier, it is increasingly important for test users to perform actual research to determine whether or not differential validity exists. The requirement for doing such research makes it even critical that test users secure the services of trained specialists in psychological testing for purposes of selecting, administering, and interpreting the tests used for any particular company.

(2) Types of Tests: Three types of psychological tests are used in selection systems for marketing personnel; tests of ability, of habitual characteristics, and of achievement. Tests of ability attempt to measure how well a person can perform particular tasks with maximum motivation. They are tests of *best* performance, and they include tests of mental ability ('intelligence' tests) and tests of special abilities, or aptitude tests. Test of habitual characteristics attempt to gauge how prospective employees would act in their daily work normally, i.e., not when they are on their best behaviour. These are tests of typical performance, and they include attitude, personality, and interest tests. Achievement tests are designed to measure how much individuals have learned from their training or education.

(3) Basis for Evaluation of Tests: Before examining the psychological tests used in marketing-person selection, we need some criteria for evaluation. Earlier discussion emphasised the importance of a test having validity—that it measures what it purports to measure—and of detecting differential validity. But even in cases where statistical validity has been demonstrated, it is possible for a test not to be valid in a particular instance. For example, a written intelligence test in English is not a valid measure of the *mental ability* of a Spanish-speaking person with an English-language handicap. A low score does not necessarily indicate low intelligence; it may merely reflect poor understanding of the English language.

Test reliability is also important. Reliability refers to the consistency of test results. If a test has reliability, an individual should receive approximately the same score in subsequent retesting with the same or equivalent tests.

Test objectivity is important, too. If a test has objectivity, it is so administered that the score's opinion does not enter into the test results. Whenever a person giving or scoring the test can affect the test results, it is misleading to compare the results obtained by different testers.

Other factors to consider in selecting tests are cost, time, and ease of administration. Wide variation in cost exists, and even small differentials may be important if testes are given to large groups. Because, there is little relationship between cost and quality, it is sometimes possible to obtain quality testes at low cost. There, is similarly, wide variation in the time required to administer and score tests. Because time frequently is crucial in selection of marketing personnel, the employer must balance the time requirements of alterative tests against their relative effectiveness. If the best available test consumes more time than can be spared, a mediocre test that can be given and scored by persons with little or no special training. Again, employers must balance the gains associated with more complex test against their costs in time and money.

(4) Test of Mental Ability: Mental tests are used satisfactorily in a wide range of areas, and they have higher validity and reliability than most psychological tests. It must be understood, however, that they measure primarily the abilities that make for success in educational or training situations, namely, language usage and comprehensions, and abstract reasoning, or problem-solving ability. They do not measure creativeness, originality, or insight. Therefore, they should be regarded more as measures of mental aptitude than of general intelligence. Because tests of mental ability are 'timed tests,' they provide an innovation of an applicant's ability to learn quickly and to arrive at accurate answers under pressure.

Within these limitations, mental tests are helpful in the marketing personnel selection process. Where there is no other evidence of ability, such as graduation from college, the mental aptitude test serves as a screen to eliminate applicants falling below a predetermined level. A wide variety of mental aptitude tests is available.

(5) Tests of Special Aptitudes: Certain tests are designed to measure special aptitudes, such as: spatial and perceptual abilities, speed and reaction time, steadiness and controlled movement, mechanical comprehension, and artistic abilities. Aptitude tests used individually aid in marketing selection for some industrial jobs, as illustrated, for example, by the use of perception test for selecting clerical personnel. But because marketing requires diverse aptitudes, and marketing job specifications differ even among competing companies, and especially designed battery of aptitude tests is more appropriate for marketing personnel.

The procedure for developing a battery of marketing aptitude tests for a particular company is fairly straightforward. The test expert begins with the job specifications derived, as you will recall, from the job description, checking them to assure that the abilities required for job performance are correctly identified. Then the expert selects existing tests and/or constructs new tests to measure each aptitude. Finally, the tests export develops a scheme for weighting and combining the scores of individual tests. This work of preparing—and later validating—a test battery is time-consuming and costly, and calls for a psychologist's services. Thus, generally only those companies which process large numbers of marketing job applicants annually feel they can afford specially developed test batteries to measure marketing aptitude. Since, unfortunately, batteries not custom tailored for a particular marketing job frequently have little validity, companies with small marketing forces find it impractical to include marketing-aptitude test batteries in their selection systems.

(6) Personality Tests: Personality tests initially were used to identify people with psychotic tendencies—and certain tests have proved useful for this purpose. Subsequently, attempts have been made to use them for measuring personality traits in normal individuals, for which purpose they seem to have little to no validity or reliability. The basic limitation is the lack of uniform definitions for such traits as initiative or aggressiveness, which these tests purport to measure. To the extent that these tests are at all valid measuring normal individuals, validity must be determined by the total score rather than by scores for individual traits. The chief use of the personality test is that of screening device to identify persons with abnormal personalities.

Projective tests, of which the Rorschach is the best known, are a promising technique for personality measurement. However, they must be administered by skilled testers, and their results represent a subjective opinion rather than an objective measure. Further refinements of protective techniques eventually may provide useful personality measurements.

(7) Interest Tests: In using interest tests as selection devices, a basic assumption is that a relationship exists between interest and motivation. Hence, if two persons have equal ability, the one with the greater interest in a particular job should be more successful in that job. A second inherent assumption is that interests are constant, that those of a person at age 40 are essentially the same as they were at 21.

The interest test is useful for vocational guidance, but it is not wholly satisfactory as a selection device. This is because of the opportunity for faking responses—

individuals may select answers overstating their real interest in a particular field. Of the two most widely-used interest tests, the Strong and the Kuder, the Strong uses the more indirect and subtle approach and is harder to fake; but because of its greater complexity, it is more expensive to score. The US Air Force, which has experimented with a technique to eliminate faking, uses an information test to measure interest on the theory that persons should be best informed about those field in which they are most interested.

What proof is there of the value of interest tests in predicting marketing success? Unfortunately, very little! Strong demonstrated that there is a positive but low correlation between interest scores and success in insurance marketing. Significant variation has also been found in the interest test scores of successful and unsuccessful marketing-persons of accounting machines. Otherwise, there is little tangible proof of the value of interest tests as devices for predicting marketing success.

(8) Attitude Tests: Attitude tests are more useful as morale-measuring techniques than as selection aids. They are used to ascertain employees' feelings toward working conditions pay, advancement opportunities, and the like. Used as marketing personnel selection devices, they may make limited contributions by identifying abnormal attitudes on such broad subjects as big business, labour unions, and government. Their validity is questionable, since people often profess socially acceptable attitudes they do not actually have. In addition, attitude tests do not measure the intensity with particular attitudes are held.

(9) Achievement Tests: Achievement tests seek to determine how much individuals know about a particular subject. Few standardised test of this type are used by industry, because the special skills involved in each job require different types of knowledge. Tests of clerical and stenographic ability are one exception, and civil service examinations are another. For the employer who has decided that it is worthwhile to custom design an achievement test for marketing applicants, such an instrument can provide as assessment of knowledge applicants possess in such areas as the product, marketing channels, and customers relations; however, as with other psychological tests, such test designing is a job for an expert, not an amateur.

Research has produced some evidence that the existence of two basic qualities, empathy and ego drive, are essential in good marketing-people. Empathy is the ability to fell as others do, to put oneself in another person's shoes. The empathic marketing-person senses the reactions of his or her customers and is able to adjust to these reactions, achieving real interaction with customers. The second basic quality, ego drive, makes the marketing-person want to make the sale in a personal way, not merely for the money to be gained. His feeling is that he has to make the sale. His self-picture improves by virtue of conquest and diminishes with failure. The good marketing-person has a proper balance of these two qualities. The developers of this hypothesis have demonstrated in experiments that measurement of these two qualities alone (through the use of specially developed psychological tests) has greatly improved predication of success or failure in a number of different marketing jobs.

(10) Conclusions on Testing: Besides the legal requirements that tests must not be used for marketing selection decisions in ways that discriminate unfairly against minority-group applications, there are other important precautions to observe when incorporating psychological tests into a marketing personnel selection system. It is essential to have accurate job specifications, derived from up-to-date and complete job descriptions, to make certain that the specific abilities required of a good marketing-person are known. A qualified expert's services are required in the choice of tests (and in devising new ones when necessary), in determining test validity and in detecting differential validity, in administering the tests themselves, and in interpreting the significance of results. In addition, marketing executives need to recognise the fact that psychological testing, although potentially capable of making a valuable contribution, is but one element in an effective marketing personnel selection system.

❑❑❑

8

Training Programme for Marketing Personnel

Introduction

The modern marketing executive's attitude toward marketing training has changed markedly in recent years. Marketing managers typically used to believe in 'sink-or-swim' training—outing new marketing-people into the field with scanty instructions and expecting them to do their best, learning what they could in the hard school of experience. For example, one of Fortune magazine's 500 largest corporations introduced its first formal marketing-training programme in one of its major industrial products division. Prior to that time, this division gave product descriptions, a territory, and an order book to new marketing-force recruits with instructions to 'go out and sell.'

The lack of recognition of the need to train marketing-people reflected an attitude that many marketing managers held toward marketing. The older generation of marketing managers operated on the comfortable—albeit superficial—assumption that good marketing-people were 'born,' not 'made.' Admittedly, then as now there are some 'born' or 'natural' marketing people. But, given appropriate training, the majority of recruits can be 'made' into marketing persons; and both 'born' and 'made' marketing personnel improve with continued marketing training. Modern marketing executives still consider experience the most valuable marketing training but they believe strongly that formally planned and executed marketing-training programmes contribute significantly to the improvement of marketing performance. They regard formalised marketing-training programmes as important supplements to, rather than substitutes for, field marketing experience.

Organisation for Marketing Training

Placement of Training Responsibility

Organisational planners do not agree on the question of where to place primary responsibility for initial marketing training. Some consider it a line function and assign the marketing-training responsibility to the chief marketing executive; others consider it a staff function and assign the responsibility to the personnel manager, reserving only an advisory role for marketing management. In most situations, both executives should pay a role in initial marketing training—the marketing executive because he should be an expert on marketing, and the personnel manager because he should be an expert on training. How a particular firm should decide the placement of responsibility for initial marketing training depends upon comparative costs. If much of the initial training of new marketing personnel parallels that given other employees, cost considerations often result in primary responsibility being assigned to the personnel manager. If very little of the initial marketing training parallels other new employee training, then primary responsibility is assigned to the marketing executive.

Once initial marketing training is over, responsibility for continuing training definitely resides with the chief marketing executive. Introduction of new products, adoption of revised marketing policies, perfection of improved marketing techniques, and similar developments call for training action—and logic dictates that top marketing executives should be in the best position to recognise the need. In the well-managed business, marketing training is a newer ending of indoctrination, the chief marketing executive has continuing responsibility.

Marketing Training Staff

Even though chief executives may be ultimately responsible for both initial and continuing marketing training, they usually delegate actual performance of the function to subordinates. Often large marketing organisations have a full-time marketing-training director, reporting directly to the chief marketing executive. The director might personally conduct some training and coordinate that given on a decentralised (and usually part-time) basis by regional and district marketing managers. In smaller organisations, some chief marketing executives handle part of the training themselves, but in most cases, they rely upon others, such as assistant marketing managers or district managers, to do most of the training. Even companies without marketing training directors often have full-time or part-time marketing trainers, or both. The large marketing organisation generally can make efficient use of a full-time marketing-training director and sometimes even a full-time staff, but the small organisation ordinarily must rely on executives to do marketing training 'in addition to other duties'. Because of specialised knowledge requirements, the tendency is for companies to training their own marketing trainers rather than to recruit outsiders.

Training the Marketing Trainers

No marketing-training programme, however carefully designed, can be more effective than the people, who conduct it. For this reason, a growing number of companies provide special training programmes for marketing trainers. The straining point is the identification of the subjects that trainers should know thoroughly, such as the company and its policies, the products, the customers, and their problems. The marketing-person's job, and marketing techniques. If the potential trainers are not already experienced marketing-people, they should be given field marketing experience to provide a realistic feel for marketing problems. Subjects presented formally should be handled by personnel already skilled as trainers, wherever possible, using instructional techniques similar to those trainers will use later.

Not only should marketing trainers have expert and specialised knowledge, they must be effective teachers. Throughout their period of preparation, the theory and mechanics of teaching should be stressed. Trainers should be required to master these, learn how to apply them effectively, preferably through doing practice training themselves. They must also learn to plan and organise teaching material for clear and effective presentation. Although formal training alone will not prepare an individual for effective teaching, a well-planned and executed programme for marketing trainers can certainly help. For the most part, however, marketing trainers must develop their own teaching skills. To emphasise this point, management often reminds them that; "If the trainee hasn't learned, the trainer hasn't taught."

Building Marketing Training Programme

Many companies conduct several types marketing-training programme. Generally, the most comprehensive and longest programme is that for newly recruited personnel. More intensive and usually shorter programmes on specialised topics are presented for experienced marketing-people. In addition, periodic 'refresher' marketing-training programmes are considered desirable in most companies. Some marketing-training programmes in certain forms are designed especially for the development of marketing trainers or for persons whom management believes have potential as marketing executives. Each type of programme serves different purposes, and the scope and content of each should reflect its particular purpose.

There are several sequential steps in integrating marketing training with the operating objectives of the business. First, these objectives should be clearly defined and phrased in terms of the marketing force and its capability with respect to achieving these objectives. Then, it must be determined what marketing training is necessary to close the gap between capabilities and objectives. At this point a minimal system of marketing-training programmes, procedures, and projects can be designed to close the gap.

Building an effective marketing-training programme of any type requires a number of important planning decisions. The purposes to be served by the training must be clearly defined, programme content must be decided, training methods selected, arrangements made for programme execution, and procedures set up to evaluate the results. Some marketing-training specialists refer to these planning decisions as the A-C-M-E decision—aim, content, method, and execution and evaluation—each of which is considered in the following discussion.

Defining Training Aims

The first step is, to decide what the marketing-training programme should seek to accomplish. Of course, the general aim of all marketing training is to improve marketing performance—both of individual marketing-persons and of the entire marketing force. Improved marketing performance is achieved through measures taken to increase marketing-people's productivity and to control marketing costs. Without training, a marketing-person's productivity tends to increase with experience; hence, if training can substitute for some portion of the needed experience or can usefully supplement it, higher productivity levels should be reached earlier. Marketing costs per unit of products sold decline with rises in marketing productivity, so they also tend to be related to experience. Furthermore, the marketing force turnover rate for new marketing personnel nearly always is higher then for experienced people—often unexperienced staff members find themselves unprepared to do satisfactory jobs, become discouraged, and leave the company. If marketing training can help marketing-persons to increase their productivity more quickly, the marketing force turnover rate will drop, hiring and training costs should fall, and marketing efficiency will rise. Marketing performance is influenced also by the state of relations with customers and prospects, the marketing force playing a crucial role in moulding and maintaining these relations. Generally, experienced, marketing people make better impressions on prospects and maintain better continuing relations with established accounts. Here, again, marketing training can contribute through accelerating the process of 'learning through experience.' In all these ways, then, marketing training serves to improve marketing performance by providing a mechanism through which the benefits from an 'experienced' marketing force can be realised much earlier and more surely than might otherwise be the case.

It is not sufficient, however, to define only general training aims—specific aims of particular programmes also need to be identified. Although, we may be interested, say, in increasing the marketing force's productivity through training, we need to identify, what must be done to achieve the general aim of increasing productivity. General aims need translating into more specific aims phrased in operational terms before the programme can be planned in detail. These process of specific aim definition begins with a review of general aims and the means currently employed to attain them; however, the process cannot be completed until management actually perceives training needs from which specific training aim derive directly. In the next two sections, discussion focuses on factors that management should consider as it seeks to identify training needs for (1) initial marketing-training programmes, and (2) continuing marketing-training programmes.

Determining Initial Training Needs

Determining the need for, and specific aims of, an initial marketing-training programme requires consideration of three main factors: requirements of the marketing job, prior background and experience of individual of trainees, and company marketing policies.

(1) Job Requirements: Marketing job analysis provides the information required for preparing the job description, which, as you recall, consists of a statement of job objectives and an explanation of essential tasks involved in its performance.

Management should study the job description for clues about the points on which new personnel are most likely to need training. But, it is at least as important to consider other information relative to marketing job performance: How should marketing people apportion their time? Which duties require the greatest proportion of marketing time? Which tend to be neglect? Why? Which marketing approaches are most effective? Answers to these and related questions help in formulating the qualifications that a marketing-person should be have to fill the job satisfactorily.

(2) Individual Trainees' Prior Background and Experience: Each person in an initial marketing-training programme enters it with a somewhat unique educational background and a highly individualised record of achievement. Conceptually, then, the gap between required job qualifications for a particular trainee and those he or she already has represents the nature and amount of training needed. But in a large organisation with a fully structured and formalised programme, it is not always practical to adjust training precisely to individual differences in background and experience. Time and money may be saved by putting all recruits through identical programmes. Nevertheless, in more flexible training situations, information about trainees' qualifications makes possible to some extent the tailoring of programme to individuals, increasing both trainee satisfaction and programme efficiency. In all companies, large and small, determining recruit's real needs for training is essential to developing initial training programmes of optimum benefit to company and trainee alike.

(3) Company Marketing Policies: A company's particular marketing situations should be analysed in determining the needs to be served by individual marketing training. For instance, marketing a line of machine tools requires emphasis on product information and customer applications whereas marketing simple, nontechnical products demands more emphasis on marketing techniques. Thus, differences in products and markets make for differences in marketing practices and policies, which, in turn, point to needed differences in initial marketing training programme. The same applies to differences in promotion, price, marketing channel, and system of physical distribution—all have implications for the needs that the initial marketing-training programme should serve. In the case of promotion, for example, if advertising is not used or used relatively little, marketing training should prepare marketing personnel to handle considerable promotional work; but, if advertising is used extensively to supplement marketing-people's efforts, there is a need to teach new marketing personnel how to coordinate their efforts with advertising.

Determining Continuing Training Needs

Training a marketing force is a never-ending process. Even though the initial training programme may be excellent, its graduate are soon in need of refresher courses as the company's product lines and markets change and as they become careless in their marketing habits. Although, the concept of continuing instruction for all marketing personnel is still new in a great many companies, it is being rapidly accepted. The experience of the Armour-Dial division of Greyhound Corporation illustrates the value of such training. Armour-Dial ran a study on marketing personnel who had attended a recent session as its Aurora (Illinois) marketing training centre. The result was a boost of 12 per cent in case marketing, 62 per cent in displays sold, and 250 per cent in marketing to direct-buying or chain accounts.

Determining the specific aims to be served by a continuing marketing-training programme also requires perception of specific training needs. Problems arising from forthcoming changes in company policy, procedure, or organisation should be anticipated and studied-they may have implications for needed training. More basic changes in products and markets almost always given rise to a need for additional training. It is also helpful for management, as it seeks to perceive needs for continuing training, to take such actions as: analysing the marketing job description relative to experienced persons' qualifications; surveying marketing personnel for suggestions; scrutinising marketing-person reports for symptoms of training needs; inspecting and analysing marketing records to uncover performance weaknesses; and personally observing marketing-people in action to detect deficiencies. Marketing management must know a great deal about how experienced marketing personnel are doing their jobs in order to define specific aims for their continued training.

Deciding the Content of Marketing Training Programmes

The actual content of a marketing training programmes, whether initial or continuing, should be derived from the specific aims that management, after analysing its training needs, has formulated. Initial programmes generally are characte.ised by broader scope and coverage than continuing programmes. Initial programmes, must provide instruction covering all important aspects of performing the marketing-person's job; continuing programmes may concentrate more on specific job aspects where management believes experienced persons to have more room for improvement. Therefore, the following discussion mainly relates to determining the content of initial marketing-training programmes.

For an initial marketing-training programme to contribute maximally toward preparing new recruits as marketing personnel, it must cover all important aspects of the marketing-person's job. Content varies considerably from company to company, because of differences in factors such as products, markets, company policies, trainees' ability and experience, organisational size, and executives' training philosophies. No two programmes are, or should be, alike. Different companies tend to cover the same general topics despite the fact that variations always exist in the exact and in the relative time developed to each major topic. But it is possible to generalise to the point of saying that every initial marketing-training programme should devote some time to each of four main areas—product data, marketing techniques, markets for the product, and company information.

Product Data

Some product training is basic to any initial marketing-training programme, even though all companies need not emphasise it. Companies with highly technical products commonly devote more than half of their programmes to product training. But in many situations, especially with standardised products sold routinely, new marketing personnel need receive only a small amount of formal product training. In all cases, however, management must make certain that new marketing-people know enough about the products, their uses, and applications to serve customers' information needs adequately and promptly. Product knowledge is basic to a marketing-person's self-confidence and enthusiastic job performance.

Understanding product uses and applications is especially important. Trainees should receive instruction on customers' problems and requirements and should learn how company products can help solve these problems and meet these requirements. Training should provide them with full appreciation for buyers' viewpoints, perhaps through role-playing instructional techniques. Through such training, new marketing-persons learn to relate company products to the fulfilment of customers requirements, thus equipping themselves not only for effective marketing but for effective handling of marketing resistance met later in the field.

Creative marketing is the name given a marketing approach that places the emphasis buyers' needs. The National Cash Register Company pioneered the use of this technique around 1900. Progressive companies make extensive use of it today. In order to indoctrinate trainees in applying this approach, initial marketing-training programmes often provide a period during which trainees are in direct contact with ultimate users or consumers. Through personal experience, such as in retail marketing or product servicing, trainees gain valuable insights on the ways different users react to company products.

More and more companies require a period of initial marketing training at the factory. This provides trainees with opportunities to observe and study the products during the various manufacturing and testing phases. They have the chance, too, to talk with or even to work alongside factory personnel. The instructional benefits should be more through product knowledge and greater confidence in subsequently demonstrating to otherwise presenting products to customers. Inordinate amounts of time, however, should not be devoted to technical production detail—such detail is important only insofar as it helps the marketing-person in actual marketing situations.

Some training on competitors' products usually is desirable, particularly in highly competitive industries. Marketing-people should not only know the important characteristics of competitor's products but be well posted on their uses and applications in solving customers' problems. They should be thoroughly familiar with how the strengths and weaknesses of competitive products compare with those of their own company's products. Thus informed, marketing-persons to emphasise superior qualities of features of the company's product, and they are well equipped to answer customers' question and to deal with their objections. Training on competitors' products must be continuous, the focus shifting as changes and improvements are made in both competitive and company products.

Marketing Technique

Most new recruits need formal instruction in marketing techniques, and an increasing number of firms provide such training. Some marketing managers still believe, however, that careful selection of marketing personnel and a heavy programme of product training are sufficient to ensure effective personality, good appearance and voice, reasonable intelligence, and knows the product, he will be able to sell it easily. But the predominant view is that new marketing personnel need basic instruction in how to sell. This is reflected in individual company marketing training programmes and in industry-wide programmes offered by such groups as the National Association of Food Manufacturers and the National Association of Machine Tool Builders. In all marketing-training programmes the practical as well as the theoretical side of marketing should be covered. In many companies, as an important adjunct to learning how to sell, new personnel receive training in the development of human-relations skills. In a few exceptional companies, training provides for practical analysis of the psychology of human behaviour and motivation relative to company marketing problems.

Marketing for the Products

It is especially important for the new marketing-person that training provides a comprehensive understanding of the market. The new marketing-person must know, who the customers are, the particular products in which they are interested, their buying habits and motives, their location, and their financial condition. In order to sell, in other words, the marketing-person needs to know not only who buys what but, more important, why and how they buy. When trainees are not given adequate instruction on the market, they may take years to acquire the needed understanding independently. During this period of trial-and-error learning, through no fault of their own, their productivity is lower than it should be. In fact, left to their own devices, some trainees never gain important market information. For instance, a marketing-person who is unaware of certain prospects' potential as buyers may neglect completely to canvass them or even to canvass entire classifications of prospects. Because markets are always changing, training in this area should be continuous, the content changing as significant market changes occur.

Company Information

Certain items of company information are essential to the marketing-person on the job; others, not absolutely essential, contribute to overall effectiveness. The training programme should include coverage of all marketing policies and, preferably, the reasoning that led to their formulation. The marketing-person must know company pricing policy in order to answer customers' questions about it. The marketing-persons also needs to be fully informed on other policies, such as those relating to products services, spare parts and repairs, credit extension, and customers relations.

The initial training programme must equip the marketing-person to perform such tasks as recording and submitting customer's orders for processing and delivery, preparing expense and other required reports, handling inquires, following up on customers for handling these and similar tasks. If trainees are to perform them properly and efficiently from the very start of their field assignments, the initial marketing-training programme must provide the needed instruction. Otherwise, company systems and procedures are learned, if at all, through a costly and time-consuming process of trial and error.

Another aspects of company information that should be explained in initial marketing-training programmes relate to the marketing department's personal policies. Coverage includes selection procedures, training programmes, compensation and incentive systems, advancement requirements and opportunities, saving and retirement plans, medial and insurance plans, and the like. Having such information improves employee morale and job effectiveness. Not having it shows up in employee uncertainty and needlessly excessive marketing force turnover rates.

Another ingredient that contributes to the building of morale among new employees might be described as 'general company information.' This concerns the company's history, its importance in the industry and economy, and its policies with regard to relations with stockholders, unions, competitors, government, and other groups. Having been briefed on these items, the new recruit's early and natural feelings of strangeness and uneasiness are replaced with some sense of belonging and company loyalty. Knowing something about the personality, or image, of the company also should bolster the confidence of recruits in its products, which they will shortly be trying to sell. It is worthwhile, then, to provide formal training covering selected items of general company information. But it also should be recognised that a common failings of initial marketing-training programmes is that too much time is spent on company background, history, and prestige building. The challenge is to provide sufficient general company information, but no to allocate instructional time disproportionate to its importance in the total programme.

Training Methods

Having defined specific training aims and determined programme content, management must select appropriate instructional methods. There is a wide variety from which to choose. Professional educators and marketing trainers have re-evaluated and refined time-honoured methods, such as lectures and discussions of different sorts, and, in addition, have developed new ones, such as the business game and role playing. Psychologist have influenced modern instructional methods through their studies of the learning process, motivation, retention, and so forth. From the many instructional methods available, the problems is to choose those that will most effectively and economically achieve programme aims.

Instructional methods can be segregated into two major categories: those requiring group participation and those involving individual training.

Group Instructional Methods

These are used wherever trainees are grouped for instructional purposes. The group instructional methods most frequently used in marketing training are: the lecture, the group discussion, role playing, and the simulation or game.

(1) The Lecture: Lecturing consists of primarily oral presentations, sometimes supplemented with visual aids, by an instructor in a formal classroom situation. This ancient teaching method, in use before the invention of printing, is still widely used in marketing training. Trainees participate mainly through watching and listening, although some versions of lecturing permit the asking of questions and allow for other interruptions. Generally, however, the lecturer involves passive, rather than active, trainee participation, this feature constituting its main weakness—teaching is emphasised more than learning. But a lecture can be effective, provided the lecturer is an able and enthusiastic speaker and makes liberal use of examples, demonstrations, and visual aids. Compared with other group instructional methods, too, the lecture is economical in terms of time required to cover a given topic.

Many professional business teachers, perhaps most, regard lecturing as the least effective group instructional methods. Professional marketing trainers seem, by and large, to agree with this evaluation. Estimates are that the average trainee can immediately recall less than 10 per cent of what he hears in a non-illustrated lecture, and no more than half of what he sees and hears in a lecture using visual aids.

Furthermore, because of the absence in a lecture participant feedback, no lecturer has any immediate or objective means for gauging the effectiveness of a lecture, but must rely on a personal appraisal of its reception, or on volunteered (and generally unreliable) comments by participants.

Even with its limitations, some lecturing in marketing training is often a practical necessity. If formal training is brief, for instance, lecturing may be the only way to cover major portions of the desired content. It may also be the only practical way to handle instruction when the training group is too large to permit constructive audience participation. Given longer training period and smaller training groups, however, lecturing is probably most appropriate for introductory and orientation sessions and for proving summaries of major topics taught mainly through methods such as case discussion and role playing. It also is used extensively, and in most instances appropriately, in continuing marketing-training programmes for providing new information about the company, its policies, products, markets, and marketing programmes. Recent research learning process can be considerably improved by using a carefully planned multimedia approach. In this approach the lecture room is equipped with two to six projectors and screens, and the entire lecture is projected visually on succeeding screens across the front of the room.

Further, lecturer support is provided by projecting illustrations, charts, and graphs, and through the provision of sound effects, where appropriate. Tests have shown that this version of the lecturer method significantly increases attention, comprehension, and retention.

(2) The Group Discussion: Group discussion differs from lecturing in several important respects. The instructor or discussion leader assumes a less dominant role, the trainees are active rather than passive participants, learning receives more emphasis than teaching, and the instructional atmosphere generally is much more informal and relaxed. Considerable flexibility is possible, too, in instructional format, the two main variations being the impromptu discussion and the case discussion. Because of these important advantages, and with the increasing sophistication of marketing trainers, group discussion methods are not only being used more extensively, they are being incorporated into an ever-growing number of marketing-training programmes.

In the impromptu discussion, often called a marketing seminar or conference, the instructor, group leader, or some member makes a brief oral presentation on a problem faced by marketing force members in their everyday work. This is followed by general give-and-take discussion. Group members gain a meaningful application for and understanding of many problems that otherwise might be acquired, if at all, only through long personal experience. Many complexities and implications that might go uneducated by individuals are revealed to all; and trainees may learn an even more valuable lesson—fixed marketing rules and principles are often less important than careful analysis and handling of specific problem situation. Experience shows, in other words, that impromptu group discussion of problems improves the marketing-person's ability in handling those problems, and others arising in connection with the job.

The case discussion involves individual and sometimes group study of write-ups of actual marketing and other problems encountered on the job. Group analysis and discussion follows. This format, originated by professional for learning by experience, has been widely adapted for marketing-training purposes. Each case should either describe a real marketing or administrative problem, or be developed around a situation sufficiently real to stimulate emotional as well as objective involvement by trainees. Participants should be required to identify the issue(s), marshal the relevant facts, devise specific alternatives, and choose the one they consider most appropriate. Most users believe that securing a through grasp of the problem situation is more essential to learning than the rapid production of solutions. To derive maximum benefit from case decision, each session should provide for the drawing of generalisations of 'lessons learned.'

Group discussion methods are effective in training either new or experienced marketing-people, but certain conditions must be met to achieve maximum benefits. Because discussion easily can drift into extraneous subjects or become sterile, an effective discussion leader or moderator is essential. The discussion leader must command the participants' respect, be skilled in dealing with people, and be extremely well informed not only on the subjects under discussion but on the marketing-person's job and its problems. If advance assignments are made, as in case discussion, it is absolutely imperative that the participants be prepared—otherwise valuable instructional time is wasted. It is important, too, to realise that group discussion requires considerable instructional time to be effective. If the aim is to maximise trainee learning of specific points in depth, and not to provide a broad general survey, group discussion is an appropriate instructional method.

(3) Role Playing: The role playing method requires trainees to act out parts in contrived problems situations. As used in training on marketing techniques, the role playing session begins with the instructor describing the situation and the different personalities involved. The instructor provides all needed props, then designates trainees to play the roles of marketing-person, prospect, and other characters. Each plays his or her assigned role and afterwards they, together with other group members and the instructor, appraise each role plays effectiveness and suggest how each might have improved his performance.

In another version of role playing, one of the group is given a bit of information on, for example, a buyer's objection to a particular product, and then is asked by the instructor to extemporise a solution. Sometimes called a 'sweat session,' this provides individual trainees a chance to apply what they have learned. 'Postmortem' critiques afford opportunities to reinforce what has been learned through participating in, or viewing, the role playing.

Role playing, as an instructional method, presents comparatively few problems. But there are some. Those playing assigned roles must become not only actively but emotionally identified with the characters they portray; audience interest must be maintained throughout, even though spontaneous reactions should be suppressed. Achieving these conditions is not easy. It becomes even more difficult when role players 'ham it up' or there is laughter or other involuntary audience reaction. Non-participants' comments should be saved for later, usually until the role playing is completed (although occasionally during 'cuts' called by the instructor). If note-taking is permitted as the play unfolds, some players tend to be distracted. This tendency, however, is overcome with repeated use of the method. These and similar problems can be minimised, provided that trainees are thoroughly briefed on what is and is not permissible, the group is limited in size (perhaps to no more than ten to twelve trainees), the instructor exercises discipline and control throughout, and role playing assignments are realistic enough to make their learning potentials clear to all.

More than offsetting the few administrative problems are the many raining benefits flowing from successful use of this instructional method. It provides realistic practice in applying what has been learned in other formal training or by experience. It is highly flexible training method in that there is extreme diversity in role playing situations. Experience shows, too, that role playing instruction lends itself to easy adjustment for training new personnel, experienced marketing-people, or even mixed groups. Among other benefits incidental to or derived from role playing instruction are the following:

(i) Most persons learn to accept criticism from others, and the group soon recognises that sound suggestions benefit everyone.

(ii) When a person criticises another's performance, that person has an incentive not to perform similarly later.

(iii) Role players practice introspection through participating in the appraisal of their own performances. The increasing use of tape-recording and playback equipment makes self-criticism even more beneficial and objective.

(iv) The 'free-wheeling' nature of role playing is highly conducive to the generation of new ideas and approaches. Defects inherent in many stereotyped and 'school' solutions soon become apparent.

(v) In role playing sessions for mixed groups, junior people have a chance to learn valuable 'tricks of the trade,' and experienced personnel are 'kept on their toes' as a matter of personal pride.

(vi) Role players gain acting experience, which may be of great value to them later in handling difficult marketing situations.

(4) The Simulation or Game: This instructional method, which somewhat resembles role playing, uses highly structured contrived situations, based on reality, in which players assume decision-making roles through successive rounds of play. A unique feature is that players have the benefits of information feedback. Trainees may play the roles of decision makers in customers, organisations, using data ordinarily available to make decision on the timing and size of orders, managing marketing forces and advertising efforts, and so on. The 'results' of these decision then are calculated by referees (sometimes using electronic computers) and feed back for the players to use in their next round of decisions.

Thus far, simulations or games used in marketing-training programmes have tended to be restricted to groups being prepared for management positions; but no insurmountable reason exists for not using them in other types of programmes. Perhaps, the main reason for not using games more extensively is the initial difficulty of preparing them. Preparation requires considerable research to dig out the needed facts, expert skill in incorporating these into a game model, development of detailed instructions for players and referees and the writing of a computer programme. Expertness and substantial investments in time and money, then, are required; but partially offsetting this is the fact that, once prepared, a game may see repeated use in many training programmes.

The game or simulation has several attractive advantages as an instructional method. Among the more important are the following: (1) participants learn easily because they involve themselves enthusiastically in game play; (2) players develop skill in identifying key factors influencing decisions; (3) games readily lend themselves to demonstrations of the uses and values of such analytical techniques as inventory and other planning models; and (4) in contrast to other instructional methods, games, with their built-in information feedback features, are highly effective in emphasising the dynamic nature of problem situations and their interrelationships.

Among the main instructional limitations of the game are the following: (1) some minimum time is required for playing, usually at least three or four hours, to generate sufficient decision 'rounds' to provide the desired learning experience; (2) since game designs generally are based on ordinary decision-making processes, their rules often prevent payoffs on unusual or novel approaches; and (3) players may learn some things that aren't so, a limitation applying especially to carelessly prepared and/or poorly designed games. Most of these and other limitations may be partly or wholly overcome through careful game design and administration. Thus the game, or simulation instructional method, still in its infancy, possesses great potential for marketing-training purposes.

Individual Instructional Methods

Some methods are used for training marketing-people on an individualised, one-person-at-a-time, basis. These techniques are used by large companies and are particularly appropriate for those with small marketing forces, low personnel turnover, and small numbers of trainees. The more important individual methods are discussed below:

(1) On-the-Job Training: The method, sometimes known as coach-and-pupil training, is a combination of telling, showing, practising, and evaluating. The coach, who may be a professional marketing trainer but is more often a seasoned marketing-person, begins by describing to the trainee particular marketing situations, explaining various techniques and approaches that might be used effectively. Next, accompanied by the pupil, the coach makes a number of actual marketing calls, discussing each with the trainee afterwards. Then, under the coach's supervision, the trainee makes marketing calls, each one being followed by discussion and appraisal. Gradually, the trainee works more and more on his or her own, but with continuing, although increasingly less frequent, coaching sessions.

The instructional effectiveness of this method depends mainly upon the coach's qualifications. Given a qualified coach, the trainee starts off on the right foot, using marketing techniques that the company wants used. Early deficiencies are corrected before they harden into difficult to change. If, however, the coach is not qualified, the trainee probably will learn the coach's bad habits as well as skills. Furthermore, many seasoned marketing-people, otherwise well qualified for coaching, are unwilling to devote the necessary time and effort. This is especially true in companies whose marketing personnel are paid commissions on marketing. The problem of recruiting competent coaches, nevertheless, can be resolved through such means as paying bonuses for each person coached, or 'overriding' commissions on pupils' marketing for a certain period.

On-the-job training should form an important part of every initial marketing-training programme. There is no more effective way of learning about a job than by actually doing it. This method is uniquely appropriate for developing trainees' skills in making marketing presentations, answering objectives, and closing marketing. Training in these aspects of marketing requires practice, and this method provides expertly supervised practice.

(2) Personal Conferences: The potential of this instructional method commonly goes unrecognised probably because many marketing executives assume that learning occurs only in structured situation. Psychological research, however, has demonstrated repeatedly that learning may occur in structured and unstructured, formal and informal situations. In personal conference instruction, the trainer (often a marketing executive) and trainee jointly analyse problems of mutual concern, such as effective use of marketing time, route planning and call scheduling, and handling unusual marketing problems. Because such training is expensive in terms of the trainer's time, idle chit-chat and purely personal conversion should be minimised. Maximum advantage should be taken of available time for instructional purposes.

(3) Correspondence Courses: This instructional method is used both in initial and continuing marketing-training programmes. In the insurance field, for instance, it is used to acquaint new marketing-people with industry fundamentals and for instruction in basic marketing techniques. In companies with highly technical products and small but widely deployed marketing forces, correspondence course sometimes are use to acquaint experienced marketing-people with new product developments and applications. Occasionally, too, this method is used for training non-company marketing personnel, such as distributors' marketing-persons, with a view toward improving their knowledge of the manufacturer's product line and marketing techniques. But, despite these varied applications, effective marketing training is difficult to achieve solely through correspondence, and few companies use the method exclusively.

For most companies, correspondence training is most appropriate as an interim method of instruction when trainees are scattered geographically, but groups are assembled periodically at central points for lectures, seminars, role playing, and other instructions. Initial marketing training, for example, might be by correspondence course begin at different times and places; continuing, or follow up, training might come later through group instructional methods at a central location. Preparing a standardised correspondence course covering technical product data, general company information, marketing techniques, and markets presents few difficulties other than those of choosing, organising, and writing up the material.

Successful use of the correspondence method of instruction requires considerable administrative skills. The greatest problem is that of providing motivation of trainees to complete assignments on schedule. Not only are enrollees engaged in full-time work requiring that correspondence lesson lessons be completed after hours, but few people have sufficient self-discipline to study without some direct supervision. Usually it is necessary to provide regularly scheduled examinations, prizes for completing work by given dates, or other incentives. Nor does this instructional method provide answers to individual enrollees' question; hence, the most successful users arrange for periodic face-to-face discussions. Similar problems are met in processing trainees' completed assignments, in evaluating their work, and in correcting errors. If these and related administrative problems are solves, correspondence instruction servers as a useful supplement to other marketing-training methods.

(4) Programmed Instruction: This instructional method represents a considerable advance over the correspondence course. It involves breaking down subject matter into numbered instructional units called 'frames,' which are then incorporated into a book. Each frame contains an explanation of a specific point, plus a question or problem for the trainee to use in testing his or her understanding. Trainees check their answers by referring to another designated frame. If answer is correct, the trainee is directed to new material; if it is incorrect, additional explanation is provided, and the trainee is retested on the point before going on to new material. Thus, trainees check their own progress as they work through the materials and may move through them at their own speed. Companies using programmed instruction, however, generally regard formal examinations as necessary incentives for the trainees.

To date, programmed instruction has not been widely adopted for marketing training purposes. Most applications have been aimed at providing needed information. The Schering Corporation, for instance, provides programmed instruction on the clinical and pharmacological background of its drug products. This method is not used widely for training in marketing techniques and market information because of difficulties in preparing appropriate programmed instructional materials. Preparation requires expert skills and thorough grounding in the psychology of learning. One ready-made programmed instructional course focusing on marketing techniques, however, is available—prepared by Jack Schiff of Pace College, for Marketing and Marketing Executives-International.

Balancing Group versus Individual Instruction

Generally group instruction is used in formal training programmes, and individual instruction is given in the field. Both have contributions to make to the overall training programme, so management must decide the role and the timing of each.

When there are large numbers of new personnel, group instructions is the most practical way to provide marketing training at the least cost per person. In planning the curriculum content of the marketing school, however, management must also determine the content that should and can be taught in the field-group instruction is often more effective when supplemented by individualised field training. To minimise needless overlap, and to maximise instructional results, careful attention must be paid to integration of what is taught by group methods in marketing schools: product data, company information, market information, and the theoretical and practical fundamentals of marketing. Advanced instruction in marketing technique usually is best handle individually, in the field.

What is called 'field training' is essentially on-the-job training, but it is conducted in the office as well as in the field. The trainee, under supervision, apportions his or her time between a branch, district, or regional office and a marketing territory. Because field training is individualised instruction, it is quite informal. In the field, the trainee learns by watching an experienced marketing-person in action and by practising marketing techniques under that individual's tutelage.

Opinion among marketing executives is divided with respect of the best timing of group versus individual instruction. Most believe that the trainee should receive formal group instruction and indoctrination before meeting the customers and starting to sell. A sizable minority, however, believe in assigning trainees to marketing jobs for individual instruction before sending them on to marketing schools. In support of the minority view, three things can be said: (1) new personnel have a chance to prove that they have what it takes to sell before money is spend on their formal training; (2) new persons are not always, not even usually, hired in groups large enough to justify immediate formal training-people hired between programmes can be put to work until the next school begins; and (3) there is considerable evidence to indicate that prior on-the-job experience not only furnishes needed learning motivation but makes formal instruction more meaningful. The minority position, nevertheless, clearly is inappropriate when highly technical products are sold to sophisticated buyers. In such cases, product training is not only highly important but best provided through formal group instruction at the outset of trainees' marketing careers.

Executing Marketing Training Programmes

A great deal of planning work and attention to detail is prerequisite to successful execution of a marketing-training programme. Important decision must be reached, as we have previously noted, on training aims, programme content, and instructional methods. Organisationally, the executive must make certain that the trainers—whether full time or on special assignment—are themselves trained and fully understand their programme responsibilities. Members of the group selected for training must be notified, necessary travel reservations made, and living accommodations arranged. Location of instructional facilities must be decided, instructional materials prepared, and training facilities must be decided, instructional materials prepared, and training aids assembled. Once these things are done, the stage is set for actual execution of the programme.

Effectiveness of programme execution, of course, depends upon instructional skills as well as skilful coordination of different planning phased and 'housekeeping' details. Successful programme administration is very much an art, but, in essence, it involves doing everything that can be done to produce a training atmosphere as conducive as possible to learning. Discussion in the following centres on (1) the timing of training programmes, (2) their location, and (3) instructional materials and training aids.

Timing Initial Marketing Training Programmes

The number of persons recruited annually directly affects the timing of initial marketing-training programmes. More precisely, timing depends upon the number of new persons who must be trained each year, and this, in turn, depends upon factors such as the size of the marketing force, marketing-personnel turnover, and management's plan for changing the size and composition of the marketing force. When the number is large, comprehensive highly structured programmes may be scheduled several times a year, the exact dates being set after consideration of recruiting quotas and deadlines. When the number is small, formal training programmes, if held at all, necessarily are scheduled more infrequently, perhaps only once each year. Thus, for example, one company with a small marketing force recruiting June college graduates schedules their training to begin in late June or early July.

There is an optimum number of trainees who may be effectively trained during a particular programme. It depends upon such factors as training aims, subject matter content, amount and availability of training talent, and instructional methods. Individualised training may be indicated in some situations, although it is expensive per individual trained, its timing can be highly flexible, depending only upon availability of trainees and trainers. In most situations, however, limitations of training funds and talent dictate that recruits be trained in groups, programmes being scheduled whenever the backlog of untrained people approximates the optimum. No precise answer can be given to the question: How large is an optimum-sized training group? Experience indicates that, for most companies, groups smaller than 12 to 15 involve inordinately high cost, while those larger than 30 to 40 incur losses in training (that is, learning) effectiveness too great to be tolerated.

Training Continuing Marketing Training Programmes

Modern marketing management regards marketing training as a never-ending process. This view recognises that initial marketing-training programmes cannot prepare the marketing-person for indefinitely effective job performance—the beneficial effects of training gradually erode away. This view also stems from modern management's conviction that all training and all learning must be continuous—new information must be assimilated, and older concepts require modification in the light of new developments. New products, new refinements of marketing techniques, new product applications and uses, new customer problems, new types of marketing aids, new marketing suggestions—all these and other developments requires that each marketing-person's training continue as long as he or she is on the job. In many situations, marketing personnel may be kept abreast of new developments informally, perhaps through field distribution of information bulletins. But when new developments accumulate, are unusually important, or imply a need for significant changes in marketing-persons attitudes and behaviour patterns, a formal retraining programme should be scheduled. Many companies integrate a short retraining programme into a series of marketing meetings or even into a single marketing convention.

In some marketing forces some but not all marketing-persons have deficiencies that many correctable through training. If their weaknesses lie in different areas, the most practical and economical solution is to use on-the-job coaching. If several people are weak in the same general area(s), it is both practical and economical to use group instructional methods in an organised formal programme (often scheduled for an off-peak marketing period).

Even, when marketing management has no clear indication of the need, regular scheduling of training programmes seems advisable. A survey of nearly 500 purchasing agents revealed that 60 per cent felt that the majority of marketing-people calling on them either had never learned or had forgotten how to sell. The same survey strongly implied that continuing training should provide marketing personnel with more adequate product information and teach them how to present it in terms of user benefits.

Management's assumption should be that marketing-people will welcome the opportunity for further training. Experience shows that most marketing personnel are eager for help in improving marketing techniques; most feel entitled to explanations of policy changes; most want to learn how to tie in their efforts more closely with advertising programmes; and most are anxious to learn more about new products, model and design improvements, and shifts in market conditions. The majority of marketing people, in other words, want to be kept abreast of current developments and welcome effort to interpret the significance of these developments in terms of their own job performance. If formal retraining programmes are designed and 'sold' as means of helping marketing-people do their jobs more effectively, they should not only be receptive to instruction but should derive benefits from it. Unless marketing personnel are convinced of the future value of continuing training, its results will fall short of what could be reasonably expected. If it can demonstrate that training results in more take-home pay and increased job satisfaction, most marketing-people will demotivated. And when marketing-people believe that these benefits may be obtained through a continuing marketing training programme, the programme's chances of successful execution are greatly enhanced.

Location of Marketing Training Programmes

Some companies hold formal initial marketing-training programmes at the central offices and plant; others conduct separately executed programmes at some or all branch offices. Each plan has advantages and disadvantages. The centralised programme held at a manufacturing plant generally provides better product training, but higher costs are incurred in brining trainees to the central point and housing them there. In many companies, too, the small number of people to be trained does not justify decentralised formal programmes, and central location is a practical necessity. Many large companies, by way of contrast, do have the option of using decentralised training programmes. They can train new marketing-people in or near the territories to which they are later assigned, and thus can acquaint them early with field marketing problems. However, since decentralised product training often requires the substitution of motion pictures, slides, and working models, it may be less realistic, less interesting and less effective than training given at a factory. But decentralised programmes suffer from even more serious defects. Unless closely supervised by higher management, their execution tends to be poor; and the trainers, who commonly have other responsibilities and regard training as a diversionary sideline, often turn in poor teaching performances. Generally, then, except in the very large company, with its vast pool of administrative and instructional skills and other resources, formal initial marketing-training programmes should be held at central locations.

Retraining programmes for seasoned marketing-people also may be held either at centralised or decentralised points. Because these programme often are short, the decision may hinge almost entirely upon where the needed instructional talent is available and whether it is more convenient and economical to transport and house the trainers or the trainees. If retraining programmes are timed to coincide with marketing conventions, they may be held nationally (either at the home office or convention headquarters elsewhere), or regionally, on decentralised basis.

Instructional Materials and Training Aids

Critically important to successful execution of a marketing-training programme are the instructional materials and training aids. The exact nature of these will vary, of course, not only for different companies but for programmes with different aims and content. Discussion in the following sections focuses on pertinent features and uses of the main types of instructional materials and training aids.

(1) Manuals: Often known as 'workbook,' manuals are used in most formal group-type marketing-training programmes. The best manuals generally contain: outlines or summaries of the main presentations, related material, statements of learning objectives for each session, orienting questions or 'thought provokers,' cases and problems for discussion, plus directions for certain sessions, such as those involving role playing or other simulations. Many manuals also include concise statement of marketing, pricing, marketing personnel, and other policies, together with details on company systems and procedures as they apply to the marketing-person's work. A few contain detailed information on the products and their applications. Discretion should be exercised in selecting items for inclusion. It is all, too easy to clutter up a manual with information of little or infrequent value to the trainee. Manuals often are designed with a dual purpose in mind; to serve as study guides during formal training, and as references later, thus, many appear in loose-leaf form of facilities subsequent and changes.

(2) Other Printed Materials: Other printed matter includes regular company bulletins, marketing and product handbooks, and industry and general business magazines and journals. Company publications are used chiefly to furnish field marketing personnel with up-to-date and needed information. Keeping field marketing personnel informed is also the main reason that many companies provide their marketing-people with subscriptions to industry and general business magazines and journals. Texts and technical and trade books are used to supplement workbook material, although trainees are rarely required to read them thoroughly during formal training. The usual practice is to assign or merely suggest selected readings, with the exceptions that the books will be used later as references.

(3) Training Aids: A training aid is an auxiliary device capable of contributing to instructional aim through transmission of sight and/or sound stimuli. Probably the most used and indispensable training aid is blackboard—no training facility should be without one on which to illustrate points, summarise discussions, and the like, adding visual to vocal appeal. Modern substitutes for the blackboard (for example, the Vue-Graph projector, transparency roll, and screen) offer such improvement as making it possible for the instructor to face his class even while his or her writing appears on a screen, and conserving instructional time through using professionally prepared diagrams, charts, statistical tables, and so on. But no substitute is as fail-safe as a blackboard, none so free of possible mechanical or power failure. Even, when main reliance is placed upon the Vue-Graph or other mechanically operated device, blackboard and chalk should be available for standby use, and to illustrate and explain points that arise in informal discussion. Although mechanical training aids supplement or support the blackboard as the basic training aid, none supplants it entirely.

The motion-picture projector and film form an appropriate training aid, especially when the instructional aim requires the depicting of motion or description and explanation of complex situations. In conveying technical information concerning installation and operation of new machine-tool models, for example, nothing short of actual demonstration is as effective as a movie. Substantial costs are incurred in producing special training film of high quality, since professional cameramen, actors, a director, and often specially constructed, sets are needed. In deciding whether to produce tailor-made films then, management must seek to appraise their probable instructional effectiveness against the cost. Most marketing-training films seek to convey information on products and their applications, but some aim at the refinement of marketing techniques. One firm, for example, used an amateur-produced (hence, low-cost) 'candid-camera' film of its marketing personnel in action as an aid to improving their job performance. For the firm with limited funds, not wanting to resort to amateur-produced films, marketing-training films of varying quality, most relating to marketing fundamentals, are available commercially. It goes almost without saying that any training film, whether company-produced or commercially produced, should be previewed before it is used for instructional purposes.

Much of the motion picture's effectiveness can be achieved at lower cost with still pictures projected from slides or filmstrips. A sound disc may furnish a commentary together with 'timed' changes in still pictures; or the instructor may make comments, varying the change interval between pictures by using a remote-control device. Many companies produce their own training slides and filmstrips, but a wide variety of commercially produced items also is available for purchase or rental.

Tape-recording and playback equipment is ideally suited for training aimed at improving marketing techniques. Actual or simulated marketing presentations may be taped and played back for individual or group appraisal. Recent advances in miniature (and sometimes concealable) tape-recording devices even make it easy for marketing-persons to tape their own marketing interviews and play them back later. Thus, they gain greater objectivity in appraising their own effectiveness, and in finding ways to improve their performance. Larger records are used in formal programmes to tape group discussions and role-playing sessions, the tapes being played back later with appropriate commentaries and appraisals by participants and the trainer. Increasingly, too, instructions in marketing-training programmes tape their own sessions routinely. Later playbacks are helpful in improving teaching effectiveness and in conserving preparation time for repeat performances.

Closed-circuit television, not ordinarily classified as training aid, is used in place of training films, especially where instructional timing is important. It is particularly appropriate in decentralised programmes, such as those in which new product lines are being introduced to marketing-persons and/or dealer marketing personnel. Other training applications of closed-circuit television include its use in short, decentralised retraining programmes focusing on important policy changes, and as a substitute for national marketing meetings devoted primarily to training.

Evaluating Marketing Training Effectiveness

All marketing training represents investments of time, money, and effort—and marketing management should expect return commensurate with the investment. Evaluating returns from marketing training is not easy, however. Results, such as improved marketing performance, may not show up until long after programme completion. Despite such evaluation problems, it is possible to measure, somewhat roughly, training effectiveness. Management can make certain comparisons, such as the following: the length of time new marketing personnel take to attain the productivity level of the average experienced person; marketing results of trained versus untrained personnel; and the respective training histories of the most and least effective marketing-people. A few companies plot each marketing-person's marketing records on a 'before and after' training basis, generally converting these records to share-of-the-market comparisons. It must be recognised, however, that any evaluation of training effectiveness based mainly on marketing records can be, at best, only an approximation. Territorial marketing volumes are influenced not only by marketing-people's efforts but by such important factors as competitive activity, economic fluctuation, and advertising pressure. No method yet devised is fully satisfactory for precisely isolating the influence of any one of these factors. It should be noted, too, that any quantitative evaluation of marketing-training effectiveness necessarily fails to take into account many intangible benefits from training (for example, improved marketing-force morale.) In spite of their technical deficiencies, however, comparative studies involving rough quantitative measures should provide management with a basis for evaluating training results.

Management should attempt to measure the effectiveness of individual marketing training programmes both while they are in programme and upon completion. The purpose should be to obtain needed insights for improving the effectiveness of future programmes. Tests and examinations of various kinds are used for measuring trainee retention of materials presented. These are used most appropriately when trainees are expected to memorise information, as in the case of product specification and applications. Most marketing trainers see little value in using tests and examinations for evaluating the effectiveness of training in marketing techniques. Trainees' performance in role-playing assignments may be a better means for appraising whether trainees have learned and, more important, are able to apply what they have learned. Trainers in some companies are required to rate each trainee's performance in sessions such as in role playing, panels, and other group discussion in which he or she takes an active part. Necessarily, such ratings are subjective, but they do provide trainees with learning trainees to rate each trainer's performance, either in each session or in the total programme, is spreading. This may help in stimulating trainers to improve their instructional effectiveness. More than a few marketing executives, however, argue that trainees are in no position to judge the trainers' effectiveness until they gain additional field experience. Nevertheless, 'comment sheet' similar to that shown in Table-6 are being used in increasing number of marketing-training programmes. Many companies now also ask trainees to evaluate training programmes after they return to their territories and have had a chance to put what they have learned into practice.

Table-6

Form for Trainee Rating of Marketing Training Session

Session Review

A brief, candid review of this training session will help you to evaluate what you have learned and help us in our efforts to improve the programme.
Please answer all questions. Do not sign your name; the results are anonymous.
Place an X where appropriate to describe your reactions to each of the following:

1. Materials covered	Exciting	☐	☐	☐	☐	☐	☐	☐	Dull
2. Instruction	Excellent	☐	☐	☐	☐	☐	☐	☐	Poor
3. Worthwhileness of material	Great	☐	☐	☐	☐	☐	☐	☐	Little
4. Completeness of coverage	Very Complete	☐	☐	☐	☐	☐	☐	☐	Totally Inadequate

5. How might the session have been improved?

____

____

____

❑❑❑

9

Promotion of New Product for Sales

Introduction

Along with product, pricing and distribution, promotion is the fourth important factor in the successful marketing mix equation. Its importance lies in the fact that it helps the product to sell and, but for a proper promotion plan, even a good product, reasonably priced, and extensively made available in suitable outlets in the target market, will not receive the support of the customers and will not reach its full potential to make its maximum possible contribution to the commercial success of the organisation marketing it. One of the accusations repeatedly hurled at marketers in the advanced countries of the West is that their activities are designed to manipulate the market and promote products and services without regard to the real needs and interests of the customers. This accusation, too, is directed primarily against the promotional activities of commercial organisations and, therefore, indirectly acknowledge the importance of such activities.

Adoption—The Promotion Goal

The primary object of all promotion is to help the adoption of a product by the customers. Adoption, which signifies routine acceptance as a matter, of course, of a given product as a means to satisfy a particular need, is the end result of the linear sequence of awareness, interest, evaluation, trial and finally adoption. The stage of awareness is reached when a reasonable cross-section of the target market is aware that a particular product exists or has been newly created but, by and large, the target audience is not in the possession of more detailed information nor is it motivated to seek such information. When, as a result of such awareness repeatedly invading their minds, they are motivated to obtain further information on their own or, which in other words amounts to the same thing, they take the trouble to carefully peruse, scrutinise or study such information placed by the communicator in different media, the stage of 'interest' has been reached. Thereafter, relevant information obtained through such sources as advertisements, sales literature or advice of salespersons, retailers, or users is evaluated with a view to deciding whether the product is useful, within reach, desirable, fits in with one's life-style, etc., and whether it deserves a trial. A final decision about whether to adopt it for use in a routine manner follows if the trial leads to sufficient satisfaction expressed in terms of cost-benefit ratio or comparative preference or superiority over the product in current use. Both trial and adoption take place over a length of time, some adventurous consumers making the initial move and others following thereafter. No product will succeed commercially unless a sufficiently large number of buyers try and then adopt it within a reasonable time. Here, it must be emphasised that the first step of awareness does not invariably and unexceptionably lead to the remaining steps in course of time but there is a very strong possibility that the product may be rejected by a consumer or group of consumers at any one of the stages including the first stage itself. Unless there is a sizeable group of customers which proceeds in the direction of at least trial order for the product within a reasonable time, the product will be doomed to commercial failure and may be temporarily withdrawn, modified or permanently scrapped.

Communication—The Promotion Tool

The promotion is based on communication by the manufacturer with the target market. The object of such communication is not "simply to inform, educate, and entertain" but "to directly or indirectly facilitate exchanges by influencing one or more of the audiences about a firm and/or its goods, services, and ideas. Promotion can play a comprehensive communication role because some promotional activities can be directed toward helping a company to justify its existence and to maintain positive, healthy relationships among the firm and various groups in the marketing environment." Since communication forms the basic tool of promotion, it would be fit and proper to understand the communication process in its broad outline.

Communication is the process of conveying to the target audience, may be an individual or a small group or even the country as a whole, some message or messages initiated by a communicator, called the source. The process of converting the idea, concept or message intended for being so communicated into a suitable format consisting of appropriate words, visuals, sounds, etc., is called encoding of the message. Such a message is transmitted through a suitable medium which, in the opinion of the communicator, duly assisted by a communication expert like, e.g., an advertising agency is likely to be most effective in carrying the message and delivering it primarily to those for whom it is meant by the communicator, with as little wastage, distortion or dilution as possible. On receipt of such a message, the receiver reconverts the words, visuals, sounds, etc., into ideas, concepts or action and this process is referred to as decoding of a message and the person(s) towards whom the message is directed is/are called the receiver or audience. While, in one way, it can be said that the process of communication becomes complete on receipt of the message by the receiver, it must be remembered that promotional communications are not intended merely to inform, educate and entertain but to facilitate exchanges and, therefore, the completion of the process, as far as the marketer is concerned, takes place only when he receives a feedback about the successful creation of the awareness, interest, etc. In the minds of the target audience for whom the communication is meant. The degree of success of such communication will, therefore, be measured not only in terms of the percentage of the target audience reached but also the degree of intensity with which the target audience responds to the communication message. Diagrammatically the communication process can be presented as under:

Source	Encoding	Transmission	Decoding	Audience
Concept Idea	Words Visuals Sounds	Medium Message	Understanding, Acceptance or Rejection	Response
		FEEDBACK		

Harold Hasswell in his *Power and Personality* has suggested that all communication centres round answering the questions as to "who . . . says, what . . . in what channel to whom . . . with what effect?"

Several steps must be taken by the communicator to maximise the effectiveness of the message and minimise the wastage of effect. Broadly, these steps include deciding the objective of communication, selection of the appropriate medium or media to convey the message, determining the contents and format of the intended message in terms of the target groups for whom the message is meant and the time or season when it can be most effectively and economically communicated and so on. A brief explanation about these aspects of promotional communication strategy will help to understand their significance and role.

Communication Objectives

The problem of deciding the objectives of promotional communication needs to be considered at two levels. There must be a common direction and purpose for all the promotional communications of an organisation for the period of, say, a year or even longer. This long term objective will decide the *inter se* priority amongst various products, markets, messages, etc. Within this overall strategy, every single communication campaign must select the primary objective of such communication. These objectives can include, for example, creating awareness about a new product or changes in the existing one, educating consumers about new features, services, concessions, etc., offered in respect of any existing products, improving market share of a line of products or an individual product in a specific market or on a total basis, or as a support to the efforts to maximise the immediate sales of a product undertaken through better distribution, reduction in price, etc.

In deciding the communication objectives, due attention must be paid to the availability of resources, the stage of the product concerned in its life cycle and other relevant factors concerning the product and lastly, the distinguishing characteristics of the target market such as industrial or general consumer, urban or rural, speciality or general utility, concentrated or dispersed, etc. Other relevant product-related considerations which influence the communication objectives of a company are the price, the present market share and position, present and intended use of the product, etc. To cite an example of product-oriented considerations, the promotional communication objective for a pain relieving drug will be substantially influenced by whether the drug is a special product to be administered by dentists or an over-the-counter analgesic like, say, aspirin meant for wide distribution not only through drug stores but even other permissible outlets. Similarly, the communication objectives for the promotion of, say, Air cargo or All-Risks (Jewellery) Policy must be quite different from those of, say, Cattle Insurance or Workmen's Compensation Insurance. Proper planning, coordination, implementation and control of promotional communications is an essential pre-requisite of their success.

Media Selection

In advertising, it is often said that the medium is message, which means that the proper selection of the medium through which a message is to be projected goes a very long way to help the message to reach the target audience and to maximise its impact. Each of the media has its own strengths and shortcomings, a proper understanding of which on the part of the communicator will be of paramount importance.

Communication media can be classified in several different ways. Firstly, they can be classified on the basis of physical senses to which they relate. Thus, some media like newspapers, sales literature, hoardings, car stickers, cinema slides, etc., can be called visual media, radio advertising as audio medium and Ad-films, TV advertising, Publicity Van film shows, exhibition stalls through which the visitor is conducted by a guide, etc., as audio-visual ones.

Another way to classify media is on the basis of those which reach the target audience at his home or place of business as against those to which he is exposed only if and when he makes a visit to the specific place where they are located. Newspapers (including magazines and periodicals) and TV advertising is of the first type, whereas exhibition stalls, advertisement film's shows in the cinema houses or point-of-purchase displays or demonstrations, distribution of samples, etc., at the retail outlets belong to the latter variety. Some media like radio and TV advertising or Ad-films are of a flitting type wherein the message is transitory and can be missed by those whose sets are not switched on at the appropriate time or whose attention is distracted at the precise moment or who may not be physically present in the cinema house at the exact time. On the other hand, newspaper advertisements, sales literature, etc., can be perused and, if necessary, referred back to at the convenience of the reader or when some situation subsequently develops when the message may have relevance to the person concerned. Some media can use only black and white colours; whereas some others can project multicolour messages, thus, considerably heightening the impact. An example of this effect has been provided in a book on marketing by pointing out that the black and white picture of a pizza in an average newspaper would look like a big smudge of ink and fail to attract or impress, whereas a multi-colour picture of the same pizza in a glossy magazine would look mouth-watering and tempting. Similarly, the black and white visual of a textile would not give any idea of its texture, design, colourfulness, whereas a multi-colour presentation on, say, TV would look very attractive.

Message Contents and Format

Promotional communication concerns not merely transmitting of a message but its understanding on the part of the target audience in the same or as nearly the same meaning as was intended by the communicator. Very seldom is there a complete identity and congruity of the message as encoded by the communicator and as decoded by the receiver. There are several reasons which account for this phenomenon. Firstly, assimilation of any experience by different individuals does not merely depend upon the experience to which they are exposed but their own perception, which is a cumulative effect of their entire personal background, education, upbringing and a host of other factors. Thus, the same story read or stage drama witnessed by any group of people may convey different messages to different members of the group. Even the same person may react in different ways to the same communication at different points of time. One telling example of this truth was provided by a famous actress when she mentioned that when, in her younger days, she attended a performance of *Romeo and Juliet,* she was moved by the tragedy of these two lovers but when she saw the drama at an advanced age, she found herself more touched by the tragic situation faced by their parents.

The communicator tries to resolve this problem by using different messages about the same product or the same characteristics of a given product, to suit the profile of the target audience exposed to the media projecting the massage. Alternatively, he selects those media which have a direct relevance to his market segment for projecting his message. The contents and format of the message will then be designed in such a way as to be best suited to the average reader or viewer of a given medium. Thus, advertisements designed to be published in a magazine popular amongst the teen-ager group and with another overwhelmingly read by a much older group of people will have to vary vastly in terms of words and visuals used therein, so as to be sufficiently effective in communicating with each of the two groups. Similarly, two separate messages about the same product may profitably be designed for national newspapers and regional or local papers, using local idiom, language, etc., in the latter case.

Examples of seasonal variation in the contents and format of a promotional communication message may be provided by the advertisements of, say, footwear, textiles or beverages. In the first two cases, different types of footwear or materials, designs, etc., may be promoted during different seasons whereas in the case of beverages the size, frequency, etc., of the message projection may be very high during summer and in a low key during the other parts of the year.

Promotional Mix

All promotional communications use one or more of the five ingredients of advertising, publicity, packaging, personal selling and sales promotion. Whether all the five or any lesser number of them will be used and in what combination depends upon the marketing objectives, the type of product and market, etc. Arriving at a good combination calls for careful consideration and continuous interaction between the marketing executives and external communication experts like, e.g., advertising consultants wherever they are used.

(1) Advertising: Advertising is defined as a paid form of non-personal communication, about an organisation and/or its products, that is transmitted to a target audience through a mass medium. It is, perhaps, the most commonly used of the ingredients of promotional mix and there may be hardly any commercial organisation which can afford not to use it in one form or another. It also used more different media than other ingredients and in respect of an overwhelmingly large number of promotional campaigns, becomes the most frequently and extensively used tool. For the communicator, it combines the advantages of being versatile, lending legitimacy and respectability to the products advertised, and inexpensive in terms of cost per person reached. However, it is not as effective and adaptable as, for example, personal selling or as credible as, say, publicity. Advertising is most suited to communication message which are basically information-oriented, where the market is dispersed and for a product which is meant for use by a sufficiently large number of persons. For more details, please refer to earlier chapter on advertising.

(2) Publicity: Publicity differs from advertising primarily in so far as the communicator does not make a direct payment to the media carrying the communication message. The media used by advertising and publicity may, in most cases, be the same but in the former case, since the advertiser is paying for the space or time he 'buys' from the media, it is possible for him to control all aspects of delivering the message to the target audience. In publicity, however, the communicator feeds newsworthy information to the medium concerned and has no control on whether it would be used and, if used, how and to what extent it would be made use of. Since an average reader or viewer assumes that the information conveyed emanates not from the commercial communicator but from the staff of the medium itself, the credibility and acceptability of such information is likely to be more than in the case of advertising. Morever, since such information becomes on integral part of the 'editorial contents' of the medium, the possibility of its being noticed is also considerably more. Thus, while reading a newspaper or viewing a TV programme, it is possible to entirely skip the advertising but some information about an organisation which appears as a news story, may be read or viewed automatically.

(3) Packaging: Packaging a product was initially undertaken for the convenience of sorting, dispensing, handling, carrying, and use, but its potential to become an important promotional tool led to its further development to fulfil this role. Use of different materials (like glass, plastic, ceramics, metal), colours, size, shape, texture, help to convey a distinct profile of a product and assist in its promotion. Distinctively packaged goods which are more likely to attract the prospective customer's attention from amongst an assortment of different goods on a store shelf, stand a better chance of attracting inquiries or trial orders.

(4) Personal Selling: It consists of an individual representative of the marketer or his distributor having a face-to-face contact with an individual customer or a group of persons belonging to a customer organisation, to explain, discuss and, if necessary, to demonstrate the product with a view to favourably influence the buying decision. It has the advantage of being versatile, adjustable and amenable to an interaction and two-way exchange of ideas which can help satisfy the queries of the customer. In personal selling, it is also possible to solicit a trial order or to get a feedback about the customer's perception of the product with a view to help modify and unfavourable features. However, it is difficult to control, expensive, and likely to lead the customers to become so used to the calls of sales representatives as to take no action except with the prodding by the salesman. World over, personal selling occupies a very important place in the promotional mix strategy of insurance organisations.

(5) Sales Promotion: All such activities as sampling, demonstrations, point-of-purchase displays, coupons, bonus or prize offer schemes meant for customers and discounts, sales conventions, incentives, etc., meant for the distribution channels or sales force come under the purview of sales promotion activities of an organisation.

Most such activities are seasonal, time-bound and can be used selectively in those areas or markets, which need special attention of the marketer. They help even out seasonal or regional imbalances or achieve short-term marketing objectives. Unless, however, sufficient advance care is taken and planning is made, the increase in sales during a given period may be followed by a setback in the immediate succeeding period. Development of a tendency in the sales force and distribution channel to keep waiting for a sales promotion campaign and to postpone even normal activities till such promotion campaign and to postpone even normal activities till such campaign is announced, cannot be ruled out in case of organisations, which may indiscriminately resort to the use of sales promotion activities.

Sales promotion and packaging are two ingredients of the promotion mix, other than advertising and publicity.

Out of these two, sales promotion has a greater importance in marketing in general and more so in respect of marketing of insurance.

❑❑❑

10

Marketing Management in Various Situations

Thus far, we have covered various aspects of sales management so as to help develop as in understanding of the basic concepts and process of selling. While doing so, the relevance of these aspects as they apply to various marketing situations in our country and more especially to our insurance marketing has also been brought out to the extent possible. It is now proposed to briefly deal with some specific issues and also to bring together at one place some of the applications of marketing percepts to insurance.

Non-business Marketing

Marketing is an activity, which is normally associated with business organisations run with the objective of making a profit in the long run. However, basically it is an activity of exchanging some goods or services in return for money paid by the buyer or customer. Thus, there are several organisations which provide such exchange transactions, without making any profit or even intending to make it. Moreover, there is no desire or effort to run them as a business enterprise. Such organisations which will be mostly found to be providing services and not tangible goods, can be broadly classified as under:

(1) Educational: Schools, colleges, and universities are not normally run with the motive of making any profit but for providing educational facilities. However, to be successful, they have to 'market' their services in a systematic manner.

(2) Health: Trust and charitable hospitals as well as health organisations like, e.g., Indian Cancer Society is an example of this type.

(3) Others: Cultural organisations like museums, religious organisations like temples, mosques, gurudwaras, churches, etc., charitable organisations like Red Cross, social organisations like Women's Lib, Scheduled Castes and Tribes welfare organisations, sports and games bodies like clubs, national associations for various sports or jointly for all sports like, e.g., Indian Sports' Council or Indian Olympic Association, and lastly political parties at local, regional and national level come under this category.

These organisations have to deal with two distinct types of markets, viz., those that provide funds to them and those use their services. Like business organisations they, too, deal with various publics like employees, government agencies, community and opinion leaders, press and other media, etc. Use of marketing concepts can help them to manage their affairs more efficiently, avoid wastage of efforts and resources, win public understanding and goodwill and, in general, function more effectively and improve their cost-benefit ratios.

Unfortunately, most of these organisations had, till recently, several misunderstandings and consequently, hesitation about running, much was left to be desired about the adequacy of their accounting systems, financial controls, personnel policies etc. Very often, they did not have a sufficiently senior officer more or less exclusively looking after these functions and they were expected to be looked after by some functionary whose primary responsibility and interest lay elsewhere and who did not have either the competence or the involvement to perform these functions efficiently. The marketing function of such organisations suffered from the additional handicap that the organisational managers harboured a feeling that any 'marketing' activity on their part is undignifying and demeaning. They did not also have sufficient knowledge or competence to handle marketing functions efficiently though, in fact, many of them needed and continue to need an effective marketing programme very badly. To some extent, this is changing primarily because of the double digit inflation which impels organisations to better manage their affairs and also because of greater involvement of enlightened institutions in following and adopting the marketing precepts. The essential features of a marketing programme for non-business organisations are:

(1) Market Analysis: The organisation should carefully analyse their markets and find out, with reference to those who provide the resources as to what is their primary motive in doing so. Such primary motivation could be philanthropic, influenced by considerations of caste, community, region, or religion, or it can even be that of gaining name and fame or saving taxes. The basic motivation of those who use their services can be either because they are inexpensive, close at hand, or carry excellent reputation, confer some status or other privileges (as in the case of, say, clubs or political parties). In case of those who use the facilities connected with the field of arts, an additional motivation can be the liking and love for the given art form like, e.g., music, painting, photography, etc.

(2) Product Definition: The organisation must clearly define the product, how it differs from similar other products in the market, what is its unique sales proposition and the market segments for which it is meant. For example, a school may have to decide whether it will have a high achievement profile and attract students from far and near or would function as a community school, attracting students from the vicinity.

(3) Pricing: Though pricing is less important in non-business marketing, it must be remembered that no non-business organisation is marketing its product without a price—either in cash or, in some rare instances, in kind like giving soul satisfaction as in respect of temple or church donations. In case of, say, surgical operations for family planning the reverse of price consideration, viz., incentives to be provided may apply. Thus, there is both the need and scope to define the pricing policy.

(4) Distribution: No middlemen are normally used by non-business organisations for distribution of their products but, even then, how and where the products will be available and what would be the method to be followed by intending 'buyers' to acquire them will have to be decided. Thus, an educational trust must decide as to where they will open new schools or colleges and whether they will give preference to intending students from a given area, community, religion, etc.

(5) Promotion: Promotion is perhaps the only ingredient of marketing mix which is commonly used by many, if not most, of the non-business organisations. Advertisements and direct mail letters appealing for donations supplemented by personal approaches to 'sell' various projects to the donors are efforts directed towards one of the two markets mentioned above. As regards the users' or clients' market, drives for encouraging people to join mountaineering institutes, boy-scouts and girl-guides, advertisements about various courses offered by various educational institutions as well as designing new courses to suit changing market demand, are examples of promotional activities of the non-business organisations in the users' market.

For successful marketing by non-business organisations, there is scope to pay more attention to generating adequate research into the present canvas and future scope of various 'products' as well as marketing programmes at present undertaken and required to be undertaken by such organisation. This again calls for the deployment of a marketing research approach and evaluation techniques so widely used by marketers. There is also scope for better coordination and direction of the various marketing activities being carried out by the concerned organisations. While it may take some time for most non-business organisations to formally recognise the role of marketing in their activities by creating a separate marketing organisation under an independent authority like, e.g., Director (Marketing), a start can be made by organising some committees with properly defined responsibilities as well as authority to perform such functions in a continuous, on-going manner.

Rural Marketing

Approximately 75 per cent of the total population of our country lives in the villages. With the progress and planned improvement in agricultural production, this population which mainly depends upon agriculture and agro-based occupations for its livelihood is acquiring increasing importance in marketing. While basic considerations of marketing management apply equally to the rural markets also, there are several distinct features of these markets which need to be more carefully considered in planning the marketing operations for the rural areas. These special features briefly are:

(1) Rural Markets are Underdeveloped: While the use of various goods and services is being made increasingly in rural areas, the population mainly depends upon the urban markets for the satisfaction of its needs. Thus, during the last 2/3 decades, the use of TV has increased manifold in rural areas but there are hardly any shops in these areas setting them. The buyers depend upon the nearest urban centres for purchase of such goods. The dependence upon the nearest urban centre also extends to such common-place goods like textiles, text books, fertilizers and so on. One psychological factor which contributes to this phenomenon is that in his day-to-day life, the villager lives an uneventful, routine life and, therefore, looks forward to visit to the urban centre with eager anticipation for some excitement and escape from drab routine. The time is also comparatively much more easy to spare and this, too, helps in an average villager's performance to buy goods in the urban centre. He many times rationalises such decision to himself and others by saying that better choice and lower prices are available in the urban centres but this is only partially true.

(2) Rural Markets are Scattered: While there is no denying the fact that more purchasing power is becoming progressively available in the rural areas, the number of persons who can buy any given product at any given time in any particular village is quite limited. The distances between two villages appear to be too long for being covered on foot and too short for the use of public transport system. Thus, the residents of one village prefer to go to the nearest urban centre by bus rather than on foot to the nearest rural centre where a product may be available. The magnitude of the dispersal problem may be gauged if it is realized that in any suburb of a metro town like Mumbai or Kolkata, more population may be found in 1 sq. km. than in the villages spread over, say, 50 sq. kms. and that comparatively to the amounts spent on the purchase of most goods may outstrip even this ratio. This militates against development of markets in the rural area.

(3) Rural Communications are Complex: The job of communicating with buyers in the rural areas is a difficult one. The very high percentage of illiteracy makes the use of many of the normal communication media rather impossible. Thus, newspaper advertising, sales literature, direct mail and other communications based on the written word are almost entirely ruled out. Advertisement films are not normally accepted for screening by the 'touring talkies' – the fair-weather film screening outfits – and even if they were accepted, it would be well nigh impossible to ensure that they are really screened. Even if they were screened, the visuals and spoken words used in these films are such as to make them rather unacceptable to the rural audiences. Commercial radio advertisements score a little better as far as the rural audiences are concerned but most of the present communications suffer from the handicap that those who prepare the messages as also those who approve them are so far removed from the rural scene that they fail to effectively understand the rural psyche and the communications do not become really meaningful. The more effective communications do not become really meaningful. The more effective communication media for rural audiences can, therefore, be the screening of specially prepared films through publicity vans and arranging interface between villagers and sales organisation of a company through the latter's participation in village fairs, melas, etc. Even here, it must be mentioned that the dresses and behaviour patterns vary so widely that an exhibition set or poster with which people in one area may be able to identify, does not become equally acceptable to those in a different corner of our land.

(4) Rural Life-style is Based on Minimising Needs: Till only a few decades ago, most villages had one or at the most a few families which could afford a moderately decent standard of living and the others led a hand-to-mouth existence. With the passing of various Land Reforms Acts, improved prices available to agricultural produce, creation of various agro-based income opportunities through additional sources of income like, e.g., poultry and milk production as well as processing of commercial crops like sugarcane, and last but not the least, substantial improvement in crop yields through better seeds, more fertilisers, use of mechanical aids and improved agricultural methods, a larger and larger cross-section of village population is now in a position to afford a better standard of living. There is, however, a tendency to use this additional purchasing power, like a typical *nouveau riche,* in ostentatious consumption rather than on mundane products of daily use, which really contribute towards making up a standard of living. Having been accustomed, for centuries, to do without anything and everything, there is an inborn tendency to minimise rather than maximise items of consumption. Overdependence on monsoons leading to uncertainty of incomes aggrevates this tendency. Therefore, in articles of common daily use, there is a marked tendency to make do with cheaper rather than quality products. To cite an example a villager of, say, four decades ago, may have been using tea quite infrequently because he could not afford it. Now, when his son or grandson can easily afford to drink tea as often as he likes, he may be drinking and, offering to his guests, any number of cups of tea; however, the quality of tea used may show only a marginal improvement.

(5) Several Cultural Constraints Militate against Rural Marketing: Though many of the cultural constraints referred to hereinbelow are now progressively vanishing, as of today, they still hold a sway in deciding the buying behaviour of a typical villager. He would not, thus, like to be the first or amongst the first to try a new product but would expect to be given a lead by one of the traditional centres of power and authority like, say, the village landlord, religious, social or political heavy-weight and so on. It may be recalled that only a few short years ago, resentment had been aroused in one part of the country because the untouchables started wearing footwear and in another because the womenfolk belonging to a particular community decided to wear blouses, both against accepted social norms. The cultural ties influence such decisions as whether to practice family planning (Children are God's gift), taking medicine in case of some diseases (they are a result of the displeasure or wrath of a particular deity), or buying life insurance (it is inviting premature death).

These cultural constraints and other norms of village existence the marketing of insurance much more than that of many other products. In case of life insurance, the villager is emotionally attached, against all logic as well as practical experience derived from the actual examples he sees around, to the concept of the undivided family and would like to blindly believe that if he was to die, his wife and children would be liked after by 'the family.' With traditional fatalism, he even refuses to acknowledge the concept of protection, holding the Almighty responsible to 'feed the mouths he created.' Similarly, the very concept protection fails to sufficiently motivate him because he feels that, were he to die, his land (if any) is not going to die with him and would continue to provide sustenance to his family. Even where he does not possess any lands, he sees his wife and even teen-ager children contributing their labour in various occupations such as cattle-herding, doing miscellaneous odd jobs on the farms, etc., and does not feel that they depend upon his earning capacity for their livelihood. In case of general insurance also, their possessions being meagre and their dwellings being in most cases substandard, the villagers do not feel the need for or are not qualified to get fire insurance protection or other covers like, e.g., theft and burglary. It is another truism of cultural norms that an agriculturist attaches great importance and takes good care of his cattle wealth and, therefore, cattle insurance naturally becomes more acceptable to a villager than some of the covers specially evolved for the *janata*.

(6) Rural Markets have been Neglected: Due, perhaps to the complex problems of tackling rural markets, rural marketing has been badly neglected by most of the good organisations. Their approach to rural marketing has been rather too indifferent and cavalier. This has often led to havoc played by the free and unrestrained operations of confidence tricksters and operators with questionable credentials. They have exploited the markets by passing substandard goods and services, often posing to be what they are not or using the brand names of quality products. They often adopt the strategy of intensively operating territory for a short while and leaving it in a hurry for new, greener pastures, leaving behind them a trial of disillusioned, disgruntled costumers who thereafter become tough problems for bona fide marketers. This, in turn, strengthens the belief of such good marketers that the rural markets are not worth being tackled systematically. Neither the government agencies not customer pressure groups and organisations appear to be doing much to tackle this situation, which is likely to pose serious long-term problems more especially to the marketing of financial services like insurance.

Against the special features and constraints of rural marketing mentioned above, it can be seen that there is a felt need paying particular attention to the special problems of rural marketing and to apply the various concepts of marketing management discussed in the earlier chapters to evolve a marketing strategy suited to rural marketing. Some of the points to be considered in evolving such a marketing strategy are:

(1) The products to be developed for the rural market should be rugged enough to withstand rough handling, simple enough not to confuse an average villager who does not basically lack intelligence or skill but is not accustomed to following complicated instructions or remembering a number of linear steps. The products should have, to the extent possible, an attractive package and yet should not be very expensive.

(2) Distribution network may have to be evolved taking into consideration the special problems of both rural traders as well as rural customers. The strategy followed by some of the tea companies specialising in selling of packaged teas in the sixties and early seventies is worth quoting to illustrate this point. Very small packets costing a few paise each were supplied to village shopkeepers through the company sales force, who would without fail visit a given centre on a given day of every week, carrying adequate stock of different brands along with them. This strategy had the multiple advantage of ensuring that good quality, branded goods found an entry in the rural market, encouraging the village shop-keepers to recommend the company's product for their convenience as well as quality and also building amongst the customers and dealers alike an image of dependability in addition to that of quality.

(3) Sales promotion will have to be directed primarily towards the sales force and dealers rather than customers. Demonstrations, sampling, point-of-purchase displays, exhibition stalls in village fairs and melas as well as film shows are

some of the consumer-oriented sales-promotion methods which may pay good dividends.

(4) The sales force must be trained and motivated and should regularly meet and explain the product features to the leading village personalities. If and when such opinion leaders start using a product, others are likely to follow suit. Very often, they also become the focal point in persuading others to make atleast a trial purchase of a given product. This phenomenon is even more marked in adopting services like, e.g., life insurance or family planning surgery. It is the experience of many rural life insurance agents that when a village opinion leader (*mukhiya*) is motivated enough to insure his own life, he calls others and becomes instrumental in prevailing upon them to insure their lives also. Similarly, cattle insurance has spread in several rural areas thanks to the significant role played by some of the village opinion leaders.

Insurance Marketing

While rural marketing has some distinct aspects of its own, marketing of insurance – both life and general – does not essentially differ from the marketing of other services. Therefore, efforts have been made throughout the book to explain any aspects relating to insurance that need special attention or emphasis, as and when the basic or general concept has been covered. This section primarily brings together at one place some of those points dealing with insurance marketing which have already appeared earlier under appropriate sections and briefly deals with some special features applying to the marketing of services in general and insurance in particular. Broadly, the special features of insurance marketing are as under:

Marketing Concept has not Gained Adequate Acceptance

Even in other parts of the world, where marketing concept has gained wide acceptance in precept and practice, insurance industry has been one of the last to convert itself to its acceptance and even today lags behind many other service industries including banks in its practice. Conditions in our country are no exception to this world experience. Thus, the marketing approach has not replaced the mainly sales-oriented activities in both life and general insurance. Views like "there is immense scope for the growth of insurance business in our country and we have not even touched the fringe of the potential" are freely expressed to signify that what is needed is merely that the sales force and operational offices should 'push' the existing products more vigorously. The adoption of a systems approach to marketing which includes careful study of external and internal environments including competition, assessment of market needs and development of products to satisfy the demands, developing suitable marketing mix for every identified market segment, and, above all, imbibing the marketing approach and philosophy by the top level managements has not yet taken sufficiently deep roots.

The statement that in our country both life and general insurance marketing enjoys a monopoly position is quite often made to signify that the commercial success for them can be taken for granted. However, this is far from the truth. It is true that if a person decides to insure his life, he may have to approach LIC or if a person decides to obtain comprehensive cover for his car or scooter, he will have to get it from one of the four subsidiaries of GIC. But, what is often lost sight of, is that unless a prospect is reasonably satisfied that his claim will be paid promptly and fairly, he has the option of not insuring his life or obtaining 'Act only' policy for his car or scooter and be his own insurer against death or serious damage to his vehicle, as the case may be. Whether he will buy his policy from LIC or GIC or be his own insurer will be decided in the final analysis by the successful marketing of their products by these corporations which, in other words, depend upon their adopting a marketing approach in their operations.

Selling of Insurance Needs 'Creation' of a Demand

In our country, the need for insurance benefit is, most of the times, not sufficiently understood and appreciated. In both life and general insurance, the sacrifice (payment of premiums) is real and immediate, whereas the benefits are distant and contingent. With our cultural tendency towards fatalism coupled with paucity of incomes in an overwhelmingly large number of cases, there is a tendency to indefinitely postpone the buying of insurance. In respect of most of the individual, as distinguished from institutional, prospects, the salesman has to begin by convincing the prospect about the existence of the need before he can enter upon the process of selling the requisite service. This can be contrasted with, say, the purchase of medical service in which case, the buyer is aware of the need and makes up his mind about purchasing the service without the prodding of the doctor or hospital concerned. The dependence of insurance marketing on sales-persons arises out of this.

Market Analysis and Segmentation is not Adequately Undertaken

The progress of both GIC and LIC has been reasonably good from year to year and both the organisations have been content to operate the traditional markets in an unplanned manner. Sufficient steps to make a detailed analysis of the markets, to evolve proper marketing strategy for each one of the identified market segments and to establish adequate sales facilities in each of them in a systematic manner have hardly been undertaken. It is both possible and necessary to establish better pre-sale and post-saler servicing organisation. Without exaggeration, it can be said that both these institutions are selling insurance rather than marketing it. In the case of general insurance, while efforts are made to penetrate new segments of organisational markets through covers for oil rigs, satellites, etc., there is much scope to plan for plan for better segmentation and penetration of individual customers' markets through improved promotion of existing covers and development of new covers to suit the changing market needs.

Product Development has not Kept Pace with Changing Market Needs

An inevitable corollary of the failure to undertake market analysis and segmentation successfully is that the product development and modification activity has also been in the low key. Most of the new plans introduced by LIC have not won sufficient market acceptance and support primarily because they have not gained acceptance of its own selling organisation. While the experience of GIC in respect of plans like cattle or crop insurance is better, there is still scope for more concerted efforts to identify specific needs, devise plans to meet the requirements, undertake efforts to promote these plans systematically and open new markets for non-traditional business. There is scope to undertake motivational as well as marketing research for this purpose on a more regular, systematic basis. It appears that adequate use of the sales organisation is not being made to obtain the market intelligence and to ascertain the market needs. Development of new products is done mainly on the basis of the impulsive perception of the management about what the market needs. This perhaps accounts more than anything else for the inadequate success of some of the new plans and covers introduced both by LIC and GIC from time to time.

While discussing the role of market intelligence and assessment of the opinions of the sales force in development of new products, it must be admitted that by and large the sales organisations of both LIC and GIC do not possess adequate insight into the technical bases of developing plans or determining premium, rates. Therefore, even if efforts were conscientiously made to ascertain the needs of the market through the sales wings, there is every likelihood of such efforts proving unproductive and, in the bargain, giving rise to the criticism from the sales wing that though many worthwhile suggestions were offered by them, they were not considered sufficiently seriously. This does not, however, mitigate the need to evolve a better machinery to develop new products and modify existing ones, on the basis of assessed needs of the market segments.

Pricing Considerations Need Clear Definition

Prices for most goods and services are determined by those who market them. Thus, for example, a particular consulting physician may charge, say, Rs. 50 per consultation while another may charge only Rs. 30. One brand of toothpaste or shaving cream may be available at a price which is considerably higher than that charged by several other brands and such a product may come to be accepted by some particular segment of the market as a premium brand. The mechanics of fixing prices depends, as we have seen earlier, on several considerations. There should, therefore, be no surprise or resentment about the wide variation in the prices fixed by any given marketer. The variations in the price range are often more marked in the case of services than goods. Thus there may be, say, a medical practitioner whose consultation fees may be twice or more than those of the average practitioner. However, this general freedom of action is not equally available in respect of such services as, say, electricity and water charges, railways and bus transport rates, etc. The same is also largely true about the fixing of premium rates by insurance organisations, more especially in our country since the buyers are not in a position to look around for another insurer who may be charging lower rates. There is, thus, no free play of marketing forces to evolve an acceptable market rate for the services offered by both the life and general insurance organisations. There is, therefore, a special need and responsibility to fix the premium rates in a fair and equitable way. Moreover, like the proverbial Caesar's wife who must not only be above suspicion but appear to be so, the rates must win the confidence of the market. There is no denying the fact that the fixing of premium rates is much more complex than fixing the prices for most goods and services. They are based on certain estimates about future trends of several uncontrollable variables, the estimates in turn being based on past experience, which also is influenced by the behaviour of these uncontrollable variables.

It is also true that insurers keep reviewing the premium rates and take steps to change them, whenever necessary. In the case of life insurance policies sold on participating (with profit) basis, there is also a built-in mechanism to pass the benefit of any improvement in the trends of actual experience as compared to the assumed one, to the policyholders. The 'No Claim Bonus' provision in many property insurance contracts also assists in maintaining equity by passing on to the policyholder the benefit of his careful use and maintenance of the insured property.

Even after accepting the above facts, marketing considerations demand that the buyers must feel that the price (premiums) is fair and efforts must be made to enlighten the customers about such fairplay. As far as insurance marketing is concerned, it can be maintained that better education and enlightenment of the consumers about the pricing of insurance policies deserves to be undertaken to meet the market criticism of the industry.

Better Attention to Promotional Inputs is Needed

In respect of every one of the promotional mix, the accomplishments of the insurance industry leaves much to be desired. Detailed observations have been made in respect of each ingredient in the concerned chapters. Briefly, the scope for improvement can be summed up as under:

(1) Advertising: The overall objectives should be clearly defined and discussed between the top management and the concerned department on the one side and between the top management assisted by the department and the advertising consultants on the other. A broad strategy has also to be worked out at the beginning of each year so that the advertising efforts do not become dispersed and uncoordinated. Efforts also need to be made to evaluate various campaigns as well as the different media used to convey the various messages as, otherwise, much of the expenditure is likely to prove infructious. For example, press advertising meant for rural markets may be ineffective in large tracts of our land wherein the newspaper reading habit in rural areas is limited almost exclusively to reading them a loud publicly at a common meeting place like the Panchayat Office, advertisements getting omitted altogether during such public reading. Similar evaluation also needs to be made about the efficacy of flitting media like radio and TV in conveying information, heavy messages about, say basic need for insurance, specific covers or plans and so on.

(2) Publicity: Adequate use of publicity is not being made either by the LIC or GIC though there is much scope to do so. The area, regional or divisional offices in case of GIC and zonal divisional offices in case of LIC need to be trained and encouraged to make better use of local media to communicate more frequently and more systematically with their respective markets through progress reports, human interest stories, achievements in insurance as well as non-insurance fields like sports, civic life problems, etc.

(3) Selling: There is an urgent need and good scope to improve the competence as well as involvement of the sales organisation in performing their duties. Many first line salesmen and sales-supervisors, viz., agents and development officers/inspectors lack in adequate knowledge about the product as well as practical training in systematic selling and are responsible for creating consumer dissatisfaction by their errors of omission and commission. While efforts are made at the time of initiation it impart some basic training, the need for further training and retraining at periodical intervals should be satisfied by a proper action-plan more clearly defining the training objectives and methodology and improving the infra-structure facilities than heretofore. As an integral part of gearing up the sales-organisation, the role of the sales-force in providing both pre-sale as well as post-sale service must be highlighted and enforced through education, persuasion and incentives. Better use of marketing information systems to motivate and control the sales organisations can lead to an around improvement in the performance of salesmen.

Other aspects of marketing orientation which can be profitably implemented by the insurance organisations in our country include:

(4) Involvement of Administrative Staff in Marketing Objectives: At present, it appears that the administrative staff including officers at the various operational offices does not feel sufficiently involved in the marketing objectives of the organisation. This is leading to avoidable consumer dissatisfaction and is likely to prove a serious handicap in exploiting the full marketing potential, unless speedy steps are taken to effectively remedy the situation. There are several manifestations of this lack of involvement which are seen almost every day. A policyholder paying personal visit to an office goes from pillar to post in getting somebody to listen to his problem and helping him to solve it.

Replies to policyholders' letters do not provide sufficiently clear guidance in simple words but are often couched in jargon abbreviations or technicalities, which may, no doubt, make it easier for the communicator to explain himself briefly, if not tersely, but fail to communicate effectively.

(5) Transaction-orientation Must Replace Paper-orientation: When a customer visits, say, a bank or post office, there may be occasions when he feels unhappy about the delay that takes place in attending to his work such as getting a cheque encashed or a letter registered. However, by the time he leaves the premises of the bank or the post office, his job has been completed and the anger of unhappiness he felt gets substantially if not entirely subsided by the time he returns to his home or place of business. This is because most of the interactions that take place at the bank or the post office are transaction-oriented. As against this, except in case of payment of premium due, the customer's interface with LIC or GIC does not result in the completion of the transaction for which he approached but rather marks the beginning of some correspondence which finally results in the completion of some transaction at some future date. During the intervening interval, the dissatisfaction of the consumer is quite likely to go up. If this is to be avoided, more transaction-orientedness must replace the present tendency to 'keep the file up-to-date.' This is not always possible because of the inherent difference between the types of transactions that take place at a bank or post office on the one hand and an insurance corporation's office on the other. However, looked at from the consumer's angle, it is difficult for him to readily appreciate the reason why LIC or GIC fails to solve his problem across the table. Every effort needs to be conscientiously and vigilantly made to give as much transaction-orientation to its dealings by the insurance organisations as possible and to explain the likely time-lag and the reasons therefore. This also needs more active role to be played by the sales force, who can and should always be available to the consumers to provide guidance at their homes or offices and minimise the need for the customers to approach the office directly. When any customer approaches the office after the initial guidance and help provided by the sales organisation, his communication is better likely to be completed so that it becomes possible for the organisation to solve his problem more easily and speedily. Apart from the involvement of the field personnel, the earnest desire and effort on the part of the administration to develop awareness of the need to provide more efficient and transaction-oriented service is necessary for the success of marketing of insurance.

(6) More Interaction with the Communities at Every Level should be Encouraged: Both LIC and GIC are providing the economy with sizeable funds for long-gestation plans in addition to providing attractive return to the government on its investment. In fact, both LIC and GIC provide very good success stories in the public sector. This is more especially true of LIC which is mobilising the common man's savings for long-term nation-building financial activities. However, when the banks lend a few thousand rupees to an individual to buy, say, an auto-rickshaw, this fact gets proclaimed to the people around through a suitable announcement displayed on the vehicle itself, whereas the facts about LIC's investments of several hundred crores in priority sectors as well as big and small commercial enterprises, are not adequately known even to its own organisation. This gives rise to a wrong impression about the role of both the insurance organisations. To counteract this situation, it is necessary that the line managers of these organisations should be encouraged to become as active as possible in the non-controversial aspects of community affairs in the areas where they work so as to make the presence of themselves and their organisations better felt. Greater thought should also be devoted by both GIC and LIC to find ways and means of projecting the positive side of their performance and the important role played by them on the national scene.

(7) Public Relations Activities should be Strengthened: It appears that both LIC and GIC need to pay more attention to their PR activities. While the need for PR is all the more in case of insurance industry more especially in a country like ours, a systematic plan for conducting effective Public Relations on a regular basis is lacking. An adequate Public Relations organisation of professionally qualified and competent people working directly under the chief executives of the respective concerns and enjoying sufficient operational freedom would help in bringing about better success of the marketing activities of the insurance industry.

Thus, while there is need as well as scope to improve the marketing of insurance in our country, there is no need to feel despondent. It has been pointed out elsewhere that insurance industry in other parts of the world has also been somewhat slow in adopting marketing concepts and it is not unnatural that our country is not an exception to this general trend. With increased insight into the role of marketing on the part of the top management as well as officers and men at all levels, there is every likelihood that the backlog will be cleared in the years ahead.

The concept of marketing has gradually evolved during the post industrial revolution era and has gone through three main stages of development as mentioned earlier. During the first production-oriented stage when mass-production techniques progressively replaced individual artisans or guilds, demand generally out-stripped supply and marketing was primarily concerned with channelising the goods to those areas where there was a market for them and deciding about their pricing. The sales-oriented stage which followed when availability of goods in abundance was accompanied by economic depression and the need to 'push' the goods successfully, changed the emphasis of marketing to high-pressure selling, searching new markets and controlling production in such a way as to help sell the goods at a reasonable profit. The third stage of system-orientation emphasised the need to look at the marketing operations from the consumers' point of view, taking into account the external and internal variables affecting the organisation's capacity to develop and market certain products and creating an integrated marketing mix to maximise the long-term success and profit of a given organisation. It is now becoming increasingly evident that a new stage of societal-orientation is being ushered in and that the truth of 'the old order change the yielding place to new' will have to be accepted and implemented. In the wake of globalisation and liberalisation, government has permitted private companies to undertake the work of both life and general insurance. This step will prove beneficial to both investors as well as insurance organisations.

❑❑❑

11

Decision Tree for Sales Management

Introduction

The management of an organisation must decide whether to build a small plant or a large one to manufacture a new product with an expected market life of ten years. The decision hinges on what size the market for the product will be.

Possibly demand will be high during the initial two years but, if many initial users find the product unsatisfactory, will fall to a low level thereafter. Or high initial demand might indicate the possibility of a sustained high-volume market. If demand is high and the organisation does not expand within the first two years, competitive products will surely be introduced.

If the organisation builds a big plant, it must live with it whatever the size of market demand. If it builds a small plant, management has the option of expanding the plant in two years in the event that demand is high during the introductory period; while in the event that demand is low during the introductory period, the organisation will maintain operations in the small plant and make a tidy profit on the low volume.

Management is uncertain what to do. The organisation grew rapidly during the 2000s; it kept pace with the textile industry generally. The new product, if the market turns out to be large, offers the present management a chance to push the organisation into a new period of profitable growth. The development department, particularly the development project engineer, is pushing the build the large-scale plant to exploit the first major product development the department has produced in some years.

The managing director, a principal shareholder, is wary of the possibility of large unneeded plant capacity. He favours a smaller plant commitment, but recognises that later expansion to meet high-volume demand would require more investment and be less efficient to operate. The managing director also recognises that unless the organisation moves promptly to fill the demand which develops, competitors will be tempted to move in with equivalent products.

The modern industries problem, oversimplified as it is, illustrates the uncertainties and issues that management must resolve in making investment decisions. (We use the term 'investment' in a broad sense, referring to outlays not only for new plants and equipment but also for large, risky orders, special marketing facilities, research programmes, and other purposes). These decisions are growing more important at the same time that they are increasing in complexity. Countless executives want to make them better - but how?

Here we shall present one recently developed concept called the "decision tree," which has tremendous potential as a decision-making tool. The decision tree can clarify for manage-ment, as can no other analytical tool, the choices, risks, objectives, monetary gains, and information needs involved in an investment problem. We shall be hearing a great deal about decision trees in the years ahead. Although, a novelty to most businessmen today, they will surely be in common management parlance before many more years have passed.

Later we shall return to the problem facing by modern industries and see how management can proceed to solve it by using decision trees. First, however, a simpler example will illustrate some characteristics of the decision-tree approach.

Displaying Alternatives

Let us suppose, it is a rather overcast Saturday morning, and you have 75 people coming for cocktails in the afternoon. You have a pleasant garden and your house is not too large; so if the weather permits, you would like to set up the refreshments in the garden and have the party there. It would be more pleasant, and your guests would be more comfortable. On the other hand, if you set up the party for the garden and after all the guests are assembled it begins to rain, the refreshments will be ruined, your guests will get damp, and you will heartily wish you had decided to have the party in the house. (We could complicate this problem by considering the possibility of a partial commitment to one course or another and opportunities to adjust estimates of the weather as the day goes on, but the simple problem is all we need.)

This particular decision can be represented in the form of a 'payoff' table:

	Even and Results	
Choices	Rain	No Rain
Outdoors	Disaster	Real comfort
Indoors	Mild discomfort, by happy	Mild discomfort, but regrets

Much more complex decision questions can be portrayed in payoff table form. However, particularly for complex investment decisions, a different representation of the information pertinent to the problem – the decisions-tree – is useful to show the routes by which the various possible outcomes are achieved. Pierre Masse, Commissioner General of the National Agency for Productivity and Equipment Planning in France, notes:

> "The decision problem is not posed in terms of an isolated decision (because today's decision depends on the own we shall make tomorrow) nor yet in terms of a sequence of decisions (because under uncertainty, decisions taken in the future will be influenced by what we have learned in the meanwhile). The problem is posed in terms of a tree of decisions."

Exhibit-1 illustrates a decision tree for the cocktail party problem. This tree is a different way of displaying the same information shown in the payoff table. However, as later examples will show, in complex decisions the decision tree is frequentely a much more lucid means of presenting the relevant information than is a payoff table.

The tree is made up of a series of nodes and branches. At the first node on the left, the host has the choice of having the party inside or outside. Each branch represents an alternative course of action or decision. At the end of each branch or alternative course is another node representing a chance event – whether or not it will rain. Each subsequent alternative course to the right represents an alternative outcome of this chance event. Associated with each complete alternative course through the tree is a payoff, shown at the end of the rightmost or terminal branch of the course.

When we are drawing decision trees, we like to indicate the action or decision forks with spare nodes and the chance-event forks with round ones. Other symbols may be used instead, such as single-line and double-line branches, special letters, or colours. It does not matter so much which method of distinguishing we use so long as we do employ one or another. A decision tree of any size will always combine (1) action choices with (2) different possible events or results of action which are partially affected by chance or other uncontrolable circumstances.

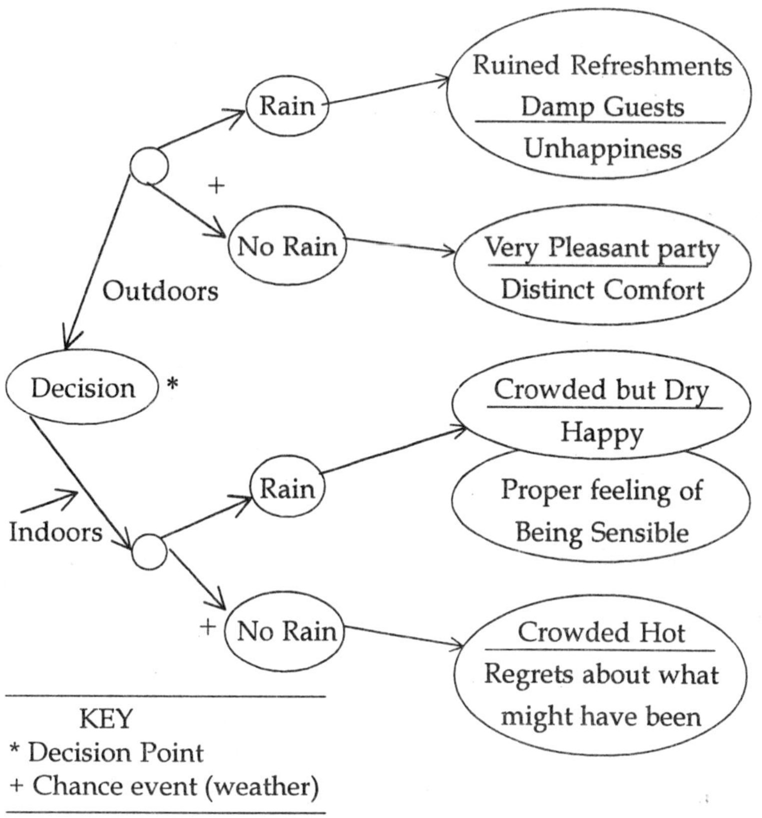

Decision Tree for Cocktail Party
Exhibit-1

Decision-event Chains

The previous example, though involving only a single stage of decision, illustrates the elementary principles on which larger, more complex decision trees are built. Let us take a slightly more complicated situation:

We are trying to decide whether to approve a development budget for an improved product. We are urged to do so on the grounds that the development, if successful, will give us a competitive edge, but if we do not develop the product, our competitor may - and may seriously damage our market share.

Of course, we do not try to identify all the events that can happen or all the decisions we will have to make on a subject under analysis. In the decision tree we lay out only those decisions and events or results that are important to us and have consequences we wish to compare.

Adding Financial Data

Now we can return to the problem faced by the N. K. Industries management. A decision tree characterising the investment problem can be sold very easily. At Decision No. 1 the organisation must decide between a large and a small plant. This is all that must be decided now. But if the organisation chooses to build a small plant and then finds demand high during the initial period, it can in two years - at Decision No. 2 - choose to expand its plant.

But let us go beyond a bare outline of alternatives. In making decisions, management must take account of the probabilities, costs, and returns which appear likely. On the basis of the data now available to them, and assuming no important change in the company's situation, they reason as follows:

Marketing estimates indicate a 60 per cent chance of a low demand, developing initially as follows:

Initially high demand, sustained high:	60%	
Initially high demand, long-term low:	10%	40%
Initially low and continuing low:	30%	
Initially low and subsequently high:	0.0%	

Therefore, the chance that demand initially will be high is 70 per cent (60+10). If demand is high initially, the company estimates that the chance it will continue at a high level is 86 per cent (60 to 70). Comparing 86 per cent to 60 per cent, it is apparent that a high initial level of sales changes the estimated chance of high sales in the subsequent periods. Similarly, if sales in the initial period are low, the chances are 100 per cent (30÷30) that sales in the subsequent periods will be low. Thus, the level of sales in the initial period is expected to be a rather accurate indicator of the level of sales in the subsequent periods.

Estimates of annual income are made under the assumption of each alternative outcome:

(1) A large plant with high volume would yield Rs. 1,00,000 annually in cash flow.

(2) A large plant with low volume would yield only Rs. 1,00,000 because of high fixed costs and inefficiencies.

(3) A small plant with low demand would be economical and would yield annual cash income of Rs. 4,00,000.

(4) A small plant, during an initial period of high demand, would yield Rs. 4,50,000 per year, but this would drop to Rs. 3,00,000 yearly in the long run because of competition. (The market would be larger than under alternative 3, but would be divided up among more competitors.)

(5) If the small plant were expanded to meet sustained high demand, it would yield Rs. 7,00,000 cash flow annually, and so would be less efficient than a large plant built initially.

(6) If the small plant were expanded, but high demand were not sustained, estimated annual cash flow would be Rs. 50,000.

It is estimated further that a large plant would cost Rs. 3 million to put into operation, a small plant would cost Rs. 1.3 million, and the expansion of the small plant would cost an additional Rs. 2.2 million.

However, we are beginning to see dramatic evidence of the value of decision trees in laying out what management knows in a way that enables more systematic analysis and leads to better decisions. To sum up the requirements of making a decision tree, management must:

(1) Identify the points of decision and alternatives available at each point.

(2) Identify the points of uncertainty and the type or range of alternative outcomes at each point.

(3) Estimate the values needed to make the analysis, especially the probabilities of different events or results of action and the costs and gains of various events and actions.

(4) Analyse the alternative values to choose a course.

Choosing Course of Action

We are now ready for the next step in the analysis to compare the consequences of different courses of action. A decision tree does not give management the answer to an investment problem; rather, it helps management determine which alternative at any particular choice point will yield the greatest expected monetary gain, given the information and alternatives pertinent to the decision.

Of course, the gains must be viewed with the risks. At many corporations, managers have different points of view toward risks; hence they will draw different conclusions in the circumstances described by the decision tree. The many people participating in a decision - those supplying capital, ideas, data, or decisions, and having different values at risk - will see the uncertainty surrounding the decision in different ways. Unless these differences are recognised and dealt with, those who must make the decision, pay for it, supply data and analyse to it, and live with it will judge the issue, relevance of data, need for analysis, and criterion of success in different and conflicting ways.

For example, company stockholders may treat a particular investment as one of a series of possibilities, some of which will work out, others of which will fail. A major investment may pose risks to a middle manager - to his job and career - no matter what decision is made. Another participant may have a lot to gain from success, but little to lose from failure of the project. The nature of the risk - as each individual sees it - will affect not only the assumptions he is willing to make but also the strategy he will follow in dealing with the risk.

The existence of multiple, unstated, and conflicting objectives will certainly contribute to the 'politics' and one can be certain that the political element exists whenever the lives and ambitions of people are affected. Here, as in similar cases, it is not a bad exercise to think through who the parties to an investment decision are and to try to make these assessments:

(1) What is at risk? Is it profit or equity value, survival of the business, maintenance of a job, opportunity for a major career?

(2) Who is bearing the risk? The stockholder is usually bearing risk in one form. Management, employees, the community - all may be bearing different risks.

(3) What is the character of the risk that each person bears? Is it, in his terms, unique, once-in-a-life-time, sequential, insurable? Does it affect the economy, the industry, the company, or a portion of the company?

Considerations such as the foregoing will surely enter into top management's thinking, and the decision tree will not eliminate them. But the tree will show management what decision today will contribute most to its long-term goals. The next step in the analysis is the concept of 'rollback.'

'Rollback' Concept

Here is how rollback works in the situation described. At the time of making Decision No. 1, management does not have to make Decision No. 2 and does not even know if it will have the occasion to do so. But if it were to have the option at Deceision No. 2, the company would expand the plant, in view of its current knowledge. We see that the total expected value of the expansion alternative is Rs. 1,60,000 greater than the no-expansion alternative, over the eight-year life remaining. Hence that is the alternative management would choose if faced with Decision No. 2 with its existing information and thinking only of monetary gain as a standard of choice.

Readers may wonder why we started with Decision No. 2 when today's problem is Decision No. 1. The reason is the following: We need to be able to put a monetary value on Decision No. 2 in order to 'roll back' to Decision No. 1 and compare the gain from taking the lower branch ('Build Small Plant') with the gain from taking the upper branch ('Build Big Plant'). Let us call that monetary value for Decision No. 2 its position value. The position value of a decision is the expected value of the preferred branch (in this case, the plant-expansion fork). The expected value is simply a kind of average of the results you would expect if you were to repeat the situation over and over – getting a Rs. 5,600 thousand yield 86 per cent of the time and a Rs. 400 thousand yield 14 per cent of the time.

Accounting for Time

What about taking differences in the time of future earnings into account? The time between successive decision stages on a decision tree may be substantial. At any stage we may have to weigh differences in immediate cost or revenue against differences in value at the next stage. Whatever standard of choice is applied, we can put the two alternatives on a comparable basis if we discount the value assigned to the next stage by an appropriate percentage. The discount percentage is, in effect, an allowance for the cost of capital and is similar to the use of a discount rate in the present value or discounted cash flow techniques already well known to businessmen.

When decision trees are used, the discounting procedure can be applied one stage at a time. Both cash flows and position values are discounted.

For simplicity, let us assume that a discount rate of 10 per cent per year for all stages is decided on by Stygain Chemical's management. Applying the rollback principle, we again begin with Decision No. 2.

Now we want to go through the same procedure when we obtained expected values, only this time using the discounted yield figures and obtaining a discounted expected value. Since the discounted expected value of the no-expansion alternative is higher, that figure becomes the position value of Decision No. 2 this time.

Having done this, we go back to work through Decision No. 1 again, repeating the same analytical procedure as before only with discounting. Note that the Decision No. 2 position value is treated at the time of Decision No. 1 as if it were a lump sum received at the end of the two years.

The large-plant alternative is again the preferred one on the basis of discounted expected cash flow. But the margin of difference over the small-plant alternative (Rs. 290 thousand) is smaller than it was without discounting.

Uncertainty Alternatives

In illustrating the decision-tree concept, we have treated uncertainty alternatives as if they were discrete, well-defined possibilities. For our examples, we have made use of uncertain situations depending basically on a single variable, such as the level of demand or the success or failure of a development project. We have sought to avoid unnecessary complication while putting emphasis on the key inter-relationships among the present decision, future choices, and the intervening uncertainties.

In many cases, the uncertain elements do take the form of discrete, single-variable alternatives. In others, however, the possibilities for cash flow during a stage may range through a whole spectrum and may depend on a number of independent or partially related variables subject to chance influences - cost, demand, yield, economic climate, and so forth. In these cases, we have found that the range of variability or the likelihood of the cash flow falling in a given range during a stage can be calculated readily from knowledge of the key variables and the uncertainties surrounding them. Then the range of cash-flow possibilities during the stage can be broken down into two, three, or more 'subsets,' which can be used as discrete chance alternatives.

❑❑❑

Index

❑❑❑